Voices of Love in the dark

44 Radio Conversations on Transforming Grief

Andrea Hylen

Heal My Voice, Inc
Santa Monica, California

Voices of Love in the dark: 44 Radio Conversations on Transforming Grief –Part 1

Copyright © 2016 Heal My Voice, Inc and Andrea Hylen

All rights reserved. No part of this book may be reproduced or transmitted in any form or by any means, electronic or mechanical including photography, recording or any information storage and retrieval system without written permission from the author and publisher.

Published by:
Heal My Voice, Inc
Andrea Hylen
Santa Monica, CA 90401
www.healmyvoice.org

ISBN-13: 978-0692814185
ISBN-10: 0692814183

Editor: Andrea Hylen
Cover design by Karen Brand

Printed in the United States of America

A portion of the proceeds from the sale of this book will be donated to further the non-profit work of Heal My Voice.

Dedication

To all of our beloved loved ones

Table of Contents

Acknowledgements   5
Introduction   7
Simple Guide to Reading Book   9

Section 1
Setting the Foundation and Understanding Grief

Chapter One: Honoring the Feelings of Grief   13
(Show #1)

Chapter Two: Grief Relief: Finding Comfort in Loss   25
Guest: Debbie Phillips (Show #2)

Chapter Three: How to Stay Open to Feelings   41
and Take Control of Grief (Show #6)

Chapter Four: The Voice That Calls You Home   53
Guest: Rev. Andrea Raynor (Show #16)

Chapter Five: Thanksgiving: Gratitude   71
(Show #5)

Chapter Six: Cell Your Soul: Owning and Clearing   83
Our Emotional Debris
Guest: Jeff Brown (Show #42)

Chapter Seven: Discovering Gifts After Loss,   103
Change, Major Disappointment (Show #26)

Chapter Eight: Spiritual and Self-Care Space   111
Guest Carin Channing (Show #7)

Chapter Nine: Thanksgiving Eve: Remembering   131
(Show #4)

Chapter Ten: The Transformative Power of Love   139
   Guest: Alan Peterson (Show #12)

Chapter Eleven: Peace on Earth and Inner Peace   157
(Show #32)

Section 2
Tools to Support Grief Transformation

Chapter Twelve: Using the Body's Wisdom   175
   to Transform Grief
   Guest Anna Stookey (Show #29)

Chapter Thirteen: Healing with Sound   193
   (Show #28)

Chapter Fourteen: Reading Stories of Grief to Heal   201
   (Show #8)

Chapter Fifteen: Dancing with the Jonas Brothers   209
   and a Teenager (Show #11)

Chapter Sixteen: Nature Ceremonies: Release Grief   223
   (Show #38)

Chapter Seventeen: Saying Goodbye to a Home   239
   (Show #15)

Chapter Eighteen: Writing as a Path to Healing   245
   (Show #13)

Chapter Nineteen: Grieving the Life You Thought   251
   You Were Meant to Live
   Guest: Elizabeth St. Germain (Show #43)

Chapter Twenty: Healing with Laughter   265
   (Show #14)

Chapter Twenty-one: Staying Balanced 273
    as You Grieve
    Guest: G. Brian Benson (Show #36)

Chapter Twenty-two: Angels in our Lives 287
    Guest: Betsy McMahan (Show #33)

Radio Show Guest Websites 305
Radio Show Links 307
Resources 317
Books 319
Films and TV and Music 321
Heal My Voice Books 323

Andrea Hylen

ACKNOWLDEGEMENTS

This is a series of 44 stories, experiences and healing techniques that were shared on a radio show between November 21, 2010 and January 7, 2011. The words in each chapter were transcribed from the LIVE shows. Twenty-seven guests shared stories of grief and healing. Seventeen of the shows were my own personal stories and experiences of how I learned to feel, heal and transform grief, loss and change over and over again.

There is a link at the end of each chapter that will lead you to the original radio show, if you want to hear the voices. As much as possible, I kept the original words and format in each chapter.

I am deeply grateful to my brother, Kenneth, my son, Cooper and my husband, Hurley who provided me with the rich opportunity to learn and grow with them in life and death. They taught me that it is possible to love someone with your whole heart and to feel everything during joy and sadness. They continue to teach me in Spirit.

I am deeply grateful to all of the people who came onto the show to share their own journey and who held a space for me to follow a heartfelt desire to provide a place for comfort, sharing and healing during the holiday season and beyond.

Thank you to the guests in Book 1: Debbie Phillips, Andrea Raynor, Jeff Brown, Carin Channing, Alan Peterson, Elizabeth St. Germain, Anna Stookey, G. Brian Benson and Betsy McMahan.

Thank you to the guests in Book 2: Asha Ramakrishna, Sherryl Lin, Jeni Shaw, Renee Barnow, Kathryn Yarborough, Jay Lee, Kater Leatherman, Cherry- Lee Ward, Ellen Kittredge, Susan Gardener, Kathy Perry, Lee Forest Knowlton, Shelly Rachanow, Yvonne Gonzalez-Baez, Claire Perkins, Connie Cornwell, Frank Mundo, Sally Laux.

Andrea Hylen

Introduction:

Grief is not a stranger to me. From the death of my baby brother to sudden infant death syndrome when I was four years old, to moving 12 times by the time I was 15, to a marriage that ended in divorce, to the death of my son, to the life threatening illness I survived, to the death of my 2nd husband, I know grief.

Grief has become my friend and teacher.

Grieving is a multi-dimensional, elusive being at times. It seems like it would be so easy to grieve. Cry, release the feelings and move on. But, grief shows up in our lives in many ways. There are layers and layers that must be honored and healed. There is no timing or prediction of where and when it will show up.

And mixed into all of the "big" events to grieve are the disappointments which we all have and where there are layers of grief. The loss of the part in the school play, the boyfriend or girlfriend who dumped you, the layoff from a job, the dreams that did not manifest. All the memories of all those events are inside of you waiting to be expressed and released.

When I talk about grief, I am talking about anything that brings you sorrow, that feels like a loss, and that is connected in some way to disappointment, sadness, hopelessness or a change in your life.

During the last 60 years, learning to embrace and become friends with grief has opened my world to feeling more of everything and learning to live a richer, deeper life of joy. The more I have allowed myself to go into the depths of feelings around grief, the more I have felt joy and happiness. I have learned that you cannot shut down one emotion and feel everything else. To feel ecstatic joy, you have to feel the contrast, deep sadness. Opening your heart to one feeling will open your heart to all.

My heartfelt desire is that you will find things that inspire you to feel more, to spend time healing and embracing all of the experiences in your life, that you will see a path to appreciate your own journey and see the gifts and light that is present in the dark. Thank you for being here.

Andrea Hylen

Simple Guide
and Suggestions for Reading this Book

All of the chapters in this book have been transcribed from the Radio Conversations. Some of the details have changed since the radio shows first aired. The changes have been updated in each chapter and in the guest biographies.

1. Begin with Chapter One. It sets the foundation for all of the radio shows.
2. Look at the Table of Contents to see if a guest or topic sparks an interest.
3. Randomly choose a Chapter by closing your eyes and letting a number between 1-22 pop into your mind. Trust your intuition and read that chapter next.
4. Keep a journal handy to write feelings or inspirations
5. Read through the conversations and content in the chapters.
6. Notice the connection you feel with some of the guests and topics.
7. Make a list of resources or exercises that you would like to try. Google the resources and explore.
8. Choose one meditation or exercise at a time. Try it for a few days or a week see what happens.
9. There are 22 radio show conversations in this book. All 44 radio show links are listed at the back of the book. Listen to a few shows or listen to all 44.
10. Check out the radio show guest websites.
11. Check out the list of books and resources. Go to your library or order on Amazon or the author websites and read some of the books.
12. Be gentle with yourself. Healing takes time and cycles around for more healing throughout your life. This is more than a journey, it is the fabric of your life.

Andrea Hylen

Section One

Setting the Foundation and Understanding Grief

Dare to reach out your hand into the darkness, to pull another hand into the light.

~ Norman B. Rice

Andrea Hylen

Chapter One

Honoring the Feelings of Grief
Andrea Hylen

Show originally aired on November 21, 2010

Welcome to the show tonight. I chose this time of the year to talk about Grief Transformation because in between all of the celebrations of the holidays there are moments of grieving. In between shopping and wrapping presents, buying food, attending parties, there are moments when we remember the past. We remember the loss of loved ones and times in our lives when things changed and did not turn out the way we thought they would.

Some people have experienced their greatest losses around Thanksgiving, Christmas, Hanukah, New Year's Eve or one of the other festivals of lights during this holiday season. And as beautiful as the bright lights are, this is also the darkest time of the year in the Northern Hemisphere. We are approaching the Winter Solstice and in the next month, it will continue to get darker and darker. That is another reflection that encourages us to pause, go within and feel all of the feelings that are present.

The 44 radio shows are my gift to you this holiday season. And as we all know, anytime you give a gift, you personally receive something yourself (even when that was not the original motivation or inspiration.) As soon as I announced my intention for this show on Facebook, women and men reached out to me. As I described my deepest desire to create a space of conversation and support, I received encouragement to share my stories. The Facebook friends connected me with people who have stories of grief to share. So, between waking up with Divine inspirations and people reaching out to me, I am being led to amazing people who have stories and experiences of sadness and hope to share with you this holiday season.

In the 44 shows, some of the topics will be loss of a loved one including a child, a sibling, a partner, a friend and a pet. There will be shows about loss through illness, suicide, and tragedy. We will talk about loss of a job, a house, your health. We will talk about grieving the changes in the world and the Earth. And we will also talk about roles that you have had to give up that you feel gave you value and without them you feel lost.

And in each story, you will hear the path that led someone to heal and love again. You will hear stories of hope, transformation, and joy. For this is truly the gift of grieving. It is the things we learn about ourselves and others. It is the path to deeper love and finding the gifts in the loss.

I wanted to create a space where we can be real with the feelings of grief. We can talk about it. In sharing stories of grief, healing and transformation we can discover our own answers.

Tonight it is my intention to set a foundation for our journey this holiday season.

"How lucky I am to have something that makes saying good-bye so hard."
~Winnie the Pooh

Today I saw something posted on Facebook. The words were: *Only time heals a heartache.* I agree that with time, we do heal and in general, the loss becomes easier with time. I know when my husband died, I had a lack of feeling and being numb for weeks. He had 10-months of chemotherapy and treatments and fighting cancer before he died. I can remember being numb and everything feeling surreal. That numb feeling does go away and it does get better. But, I am going to say something and be really honest. This may upset some people and some of you will know exactly what I mean. I believe that you never get over the loss completely. It is a part of your life experience and it is something that you learn from but, the feelings of grief can appear over and over in cycles. Forever.

When my son died, I definitely grieved and had years of grieving on and off. And then time healed. Life went on. I thought about him. He will always be a part of my life but life was in flow again. Until the day that would have been his 17th birthday. I woke up that morning with so much sadness. I felt raw. It felt like he had just died even though it had been 15 years. I cancelled everything on my schedule that day. I let myself feel the rawness and the richness of deep, deep feeling. I gave myself over to the grief all day long. If it had been longer, if I needed two days, I would have taken the time I needed. By really letting myself sink into that deep sadness, I was able to feel the feelings and cry and release it. So, when I woke up the next day, I did feel better. I felt like I had the experience of expanding my heart by allowing the grief to be there. I listened to the voice of grief and I let it speak to me.

So, for someone to say time heals everything. I say, Yes and No. Yes, it heals, but grief continues to show up at different times. If you can accept that it is a part of the cycle and honor it when it shows up, it will lead you to new awareness and healing.

One of the things that was happening in my life at the time of my son's 17th birth anniversary was a huge adventure with my youngest daughter. My heart was expanding to more love and we were about to connect with more people all over the United States. I was stirring up the feelings in my heart as the trip was getting closer. In my heart was grief and it was still there. When you feel one emotion, you open the door to feel everything. More love will connect you with more sadness.

An Exercise: Take a minute to be in this possibility with me. That you never get over grief. That grief is always there and that other experiences of loss and change can open the door to feel this again.

Breathe into this idea. Let it be what it is for you. Even if you disagree with me. It is okay if you disagree, if you are angry, if you are disappointed. Whatever feeling is there, just let that be.

For just a minute, think about something that you like, whatever comes to your mind. It could be a fresh strawberry, a sunset, a cup of hot chocolate. Something simple that you like. And get that picture in your mind.

Now, in this moment, can you experience what that is by just thinking about it? By letting it be? Can you feel a sensation, a feeling that is part of the picture?

Now think about a special event or a moment in your life. A party you attended. A really happy Thanksgiving, a vacation, a day you experienced with a friend at the beach or a carnival. Or a success, a day where everything just worked out exactly the way you wanted it to. Now take a minute to bring that into your consciousness.

Now, think about this. How long ago was that memory? Did you think about a Thanksgiving that happened last year, ten years ago or twenty years ago? Did you think about a vacation that happened many years ago?

And in that memory, that moment, that special event holds vivid feelings in the present moment. Even though it is a distant memory, an experience from the past, you can feel it now. It is something that happened a while ago. It is also something that you have a stored memory you can tap right back into with feelings you can feel right now.

I love to go to the beach. I can close my eyes and in a moment, I can feel myself there. I can hear the sounds of the seagulls and hear the waves of the ocean. When we think about a loss, it is as easy to tap back into those feelings as it is to tap into the special events of happiness and joy. So, why would we think we would ever get over the grief totally?

I believe that it is part of our experience and feeling everything brings us to live deeper, richer lives. It is learning about ourselves through those moments of grief. Knowing what it is like to love someone so much that you can feel your heart breaking at the thought of not seeing them in this lifetime again. You can tap back into the most joyful moments with that person where you can remember a moment of laughing with them. And that can lift your heart into this great place of joy.

So, with the same person you can think about different moments of feeling all of those feelings. When we allow ourselves to feel all of it and we allow ourselves to take that time to grieve and cry whenever it comes up again, something opens our heart to feel more. The fact that I was able to take that day and grieve the loss of my son on his 17th birthday and to feel all of those feelings and to feel the loss of him not being there, I had an experience the next day where I actually felt like my heart had expanded into a new place of loving even more. And that is one of the gifts of the grieving process, of letting yourself feel all of that.

I also want to acknowledge that there may be some people who are in that raw, fresh grief and you may be able to feel joy today, if you tap into those memories. I also want to give you permission to feel whatever you are feeling right now. It is very different to be in a new grieving situation. I would encourage you to be gentle with yourself, to be compassionate and patient.

Let's take another breath together. Let yourself feel whatever you are feeling.

POSITIVE AFFIRMATIONS

I want to talk about this right now because grief is one of the topics in the world where people can be uncomfortable with someone who is grieving. Some of the classic lines you may hear at a funeral.

*She lived a wonderful life.
*You will find that your life will be even better.
*Your life will be better soon.
*It was his time.
*You must have known he was going to die so you will move on quickly.

What I have discovered is, in our society, people are uncomfortable with someone being sad and there is a desire, a true heartfelt desire, to fix it and make it better. We try to

place a time frame on it or do something else to patch it up and cover it up. It is one of the challenges with positive affirmations. In this time of an increase in talking about positive affirmations and visioning and bringing positive thinking into your life, it can actually be a detriment to feeling something sad. *Let's just cover it over with some positive affirmations.*

There are movies like the Secret and Law of Attraction. Books with the words, Ask and It is Given and Positive Thinking. I do believe in the power of positive thinking and I will tell you, I am eternally grateful for the films and being able to go into a bookstore and find books that are positive and uplifting. I know that whatever we focus on is what we attract more of into our lives. I love to feel joy and happiness and experience my brilliance and be inspired.

But the challenge of putting a layer of positive affirmations without looking at how we are feeling can cover over the feelings. Before we can get to the visions and dreams, it is important to understand the need to go within our heart and have the courage to see what is bubbling up to be healed first. Without honoring this first step, positive affirmations can cover a layer of pain with a bed of roses. It is time to embrace the thorns as part of the process of life and to know that part of a beautiful rose is the thorns. It is time to understand that by embracing the pain we will deepen our ability to feel all emotion, including love and joy.

Imagine that you were cleaning your house and sweeping piles of dirt under the rug instead of looking at it, sweeping it into a dustpan and releasing it to the trash. Instead of just throwing it away, what if you also stopped and looked through it. Maybe you check and see that there is a lost earring in there. You see that there are some pennies and quarters. And in grieving, as you discover the gifts, you sweep around in your heart. You check inside and feel the feelings. You explore the feelings.

There is a time and place to sweep the dirt (the feelings) under the rug as a temporary holding place. But after a while the piles of dirt accumulate to mounds and it becomes uncomfortable to walk on the rug. You would eventually start walking around the rug to avoid the uncomfortable mounds of dirt. You might not be able to get anywhere near the rug, all that hidden dirt would be taking up too much room!

Sometimes, we have to go to work or take care of our children. We don't have time to process and feel everything in this moment. It's okay to give yourself permission to wait to feel those feelings. But if you don't go back to feel them, it is like continuing to sweep the dirt under the rug.

The point here is that if you have pain in your heart that is bubbling up to be healed and released, you can't just put a coating of positive affirmations on top of it. You can't just say, *yes, I feel better. I am all better now* and push away sadness. See it for what it is. Accept this moment. Look at it and learn to dance with the feelings. There is no timing of grief.

You may have had a loss last year and you've healed so much and you felt the feelings and you have done the work to heal and then you walk into someone's house at the holidays and you smell apple cider cooking in the crockpot and it just brings you back to a memory. And right there is the grief. So just be with those feelings and know there is nothing wrong. Accept the moment. Notice the feeling. It could just be that that feeling of sadness could switch to a moment of joy when you remember that it was your grandmother that always had hot apple cider around the holidays. In that moment, you can appreciate the memory of her along with the feelings of sadness that she is not there. You are capable of feeling all of the feelings. The dance is with the feelings not by denying what is present. Joy and sadness can exist in the same place.

Close your eyes for a minute and breathe into your heart.
What is bubbling up in you right now?
It could be a beautiful moment of joy. It doesn't have to be sadness or loss. Let it be what it is.
Honor the feelings.
What are you feeling?
Pause and feel the feeling.
Now, identify the feeling.
When you can feel those feelings, you can replace the pain with something positive.

An example: *I am a powerful, courageous person who is open and ready to receive more love into my life now.*
And that is one of the gifts of grieving.
Another idea to share.
Did you know that when you are grieving or sad or disappointed or in fear, you hold your breath? Your breath becomes shallow. You only let in enough air to keep you alive. Remember that the definition of inspiration is to breathe with Spirit. How can you be inspired when you are holding your breath? How can you put a layer of affirmations over the sadness or pain that is in your heart?

Feel the feelings first.
Breathe.
Now, place a layer of positive affirmations and breathe into them.
Doesn't that feel better?

HONORING THE FEELINGS

I have one more thing to share with you tonight. This is an article I wrote about honoring the feelings. I will read it to you now.

Some people feel the rain. Others just get wet. ~Roger Miller

The quote from Roger Miller reminds me you can stand in the rain and get wet or you can let the rain into your heart and soul. Your feelings are there for a reason. Whatever event has opened the door to grief, the loss of a loved one; a health challenge; the loss of a job or the loss of a dream; there is a gift in grieving.

The gift is in the feelings and they deserve respect. Feelings can be anger, sadness, disappointment, hurt, shock, betrayal and even relief. Why is it so important to feel the feelings? When you can feel and grieve, you open your heart to experience more love, joy and happiness.

In the Art of Loving, the author, Erich Fromm said, *"To spare oneself from grief at all cost can be achieved only at the price of total detachment, which excludes the ability to experience happiness."*

In other words, by detaching from the feelings around grief, we place our heart in a box. Nothing can touch it. We cannot feel the pain and we cannot feel love. The gift of grieving is the ability to go deeply within ourselves and to open our heart to feel more emotion. Ultimately, that leads us to feel more joy.

The greatest gifts in my life have been the moments when I loved so deeply that I felt like my heart was breaking. The truth is that the heart muscle was being stretched and expanded in this moment of pain. There is a gift in the ability to love and feel all the feelings.

My son, Cooper was born with a congenital heart defect. He had an absent pulmonary valve and an enlarged lung. After his first open heart surgery, at the age of two weeks old, the doctor told my husband and me that he might not make it through the night.

I can remember sitting in the private room with my husband and the doctor as he gave us the news. And in that moment I decided to go sit with my son. As I looked at my little boy in an infant bed, I knew that I loved him more than I had ever loved before. Even in this moment of deep grief, I could feel the love and pain at the same time. In the pain of the thought of losing him, my heart expanded to be with him and love him. With tears streaming down my face, I told my son that no matter what he chose, life or death, I would be by his side. I told him that if he wanted to fight for his life, I would be with him every step of the way. And if living was too hard and he wanted to die I would still love him with all of my heart.

In that moment of deep grief, and I am sure you, the listener, can hear it even though this happened twenty years ago. My heart expanded to love him unconditionally in a way I had never experienced before. This gift, as painful as it was
and even now, 20 years later, it was an experience of honoring the feelings and being willing to dive deeply into the core of them. He gave me a great gift of being able to feel and love and even share these deep emotions with you. Five minutes later the nurse told me his vital signs were improving. In this moment, he had chosen life.

For 19 months, I loved my son for who he was through two open-heart surgeries, shunt and hernia operations. I threw away all of the developmental books that told me who he should be at a certain age and I loved him unconditionally for who he was. Ultimately, he died from a 4th stage neuroblastoma cancer. In my heart, I knew that he had completed his mission in life and had made the decision to let go and die.

He was one of the greatest teachers in my life. One big lesson I learned was to love people for who they are and let go of trying to change anyone. Grieving the loss and feeling all of the emotions opened my heart to love everyone in my life deeply in the present moment and to live life. It is a decision point to shut down and not feel the feelings of emotional pain, but you also shut the door to feeling love and joy and happiness and all of the other feelings.

When you open your heart to grieve, you open your heart to love.

Someone left a message on the chat line. *Thank you. Yes, he is an angel now.*

I didn't expect to go so deeply into the feelings tonight. I know you can hear it in my voice. As you can see, this is something I experienced 20 years ago and talking about it tonight, I was able to transport myself back there and feel the feelings of loving my son so deeply.

He was my third child and what I found in this experience of loving him where he was and in grieving that it actually opened me up to feel more love for my two older daughters, Mary and Elizabeth.

I thought I was loving them and I WAS loving them. I was loving them with as much love as I had. But it was in the experience of feeling this wider range of feelings I had with my son, Cooper that it expanded my heart so much that there was even more love allowed in there.

One last thought tonight...

I had a conversation with a man in Priscilla's coffee shop earlier today. I was talking with Carlos, one of the employees. We were talking about Senator John McCain who was a prisoner of war and how he found joy in little moments that helped to keep him alive. While he was a prisoner, he found ways to communicate with other human beings and find joy. Carlos said that when he thinks of someone like John McCain, that he feels bad having any complaints or feeling sad, because Senator McCain's pain was so big. I told Carlos that your pain is your pain and there is no reason to compare your pain to someone else's. Honor what you are feeling.

We all have our own journey and our own experiences. As Carlos reflected about his own life, he began to talk about some places that he could find joy in his life now, even in the loneliness, even in the sadness. I encourage everyone to stop comparing yourself to anyone else. Honor your own feelings. Find moments of joy whenever you can and let yourself feel everything.

I want to honor each person who comes on the show live during the next 44 days or listens to the recordings. I want to honor you for having the courage to listen to a show about grief transformation. I want to honor you for feeling the feelings, for showing up in your life, for embracing the journey of life, for listening to the guidance that is within you. For having the courage to look under the rug, after you have been sweeping some feelings under there and for seeing what is bubbling up inside of you.

And to know that even in those moments of grieving, to believing that there are blessings of joy.

As I sat by my son's hospital bed for many days through many operations, I made the decision to cross stitch angels. I cross stitched elaborate counted cross stitch angels with multiple colors and sparkly thread. One of the pictures was a little boy laying in a bed with an angel leaning over him. When I think of the moments of sitting by his bed and cross stitching angels, I am filled with joy because those moments were so precious and beautiful and joy filled. Even amongst the tears, I can see this incredible journey he and I had together for 19 months. He had other people in his life. I had other people in my life. But I had these moments that were so precious and lovely and beautiful of life with him.

Even in the sadness, I can feel and remember that.

I am going to close the show now and hold you all in my heart on this journey. Most of the nights for this 44 evenings, I will be on the call live. There will be a variety of guests. If you would like to call in and share, there is a call number or if you would like to share questions or feelings or inspiration on the chat line, I will read your words out loud. Thank you for being here.

Andrea Hylen is the founder of Heal My Voice, a Writing. Life Coach and Orgasmic Meditation teacher. Andrea has discovered her unique gifts while parenting three daughters and learning to live life fully after the deaths of her brother, son and husband. She is currently living out of a suitcase following her intuition as she travels around the world speaking, teaching, collaborating and leading workshops. www.healmyvoice.org

Andrea Hylen

Grief Transformation Show #1
Honoring the Feelings of Grief

November 21, 2010
http://tobtr.com/1369270

Chapter Two

Grief Relief and Finding Comfort in Loss
Guest: Debbie Phillips, founder of Women on Fire

Show originally aired on November 22, 2010

Introduction: Tonight I am honored to have the fantastic, brilliant, open-hearted woman **Debbie Phillips as my guest to discuss Grief Relief. Debbie is a pioneer in the field of life and executive coaching. She became a coach in 1995.** For years she conducted Grief Relief calls and Grief Relief workshops for friends and clients struggling with loss.

Debbie and I met in Los Angeles at a conference called, The Freedom Formula. Sitting next to each other during one of the luncheons led us to a discussion about the death of my husband. Sharing the death of my husband and my experiences of grief connected us. It began a friendship that has continued. Grieving and sharing our stories and vulnerability brings people together in deeper connection.

Andrea: We are entering into a holiday period and we focus on celebrating but we don't always talk about the sadness and the loss we have underneath it.

Debbie: I think to spend all of the radio shows this season talking about grief opens our hearts to the information and is also a great way to start the new year. It is moving out of the old and into the new by hosting this series. I really applaud you.

We often feel if we share the information about loss and grief and death and really share our hearts, it is frightening for most of us. But, when we do and I am so grateful for that day we shared our feelings of grief, because it forged a relationship that has been really joyful for me.

Andrea: I feel the same way. We can have a Love Fest here about the deep connection we have just by sharing common experiences of grief and loss.

I know that you have studied grief since you were 10 years old! Can you tell us a little bit about that? I am sure you had an experience that opened that door for you.

Debbie: When I was ten years old, my grandmother died. She died young and was only 56 and I was very close to her. I actually had a little bit of a premonition the last time I saw her. I was with my family and we were at Grandma's house. She walked us to the car. I got in the car and then got out of the car because I thought, "What if that's the last time I see her." I remember waving good-bye and thinking that. Then, ten days later she died. She died of an asthma attack. She was not particularly sick. I wasn't aware of her being sick and she was only 56. But, when she died, I felt I got tuned in somehow, maybe to the spiritual world. I remember hearing noises and voices and having all kinds of feelings in those first days after she died. I also saw that it completely threw our family for a loop. I knew as a ten-year-old that everybody eventually dies but I was thinking, why doesn't anyone know how to handle this?

I was watching my grandfather behave in one way and my parents behave in another. All the while my parents were very comforting and loving to me, but I could tell that things were out of control in some way. I became very curious about grief. I got the message very quickly that it was not okay to talk about this.

That was back in the days with no Google! In order to look at grief and feelings about death, I decided to go to the library. I remember asking the librarian, where there were books on death. She was really appalled that I asked the question. I got the message right away that there was something really fishy about death.

Somehow when I was about 12 or 13, I got books about the afterlife. I brought them home and I hid them. My mother found them and asked why I was reading them. So, even then, there was a little bit of shame around this whole idea of grieving. I began to watch what happened when other people's family members died. I began to keep a little journal of the anniversary death of my grandmother. I would write to myself as each year passed. In a way, I was honoring her by doing that to keep her spirit alive.

Andrea: It is so amazing that you took the initiative with grief and followed the curiosity and reactions. My brother died of SIDS (Sudden Infant Death Syndrome) when I was four years old. When I was 30, I had my own two little daughters and I asked my mother how she dealt with the loss of her child. I didn't remember anyone talking about him. It was like he was whisked away. I wondered, what happened to my little brother. Where was he?

    I asked her how she coped with it. She said, *"He was dead. He was gone. That was it."* A part of me was shocked by her words. But, the other part of me knew what she was saying. No one talked about it then. There was no support. It would have been unnatural to talk about it. She told me that my Dad was transferred from Minnesota to Virginia for his work because they wanted to move us from the house where my brother had died. This move took my mother away from the only community support she had. No one was trying to be mean, they were just trying to figure it out and not talking about it seemed like the thing to do.

Debbie: Sometimes there is so much grief it is just hard to hold it in a container. Did your parents stay married?

Andrea: Yes

Debbie: Because the divorce rate is very high among couples who have lost a child for the same reason. There is so much grief that the container can't hold it. People do things in order to get out of the pain. It really is about finding the right kind of support to be able to let it go. People have grief trapped in them. As a coach, I was working with people who were in their 40's, 50's, even 60's and there were many people who had a child and grieved like that. It could be anything from a 6-year old neighbor next door who died. They held the grief inside of them for 30, 40, 50 years.

Andrea: I know that is true, because I had a son who had a congenital heart defect. After one of his open heart surgeries, my parents sat across his bed and talked about their son, thirty years later. It was one of the healing moments that can happen with grief.

    I am always amazed how life leads us to experiences with a common thread. Here you were ten and then twelve and you were exploring and honoring your grandmother in the way that you did and you had this curiosity. I know that part of your story is you became a newspaper reporter. Tell us a little bit about that. I know there was a connection there with grief.

Debbie: I became a newspaper reporter in the period of time when women were entering the newsrooms en masse. I went into a pretty male dominated profession with a group of other women. Because I read so much about grief and dying and I had my own thoughts and ideas about how to talk about it, as a reporter and with other women, we became superstars by being able to talk with people.

I remember being sent out on a murder kidnapping. I spent hours and hours with the little girl's family talking about their loss. As a reporter, I was able to deeply satisfy that part of me that wanted to speak about something that was so deeply painful.

At one point, I had a story on the front page of the newspaper. I had covered a murder and talked with the family, got lots of information and wrote about it. I worked for a newspaper in Columbus, Ohio. The police, the detectives, called my city editor and were upset. They wanted to know how we had so much information. The city editor said, *"You need to hire yourself some women who really know how to talk to people."* But, it really came from my understanding that people who are in pain, if given the right circumstances, need to be supported and allowed to talk.

Of course, people grieve in many, many different ways. I never had anyone who was really going through that kind of trauma or tragedy not want to talk and open up.

Andrea: When you can create an environment for people to grieve and express, I think that is the gift that you brought there. It was that you understood grief, you had looked at it, you experienced it and you had looked at it from so many different angles that you were creating an environment that welcomed people in to talk about it.

Debbie: There was also the notion that as a newspaper reporter you are to remain objective. It was kind of a dichotomy because there is a general fear of reporters and how much you share. And sometimes I would say to the family, *is it okay if I say that?* They always told me much more than I had room to share. It was a very funny situation in many ways.

It led me to further know, it is really important to have support and to be able to express in some way.

Andrea: Yes, there are all kinds of ways to experience grief and to release it.

I would love to have you share about Libby. She was such an incredible teacher in so many ways in your life. She taught you so much about grief.

Debbie: At the same time, I was working at the newspaper, I met someone and we fell in love. He took me home to meet his family. When he picked me up and we were driving over, I was terribly nervous. He said to me with a look of shock on his face, *"I need to tell you something before we go to my parent's house."* He was very nervous. He said, *"You know how I told you my mother was a nurse?"* I said, *"Yes."* In a very conspiratorial tone he said, *"She deals with terminally ill people."* I remember feeling so joyful and my nervousness flew away. I thought, *oh my gosh, I am going to meet someone who knows about grief.*

From the very moment, I met Libby she was so amazing. I always remember her opening up the back door and reaching out her hand, pulling me inside into this whole new life and world. This was in 1978. And even that night she was wearing her pin that said **Libby Bradford, Hospice**. Back then, hospice was so new in this country. It only came to the United States in the 1970's. Libby brought hospice to her area in Central Ohio. It was so new that most people called it Hoe-Spice. Libby wore her tag wherever she went so people could say Hoe-Spice and she could correct them; tell them it is hospice and tell them what hospice is.

Andrea: Talk about a society that had no awareness of grief and dying at that time!

Debbie: It is phenomenal when you think about this in our lifetime. I can't imagine now that there is anyone who hasn't heard of hospice.

So, this evening began a ten-year period. I married Libby's son. I continued to develop my career as a newspaper reporter and then press secretary for a Governor and a Presidential candidate. I was Deputy Press Secretary for John Glenn who was an astronaut and a Presidential candidate. So, I was moving along in my career and Libby was developing hospice which met a lot of resistant. Many physicians felt that this was killing people not to treat them, to allow them to die in dignity, in comfort and to treat them in a way that they had no pain. There was a huge struggle.

We had these parallel careers and she mothered me in the most wonderful mothering, mother-in-law, friendship way. I loved her dearly. I called her my best friend.

After I knew her for ten years, she became ill. I thought it was so odd because she didn't seem to be getting better. She had some tests. And one day, at lunch, it dawned on me. She's a nurse. She must know what is wrong with her. I asked her if she knew what was wrong with her. She said, *"If I die, it will be okay."* We were in the restaurant but I burst into tears and yelled out loud, *"If you die, it will not be okay!"*

She was diagnosed. This woman who had taught scores of nurses and physicians how to help people die was given a diagnosis that she would live less than a year. She lived for 8 months. During that time, she taught me how to die and how to live. Because I saw in dying and being with someone almost every day, as they were dying, helped me really learn how I wanted to live my life. It really woke me up. And at the same time, I learned so many practical tips from her, from the stand point of grieving. We talked about what would happen after she died, how I would feel, and she told me, *we all grieve alone, but we heal in community.*

Andrea: That is such an important point. We cannot grieve for someone else. As a mother myself, when my son died, I had two daughters and actually had a baby born two weeks after my son died, which is a whole other story. But, with my daughters, all I could do was be there and observe. I couldn't grieve for them. I couldn't figure it out for them.

Debbie: How old were they when your son died?

Andrea: They were eight and nine. And when my husband died, my daughters were 12, 20 and 21. And even then, there were things I couldn't do. That is such a wise statement from Libby. **We grieve alone but we heal in community.** There are things people can do in community to support us, after the initial period of feeling numb in grieving and to find ways to connect.

Debbie: One of the most common questions I hear from people is they don't really know what to say to someone who is grieving. If someone is grieving, the simpler thing is to say, "I'm sorry or I'm here for you or you are always welcome to talk to me or I love you." When we are grieving we are hyper-sensitive to noise and to things that people say.

My father died six years ago. I am aware of the world of grief, but I was reminded of how comforting it was when close friends who might not normally say it to me, but said, *"I love you. Is there anything else I'm supposed to say?"* They were so sweet. I greatly appreciated that. Periods of grief can last for a long time. Just asking people if you can help them. *"Can I send someone over to mow your lawn? Can I bring you a meal?"* That sort of thing is so incredibly powerful to people who are grieving.

Andrea: I want to highlight what you just said because I had one very close friend who felt totally helpless as to what to do to help me after my husband died. At that point, I couldn't really coach her on what to say to me because I had no idea. What I heard you say, Debbie, is to offer help by specifically offering the help you can provide.

Sometimes saying to someone, *can I help you,* is hard to even hear when feeling numbed out There were points where I was so numb I might think what does the word *"help"* mean?

But, saying, *"Can I help by sending someone over to cut your grass? Could I bring a meal over on Friday? Would you like me to come and sit with you?* Specific offerings make it easier to say yes or no. One of the greatest gifts is being willing to witness someone's pain without needing to fix it and to offer what you can.

I would also add to your wonderful list of things to say even just reaching out and squeezing someone's hand. Sometimes there are no words and a simple gesture like touching someone's hand can mean so much.

Debbie: In the Jewish culture, the idea that there are no words for this, the tradition is to not even speak but to hug for the first 24 hours. I think it is a beautiful cultural ritual.

When my sister was young, in her 40's, her husband was dying. A friend offered to take her kitties to the vet and get their shots. When you are going through anticipatory grief you can't always think of what the words mean and stuff doesn't get done. It is helpful to be very specific about what you can do. That's a great point.

Andrea: Yes, to offer a specific thing. Because it is easier to say no, I have someone who is going to cut the grass. Or to say no to a meal because we have three pans of lasagna in the freezer and we are going out for Chinese tonight.

I have lived in wonderful communities where the minute someone was sick or grieving or there was a loss going on, immediately there was a food chain. So, normally I would not turn food away! But, to offer what you can, maybe driving the children to Girl Scouts or whatever you know they need and allowing a space for the grieving person to say yes or no.

Debbie: I found it comforting when someone would say how much they miss the person. Even when you said the word Libby, it made me smile so big because it makes me feel so good when someone acknowledges that person I love so much.

When my father died, I went to the post office. One of the postal workers said **how much they were going to miss my Dad and how beautifully he dressed.** It was so funny. No one else said that and it was so true about him. I thought, what a great comforting statement. I would say to everyone, don't think if you bring up the person it is going to make someone sad. Usually it makes someone feel good if you say something specific about missing them; if you do.

Andrea: Absolutely and to take the cues from their reaction. I love to talk about my deceased husband and my deceased son; to me they are still such a part of my life. For me, I can't imagine not wanting to talk about them. They were a part of my life and will be forever.

They both had such an impact on my life. There are so many memories of love and more and I know that not everyone feels that way.

It has been 21 years ago since Libby died. Do you have moments when you feel really happy or really sad when you think of a memory?

Debbie: Yes, I do. Obviously looking at grief over such a long time, I remember every moment. I want everyone out here to know, everyone grieves differently and this idea that we should grieve and snap out of it at some point is just not the truth. In some of the wonderful Elisabeth Kubler-Ross books, she is the one who really framed the process of grief, which is not a tidy process at all. One of the ways she posited was in the end, we reach an acceptance. As much as I love her work, and respect her and feel she laid out an amazing foundation that grieving is a process, I think over time we accommodate the loss.

Christmas and Thanksgiving were really wonderful in the world of Libby. This time of year reminds me a lot of her and something will come up. I have Christmas decorations from her, candles, a beautiful glass icicle mobile. I always get a little teary. I have had rituals over the holidays. She and I always used to have a breakfast together to go Christmas shopping and we would buy cinnamon rolls. For years, I used to buy cinnamon rolls and put them out for the birds because she would love that, too.

I guarantee that something has come up in the last month or two and I got teary and then I moved through it. I have both the happy and sad of missing her. I am grateful she was in my life. It allowed me to learn so much. It allowed me not to be afraid of dying. I was 31 or 32 when she died and I am no longer afraid.

At one point she took my shoulders and said, *"I know it's really hard for you, but I will not be here."* I cried and sobbed and she held me. It was amazing and she fostered some real conversation. It was an incredible gift. Most of us don't experience that. By the time Libby died, we really had said everything that I was capable of at that point. Now, I am in my 50's and I have so much more I would say to her now.

Andrea: For me, it was my grandmother. She died when I was in my 20's and she had so much wisdom she wanted to share with me. I have wished that she was here for a conversation. I have had moments of deep sobbing over it. Like, this is the moment I could understand what you were trying to say to me when I was 10 or when I was 16.

Debbie: Do you talk to her?

Andrea: I have talked with her. I went through a period when I had a very serious illness. My immune system was attacking my muscles. I had an autoimmune condition. I can remember feeling like I really wanted her. I actually went to a hotel for a weekend. I had small kids and my husband watched the kids and I needed to have some time by myself. I brought letters I had saved that she had written to me. I read them out loud and sobbed and sobbed and sobbed. It was incredibly healing. I do feel her with me. I believe that life goes on and all of our deceased loved ones are with us.

Debbie: I want to point out that was a supreme act of self-care. You put yourself some place safe and private and you were able to really let go. There is a wonderful saying, *"Like soap is to the body, Tears are to the soul."*

When I was in the height of my coaching practice, I would say, *how many gallons of tears do you have?* If you ask yourself when you are grieving, you'll know. People will say anywhere from 9 gallons to 90 million gallons. We can greatly heal by opening that up. Some people cry, some people paint, some people dance. A woman told me she threw ice cubes in the tub or shower because it felt like breaking glass. It served that purpose of healing a deep, guttural pain. Some form of expression to move it out of your body.

Grieving is like being in an internal car accident. If you've lost someone you loved deeply, you look fine on the outside, but inside is another matter. It felt like my arms and legs were broken but I had to keep moving about. If you were able to see those internal injuries, you would take extreme care of yourself. You would go gently, you would go gingerly and people would be able to see how much you are hurting. That really is the number one prescription when you are grieving. **Be gentle.**

Grieving comes and goes and flows depending on your relationship to the person. It is so important to take care of yourself.

People expect us to get back out into the world and sometimes we have to but it is so important to double, triple and quadruple our self-care. We just can't keep going. And the holidays raise something completely different because part of it is we have to keep the spirit going or keep it up for our children and our family. Often there are multiple people in a family who are grieving and so it is essential we really take care of ourselves. It is essential we are with people who will give us some comfort.

Do you have ways that you have found during the holidays that have helped you work through your grief?

Andrea: When, my husband died and it was Christmas a few months later, I bought a special necklace for each of my daughters and I talked with them about the strength of women. I acknowledged that we were all grieving in different ways, but that the one thing we all had was each other. It really seemed to impact them. I didn't make them do anything they didn't want to do on that holiday. I just had a moment to solidify the people who were here and bringing in the memories.

Debbie: It really helps me that I have a few of Libby's Christmas things. Libby died 21 years ago and my father died six years ago. My father and I would sit up and he would tell me stories on Christmas Eve; stories about his mother and about what they would do on Christmas Eve. His mother died when he was in his early twenties.

I make sure I take some quiet time during the holiday season. Also, moving our bodies is important.

I am so glad you brought up divorce and life threatening illness and pet grief because these are all huge, huge, huge in the category of grieving. Sometimes we may feel that they are a lesser than grief and there is no such thing, as a lesser than grief. Whatever it is that pains you, pains you.

Andrea: To me, if there is a change or a loss or anything that brings in disappointment it is in the category of grieving and acknowledging and feeling the feelings is important.

Some people sent in questions through the chat line, Debbie.

How do you handle people who tell you it is time to get over it?

Debbie: My number one way for people who say *"snap out of it"* or *"how long has it been now"* or *"you should be over that."*

You can say, *"Thank you, but that's not helpful to me right now"* or some variation that you feel comfortable with because it isn't helpful.

Over the years I have actually said that a number of times because people are so awkward in our culture around grief. We need to help train them. People will usually back down and say they are sorry.

If we can tell them what is helpful, or let them know, *I am going to grieve until I feel better,* and *I'm working on it.* People want us to feel better so they can feel better.

Andrea: Yes, they are uncomfortable with it and want to fix it in some way. But, there is nothing to fix.

Debbie: I am saying this for almost all cases. Sometimes a licensed psychotherapist may assess something differently. But, as long as people need to grieve is as long as it is going to take. Nobody should tell you how long to grieve.

The worst case I ever heard was a woman who said how wonderful her office had been to her when her mother died. Then, three days after her mother's death her manager said, *we need you back at work. We've been good enough to you.* They expected her to be over it. Her mother had been ill but not for a long time, 5 or 6 months. With the death, now her grieving was just beginning in another way.

Andrea: Let's list a few things "not" to say to someone so we can educate each other. I know I have said things I wished that I hadn't said because I wanted to say something to someone and make them feel better.

Probably the worst thing anyone said to me was at my son's funeral. *"Well, you knew he was going to die didn't you?"* No, actually, I didn't. He had two open-heart surgeries and was doing well. I did not expect he would be diagnosed with a 4th stage neuroblastoma cancer and be dead a week later.

Debbie: People do this in their awkwardness. Especially when we are dealing with babies or a miscarriage.

Things not to say.

"Call me if you need anything." Instead, offer to check back in with them. Ask if you can call back in a day, or a few days and do it.

"Time will heal everything." Sometimes time doesn't heal everything. It changes things, but doesn't heal everything.

"Be grateful your loved one isn't suffering any longer." We may say that to ourselves, but it doesn't really feel good to hear it from someone else.

"Let's not talk about anything sad" Let's change the subject.

"What you should do now is…" Giving unsolicited advice. People in grief do not need to be fixed. They need love and comfort and support and care and gentleness.

I have often thought that we need to wear a button like the pink ribbon so that people know we're grieving. Maybe like a little dove so people know to treat you sweetly and kindly when you're grieving.

Andrea: And an instruction, like saying, *I'm sorry is enough.*
   We are nearing the end of the show. Is there anything you would like to say now to our listeners?

Debbie: Especially with the holidays coming up, I want to urge everyone to take good care of themselves. If you are grieving, to not feel like you need to take on the holiday season in its entirety. Pick out a few things that would be fun and comforting so you don't end up starting the New Year exhausted or sick. Or do something really different for the holidays, like work in a soup kitchen. After Libby died, I worked in an animal shelter over the holidays and it really lifted my spirits.

Move your body. Go to the Y and go swimming. Really take extra care and comfort. And don't think you have to do the holidays the way you normally do them.

Andrea: Thanks for being on the show tonight Debbie.

Debbie Phillips *is the founder of Women on Fire®, a membership organization that provides inspiration, strategies and support for women to live extraordinary lives. She authored the award-winning book Women on Fire: 20 Inspiring Women Share Their Life Secrets (and Save You Years of Struggle!), Volumes 1 and 2.*
http://www.womenonfire.com/

Grief Transformation Show #2
Grief Relief with Debbie Phillips

November 22, 2010
http://tobtr.com/1369271

Andrea Hylen

Chapter Three

How to Stay Open to Feelings and Take Control of Grief
Andrea Hylen

Show originally aired on November 26, 2010

Tonight, I will share a variety of ways to open to the feelings of grief and how to take control and manage your grief in a way that will help you with healing. We will explore how grief can resurface in your life and how to open to the feelings and discover the deeper source of pain.

    Grief surfaces at predictable and unpredictable times. Revisiting the same feelings is normal. Learning how to respect the feelings when they appear and creating the time and space to feel is important. Situations can appear from the past in relation to the present and bring up moments of grieving. A little bit later in the show, I am going to share some details about an experience I had today and steps I took to stay in the feelings and allow for new awareness.

    Briefly now, I woke up this morning stirred up about the loss of my husband's business property. I sold the property a few years after my husband died. I sold it to someone who was making monthly payments to pay for the property over the next few years in monthly interest checks and in a final balloon payment. The man declared bankruptcy before completing contract. I lost $150,000, my life savings and that loss cost me an additional $50,000 in related expenses and loss of income. Even though this was something from the past and I had grieved and moved on, I have been feeling waves of grief in the last few days. My question to myself this morning was, *"Why am I grieving this again?"*

    The truth is a situation happened in the last few days that really triggered that old memory and grief. Before I go into more detail and how I took control of the feelings today, I want to share a simple story about old grief connecting us with making a change.

A Wave of Grief

My daughter and I were watching a TV show called The Bachelorette. Some of you may have seen the show when The Bachelorette was Ali.

On the show, 12 men spend time pursuing one woman. They go on group and individual dates with the bachelorette. At the end of each show, she gives a limited number of roses to the men. The men who do not receive a rose go home that week.

During this season, I saw a lesson about how grief shows up and shows us where we have desire. It happened when two of the men left the show to return home to former girlfriends. I was really struck by one of the stories and I felt like it is the perfect example of what happens when our heart expands in love.

One of the men on the show was falling in love with the bachelorette. Week after week, Frank was falling for Ali, but he also seemed conflicted and sad. He didn't know what was wrong with him and the bachelorette was questioning why he needed so much reassurance from her. They were both falling in love with each other.

The ultimate moment came when the Bachelorette, Ali, selected the last four men and spent time with each of their families. When she was in Frank's hometown of Chicago, he began to realize that he was having feelings for his old girlfriend. He and his girlfriend had broken up right before he came on the show.

Without taking the time to analyze the whole situation between Frank, his girlfriend and Ali, I want to focus on something that truly happens for all of us. (So, let's let go of the TV drama for this example.)

The show defined a moment we all experience at times. We are going along in our lives and we feel really happy. We are falling in love with a job, a house, an idea or a person and all of a sudden we feel sad. It can be a blip of a moment or it can deepen and stop us in our tracks.

Frank and Ali were awakening to love. As part of his awakening, Frank began to feel conflict and sadness. He was remembering the love he had for his last girlfriend. When the feelings surfaced, he had an opportunity to identify them, feel them and heal them. Or act on them. He decided to go see his old girlfriend for closure. When they connected again, they both realized they still had feelings for each other. They are together now and he is off the show.

Whenever your heart expands with love, you are shaking it loose, and you are stirring memories from the past. A light is shining into your heart. It is one of the reasons we all grieve moments that happened many years ago when something happens in the present. A song, a smell, a food, or a location can trigger and awaken a memory.

I have experienced this a number of times since my husband died five years ago. We were married for 15 years and had many dreams for our future. When my husband died, some of the dreams we had together died, too.

One dream was around a house we were renovating together. I completed a few things after he died and then slowly the dream of completing the house died within me. A new dream of selling the house and all of my personal belongings emerged. Even with the clarity that it was time to release the house and all of my daughters being in agreement with the decision, as I cleared and released items in the house, I grieved over and over again. Layers of my identity with my husband were dying. When I sold the house, I was filled with joy and new possibilities and still there was more to feel and heal.

I wanted to share this story in relation to opening to grief. We might have moments when we are confused about what we are thinking and feeling. There is more to grieving than is right in front of you, even with the death of a loved one. The loss of a spouse could bring up feelings of abandonment from your childhood. The loss of a child could bring up feelings of inadequacy.

As you take the time to examine the emotion, identifying the underlying feelings, there is a gift in feeling and healing old wounds.

<u>Creating an Environment for Opening to Feelings</u>

Now, here is the rest of the story that happened today when I was grieving the loss of money and my husband's business. I was expecting a paycheck from a client this week that was delayed. When I deposited one of the other checks today, the bank put an unexpected two-week hold on it. All of the feelings came flooding over me about how I would not be living check to check, if I had the money from the sale of the business property. The feelings of losing all of my money and being forced to create an income flow while I was finishing the last few years of home schooling my daughter returned. When I woke up this morning, I felt a wave of emotion. I stopped for a minute to identify the feelings. I closed my eyes and connected with my heart. I asked myself the question, *"What is really surfacing right here?"*

    I identified anger. I dug down deeper and started to ask myself some questions. First I reflected, *"Wow, I'm feeling anger. What wants to be healed with this? Is there something for me to do or to learn or should I just sit with the feelings?"* The anger was a huge discovery for me because I was raised to be a nice girl. Nice girls don't get angry. I am still working on that one. I thought that was amazing to see that. Wow! I am feeling angry. I played with that and dug deeper.

    Sometimes I can identify an action step to take now. Sometimes I get an immediate answer. This morning it felt like it may be time to do some forgiveness work; Forgiveness of myself; Forgiveness of the man who declared bankruptcy; Forgiveness of what is happening on the Earth right now with all of the changes.

    Sometimes there is no response when I ask a question and I know I need to wait patiently. An answer will arrive in the hour, day or week. Sometimes when I ask, *"What are you feeling,"* and I don't really know what I am feeling, I just say *"Okay, I am open to knowing what I am feeling."* I enter into my day and surrender. The answers will appear by setting the intention of wanting to know. Sometimes in a minute and sometimes the answer will come in a day or a week.

    One of the ways to explore the feelings more is by journaling. I regularly write a page in a journal in the morning to do a brain dump to see what feelings I woke up with this morning. Many mornings I wake up with a song playing in my head. I reflect on the words in the song. It is another clue as to what I am thinking and feeling. By writing down the feelings or memories, I can keep exploring.

I may feel guided to e-mail a letter to a friend or to write in my journal about it. I may write about forgiveness to the man who declared bankruptcy for instance without mailing it or I may write a letter to him in my journal. I have written letters to deceased loved ones when I have been feeling things. I have even taken the writings and spoken them out loud in the room to declare what I am feeling.

Another way of opening to feelings is to allow yourself to sink into the emotions. This morning when I was thinking about the business property and the bankruptcy I really felt like identifying the anger was all I needed to do this morning. I acknowledged the anger and let it be there. I didn't really feel like I needed to process it right now. It felt like it was stirring and there would be something to learn and let it bubble. It may have surfaced because I was going to share the process of feelings on the radio show tonight. One of the gifts was to feel that and be able to talk about it here with you.

Sometimes sinking into the emotion of grief means you play music or write and you let yourself cry. It could be that you create an environment for laughter. You turn on Saturday Night Live or you read a joke book or you look through pictures that make you laugh.

It may mean that you need to stomp or shout or pound a pillow. Let yourself sink into the emotion and do what you need to do to feel and clear the emotion out of your body.

When Debbie Phillips, the founder of Women on Fire, was on the show, she shared the idea of throwing ice cubes into the bathtub to release emotions. It feels like you are breaking dishes or glass but nothing is destroyed. It is a physical release.

Another thing I did today was walk. I went for three different walks in between working today. I started the day off with a walk to the coffee shop. I ran two errands at two
different times today and decided to walk. Part of the guidance was to clear the feeling from the physical body. That is very different than denying it or pushing it away. To actually let it flow through you physically.

Take a walk. Go for a run. Swim. Do some other type of exercise. My favorites are going for a walk and cranking up the music and dancing. I dance in my apartment and right now we do not have furniture in the living room and it is a great place to dance and let loose.

Another way to honor the feelings is to feel gratitude or express appreciation. I was walking past the mirror today and caught a glimpse of myself. I stopped and looked myself right in the eye and told myself what a great job I am doing. I said, *"Good for you"*, that I was identifying the emotion of anger and that I know anger is not an easy emotion for me to express. I looked myself right in the eye and congratulated myself.

Another reminder in opening to your feelings is to be gentle with yourself and know that your heart is expanding to experience more love. That is one of the greatest gifts to me, the opportunity to feel something so deeply in this loss or in the death of a person or a situation or a relationship and to know that my heart is expanding. As you can experience the grief, you will experience more love in your life. You will have moments when the grief has moved through you in a new way and you will see life clearer and with more joy and you will open yourself up to love.

When you get to the end of this list of ideas, and you feel great, and another wave of grief comes either in the next day or a month or in a year, open the list and repeat the steps to feel, to heal and to release. It is an ongoing opportunity to keep transforming. When you feel those moments of grieving, they are here as a gift.

I talk about my son and my husband quite a bit on the show because there are so many different aspects to the losses and the relationship I had with each of them. There is richness in the reflection, the discussion and the honoring of the gifts that each has given to me during this journey.

Grief surfaces at predictable and unpredictable times. Revisiting the same feelings is normal. Learning how to respect the feelings when they appear and creating the time and space to feel is important.

I had an unexpected moment of grieving remembering the death of my son, Cooper. It was June 12th and it would have been my son's 17th birthday. He had died 15 years earlier from a 4th stage neuro-blastoma cancer at the age of 19 months. I shared some of this story in the first radio show. Here are more of the details and some of the ways I healed on this day.

Our family acknowledged his birthday every year. We would bake a cake, look at his photo album, and talk about his laugh. For a little guy, he had such a great sense of humor. It still makes us all laugh when we think or talk about his laugh of the day and the antics we would go through to score a laugh from him. On his birthday remembrances, after his death, we would prepare a feast of his favorite foods which always included Pillsbury cinnamon rolls. As the years have continued, sometimes we have not all been together but we remember by calling each other or posting a Facebook message on our walls.

On this day, his 17th birthday, I woke up with a huge pain in my heart. I woke up remembering the day we decided to turn off the life support. In 19 months, Cooper had two open-heart surgeries, a shunt for hydrocephalus and a hernia operation. In the last few days of his life, he had been diagnosed with cancer and had slipped into a coma from the pressure of the tumor. With about 10 doctors in the room sitting in a conference room around a table, my husband asked one of the doctors what he would do if it were his son. He said, *"I would ask myself how many hits does a kid need to take?"* We knew in that moment that there was nothing else that could be done and we were willing to let him go. My husband and I spent the next 24 hours talking with each other at Cooper's bedside. We asked each other what we needed to do to feel complete. Many friends came by the ICU to say goodbye.

On this morning, almost 15 years later, the memories and the feelings of letting my son go were vivid. I cleared my schedule and gave myself time to feel the feelings without any judgment or the need to uncover why I was feeling this pain. The grief had reappeared as if Cooper had died yesterday. I did not waste any energy trying to figure out why this was happening on this day. It didn't matter. All I knew was I was feeling the pain as if my son died yesterday.

I have been talking tonight about a variety of ways to open to the feelings. I used some of the things on the list that day. I created a safe environment to embrace the emotions by clearing the space. I played music. I looked at some pictures. I let myself sink into the emotion. I cried. I laughed. One of the emotions I felt on that day was gratitude for his birth and for what the loss had taught me over the years. The richness in life is our ability to love with depth. Grief is the path that will deepen the love and connect you to the Oneness of all life. Here are words from a beautiful song by the Beatles that express many of my feelings.

In My Life by The Beatles

There are places I'll remember
All my life, though some have changed
Some forever, not for better
Some have gone and some remain

All these places had their moments
With lovers and friends I still can recall
Some are dead and some are living
In my life, I've loved them all

To me one of the things grief represents, is this ability we have to love so deeply, to love life, to love our jobs, to love our homes, to love our loved ones, to love the richness of it. It is in the loving that we can feel the depth of the pain when there is a loss. By honoring whenever it comes and to create the environment for that, allows the richness to enter for the experience.

Take Control of Your Grief

I learned something very valuable by grieving the loss of my son in 1993 and the loss of my husband in 2005.

There is a fine line between the contrast of denying your feelings and immersing yourself in the grief for long periods of time. When I had the wave of grief arrive on my son's birthday in 2008, I let myself sink into it on that day. When I woke up the next morning, I felt complete. I felt I had released something. I felt clear and alive and open and loving. If I needed another day or two, I would have allowed myself time to sink into that.

But after the death of my son and my husband twelve years later, I learned to make a distinction in the timing of when and how long I would allow myself to sink into the emotions. There comes a time when you have to take control of your grief.

I had an unusual situation in 1993 when my son died at the age of 19 months; I was 8 ½ months pregnant with my fourth child. My son, Cooper died on January 15; the memorial service was on January 23; I gave birth to my daughter, Hannah on January 30. Take a minute to imagine and think of the depth of emotion, the contrasts between the deep, raw grief of losing a child and the ecstatic joy of welcoming a new born baby. That is what was happening in our house.

The details of life kept me busy during the first year of grieving. The arms I had wrapped around my son were now wrapped around my baby daughter. I grieved and cried and I began to reconnect to life. I couldn't just stop everything. Who would have taken care of my new baby girl?

With all of the operations, therapies and pain during Cooper's life, he was very sensitive to his environment. I had traveled very little with him and was isolated in the house to keep the environment calm for him. The first year of grieving Cooper and caring for Hannah, I flew from Maryland to Florida to visit my sister, went on a two-week car trip with my mother exploring our family history, and to Massachusetts to
visit family. My two older daughters were in school and stayed with my ex-husband. Part of my grieving process was to reconnect with loved ones around the country.

Then, the one-year anniversary of his death was approaching and for two weeks, I immersed myself in grief. Everyone said that the first year would be the hardest, right? The first anniversary of a birthday, all the holidays, special moments experiencing the loss and the first year without my loved one and then it would get better, right? Somewhere inside of me, I thought that if I let myself grieve and feel the depth of loss with my whole heart and soul, that I would never feel this deep pain again. I knew I would miss him and always remember him, but I was hoping I could heal the deep pain.

It was easy to immerse myself and remember every little detail surrounding my son's life. By the time my son entered the hospital for the last time, I was a walking encyclopedia for every symptom, treatment, and medication. The details were imprinted on my brain. At the one-year anniversary, I was reviewing every detail of every day, leading up to his death, the details of the last two weeks of his life in the hospital. I cried. I read every book I could find on life after death and books about the loss of a loved one. I wanted to grieve until I felt healed. I sat in the rocking chair with my arms wrapped around his favorite toys and cried. I curled up in a fetal position on my bed and cried for hours. I looked at his pictures. I sang his favorite songs. The pain I felt in my heart, the flow of tears, and the sobs of feeling the loss of his physical presence here were raw and real.

I wanted to feel it all so I could let the pain go forever. I thought that I could cry it all out and I would never have to grieve again. I didn't know that grief would always be there, not dominating my life, but present as part of the tapestry of life experiences.

By the end of the month of grief immersion, I was physically ill. For the next few months, I became weaker and weaker physically. The diagnosis was an autoimmune condition called polymiositis. My immune system was
attacking my muscles. It took me 3 years to recover from the illness and the final part of the healing was a homeopathic remedy that was connected with healing grief.

One of the greatest lessons from that experience, I learned that grief immersion for a month was too much for my physical body. I also learned that grieving is a dance with different rhythms that last a lifetime. There is no way you will remove all of the pain from your heart forever. I learned that when grief appears my heart is expanding to open to more love and to feel it.

When my husband died, I took control of my grief. In the first few days after his death, I cuddled on the couch with my daughters. We cried, watched movies, looked at family pictures, ate junk food and the healthy food people were bringing to us. On the 4th day, I made us move our bodies. I told my daughters we were going to go through the motions to move some of the grief out of our bodies. We went out to dinner, walking several blocks to the local Chinese restaurant, ordering food, packing most of it to take back to the house with us.

From that point on, every day we engaged in life with something every day. Simple things like taking a walk, climbing into the car to drive a few blocks to fill the gas tank, paying a few bills and finding something every day to create opportunities to connect with life again.

I knew that I would never forget my husband and the amazing journey we had in life together. I knew I would carry him in my heart together. Within the experience, I found the rhythm of grieving, releasing and living life again, one step at a time.

I want to end the call by saying that everyone grieves differently. I spent the last year inwardly reflecting and writing about 50 years of grieving and transformation. I process grief in words by talking, including writing in a journal. Writing brings the thoughts out of my head and puts them onto paper.

I have seen, with my daughters, how different they each grieve. One of my daughters doesn't want to talk about it at all. She has favorite mementos of her father she keeps with her and she has several of his T-shirts that she likes to wear to bed. She likes to exercise and listen to music and she has a dog she cuddles with for emotional support.

I have one daughter who is very similar to me and we process everything. We talk about every emotion, looking at it and processing it. We love it, we hate it, and we put words to it. Written word and spoken word. She also writes poetry.

My other daughter processes emotion and moves the energy into a project. She creates tangible products for her theatre company or knitting or cooking. She puts her energy, emotions and love into those things.

Grief is a personal dance that we each learn. During the holidays, you will feel a variety of feelings. You might see lights on someone's house or on the Christmas trees and you feel so happy and think, *oh, I love that.* And in that moment of feeling love, it also opens you to other memories and feelings. And that is all they are, other feelings and other memories.
It may be that you walk with them, honor them, feel them and then you wave back into the joy.

I honor you for having the courage to feel your feelings, to look at the losses and to know that all of these opportunities are leading you to a deeper and richer life.

That's all I have for tonight. I thank you for coming to the show and I hope there was at least one thing tonight that stirred your heart, opened you to an idea to live a life worth celebrating. Blessings to you.

Grief Transformation Show #6
Open to Feelings and Take Control of Grief

November 26, 2010
http://tobtr.com/1369275

Chapter Four

The Voice That Calls You Home
Guest: Andrea Raynor,
Hospice and Ground Zero Chaplain

Show originally aired on December 6, 2010

Introduction: Andrea Raynor a graduate of Harvard Divinity School, is a United Methodist minister, a chaplain, and a cancer survivor. She served as the Chaplain to the Jansen Memorial Hospice in Tuckahoe, New York for over ten years, has worked with the homeless in NYC and Boston, and was a pastor to churches in NY, CT, and MA. In the aftermath of September 11th, she served as a chaplain to the morgue at Ground Zero, offering blessings over remains and support to the many workers there.

(Andrea Raynor uses the name Andie. In the following conversation, "Andrea" is Andrea Hylen and "Andie" is Andrea Raynor)

Andrea: I want to start by talking about the mustard seed. I had a personal connection to this story in your book. My grandmother gave me a bracelet when I was 5 years old that had a heart with a mustard seed. On the back, the words read, *"If ye have faith as a grain of mustard seed, nothing shall be impossible to you."* When I look back on the moment of receiving that, it has been a core piece I have carried in my heart forever. Even though I didn't grow up in a family that studied the bible. I am always fascinated by how our early life experiences lay a path to our life work. I want to know if you would be willing to share some of the early experiences of mustard seed faith.

Andie: It is interesting. When you say that, I have an immediate image of a little necklace I had. It was a circle with a tiny mustard seed in it. I remember that being both a constant symbol that we just need to have a little faith in our lives and on the other hand, it was also confusing because the Bible also said, *if you have a tiny bit of faith you could move mountains.* When a tragedy happens like a death in your family or in my case in my earliest traumatic death, the loss of a playmate. Then, as a child, you can also say, *did I not have enough faith? Did I not have even that little bit of faith?*

These images that we tumble about from the time we were children to young adults to older adults, the themes keep coming up and up and up. It prompts us to dig deeper into what it is to have that tiny bit of faith. Sometimes that tiny bit of faith means learning to accept that God is present even when the unthinkable happens. Then, we begin to build a deeper well for faith to grow.

I was really blessed growing up. I grew up in a family that was religious in a traditional way. We went to the Methodist church every Sunday. I grew up active in my youth group but we were also a very spiritual home. By that, I mean, we did everything from having Saturday night séances and exploring the supernatural realm always in the context of prayer, to watching my parents be the first people to bring food to someone who was home from the hospital, who lost a loved one. It was faith that was both in action, in worship, and faith that was in spiritual exploration. Those threads definitely began to build my understanding of the Divine as both a mystical presence that we have to move towards with faith and with adventure and also a practical manifestation of the Divine in the actions and acts of kindness and compassion that we do offer one another.

The first memories I can think of that really shook me, I lost a playmate very early on. I was eight years old. We were picnicking with our very best friends. They had four kids. We had six kids. We were out picnicking and the six-year-old boy started complaining he had a headache. By the time we got him home, he was in a coma. A few hours later, he had died of a brain aneurism. The experience that death can come to children at any point, not just to older people, really had a huge impact on me. And perhaps earlier than some people I had to accept the fact that even to faithful people, tragedy can happen.

The positive part of that was watching my parents be friends and be parents to these children. To be the compassionate arms of support for them and to watch this family stay together despite this terrible loss.

That first traumatic loss immediately propelled me into thinking about death as something that is quite possible no matter what age. It wasn't something that happened to old people or bad people, it could just happen.

Andrea: I thought that was such a powerful story and to have that experience imprinted on you from such a young age. I was really struck by how you described your family interacting with the family that had the loss.

I lost a brother when I was four years old and no one talked about it. It was like he disappeared. And even years later, when I asked my mother how she coped with it, she said, *what was there to talk about. He was dead. He was gone. That was it.* I was startled when she first said those words and then I had a deeper understanding. She was really saying, *there was no one to talk to and people didn't talk about it.* She had two small kids to take care of and my Dad's job kept him on the road a lot. There wasn't even that support from a spouse.

To look at the contrast of that, what it could be and how we can reach out to people is important. I am talking about something that happened 50 years ago. It wasn't normal or natural to talk about it in most places. We are giving people more permission to talk about it as a part of life now and how that could be woven into community support. Another part of life is death.

Andie: Sometimes friends are afraid to say the wrong things and so they don't say anything. I have seen this. In my mother's case, what she taught me early on was that by bringing up Matthew, the little boy who had died, to her friend... By inviting the opportunity to speak about him in a way, she brought the little boy close again. She could share her dreams about him and she could share the stories she enjoyed about her son. It wasn't like she was bringing up his name at a time when his mother wasn't thinking about him because she was thinking about him at every turn.

When we are not given the opportunity to talk or to share the stories it can be isolating and it can feel like our loved ones are so far away. I experienced this, when an acquaintance who is now a very dear friend of mine, lost a baby to a SIDS death, sudden infant death syndrome. The baby was 10 months old. We didn't know each other very well. We had daughters the same age and then we had sons who were three months apart. When I brought soup to her, the day after I found out about her son's death, the mother greeted me at the door and said, "You know Andie, this is nice, she needs the soup. But she's going to need you tomorrow and the next day and the next day and the next."

What really happened was people who perhaps wanted to share their sympathy or compassion stayed away. They were afraid of the grief of that mother and afraid of saying the wrong thing. Because of the model of my mother, I called this friend. We spoke every day, probably twice a day for the first year. We saw each other almost every day because she needed that support and she needed to be with someone who let her know it was okay to speak about the death. Even now, I think it is out of fear of saying the wrong thing many of us don't say anything at all.

Andrea: Yes, and having dialogues like this about it and saying to go ahead and reach out. Sometimes it is just letting someone know you are there and you can sit in silence with them. There is nothing you can do to fix it. You can't take it away, but to just let the person know you are there. It can be a really powerful gift.

Andie: I have worked with a lot of volunteers in hospice and one of the questions is, *"What if they ask me why this has happened."* I think many of us who are in the fields of compassion are also fixers. We would love to make things better. We want so much for people to be healed and happy and well. The best advice is you can always say, *"I don't know why this has happened. I am here."* And take that hand. Sometimes it is our presence, more than our words that is really going to help someone who is in pain.

Andrea: I want to ask you two things. What led you to Divinity School and what led you to become a hospice chaplain? I know those are two big questions. If you could share a little bit about each path.

Andie: The first one, what led me to Divinity School was probably a moment of insanity and what led me to hospice was a moment of inspiration. (Laughter) I started out as an undergraduate at Denison University. I started out as a bio pre-med major. I had an interest in medicine, an interest in healing. When I met chemistry, we instantly did not like each other at all and agreed to part ways.

I came to my religion major at Denison very last minute and rather haphazardly. I had taken Theology classes out of interest all along because I was fascinated with the study of Religion. I had grown up, as I said, a very spiritual person. By the time I was finishing my senior year, I realized how much I loved the study of religion or religions of theology. I was doing an Honor's Thesis looking at Liberation Theology coming out of Latin America. When I went to Divinity School, I promised all of my friends I would never become a minister. I was simply going to study theology and to be in a helping field. That is really what I thought of as a doctor, to be in a field where I could offer help to people who were suffering. I took that same impulse of wanting to be a help and a healing presence in the world and thought I would concentrate more on the spiritual.

It was in Divinity school by my second year, I felt a calling to be ordained. Still wasn't quite sure if I saw myself in a secular or a sacred professional setting. I worked with the homeless in Boston. I worked with protective services for the elderly in Boston. Eventually fulfilled this calling to be ordained. I did serve a few churches after being ordained. It was after my children were born that I had gotten this nudge to do hospice. I was filling in for the local chaplain at the hospital who I met. She needed some vacation coverage. During my first call at the hospital, I was present with a young couple who were experiencing what is known as a fetal demise. The baby who was 30 weeks in utero had had the cord wrapped around his neck and had died. The woman had
to deliver the baby. I was with the couple during the delivery. Offered a blessing on the baby. Ended up doing the funeral
for the baby where I met a wonderful funeral director who said the local hospice needed a chaplain.

At that point, I didn't really know what hospice was. I thought of it as a place where someone goes for the last months of their lives. Whereas the hospice I ended up working for was primarily hospice care in one's own home. It is one of those things Andrea, where you think of your path as very jagged and maybe has no rhyme or reason. But, when I look back, it is almost like a clear path beginning with my interest in the medical, wanting to be a spiritual help, and then, here I am in a medical setting doing spiritual care.

Andrea: I love your willingness to share your path and show people the way. It serves us all to hear how that path happened. You didn't just show up at this place. All of the different experiences led you here.

Andie: All of our experiences really do lead all of us to where we are. It is whether we are willing to acknowledge the guidance and the little nudges that have brought us to our present situations. One of the key things is to look back and begin to see how our paths, in some way, have made sense.

Andrea: And all of my experiences is what really got me to talk about grief transformation in this year. I realized I had had experiences throughout my life and had been talking to people and counseling but not really with transforming grief as the focus. But, that was the underlying piece. Not just focusing on people dying but how to live through having had these experiences.
    I am not really sure how to segue into this. So, like a girlfriend, I am just going to say, okay we finished that and what I really want to know is…

Andie: And feel free to cut me off, if I could too long winded.

Andrea: No, this is fantastic! I love it! I would like to talk about some of your experiences and the blessings at Ground Zero. Before we get to that, I know you had a miscarriage right before 9/11. Will you share a little bit about that? Because that is a loss and there aren't necessarily places to talk about that. There aren't pictures of a baby. It is another loss that needs to be talked about.

Andie: Yes. It is amazing how many of us have had miscarriages. My heart just breaks when I think of you losing a child, Andrea, who has already been in your arms. Miscarriages are a hidden loss. In many couples, not all, but in many, it is the loss the mother experiences more deeply. For me, as soon as I had a positive pregnancy test, it meant baby and I became a mother.

I had an early miscarriage before my first child, my daughter was born. I have two children who are 17 and 15. When my daughter and my son came along, the loss begins to be woven into the fabric of your life. I could accept it because here I had my children. The last miscarriage that I had was actually right around the first anniversary of Sept 11. What made it particularly painful for me was I had been working for the year at Ground Zero. I was working as a hospice chaplain. My children were in kindergarten and 3rd grade at the time. I had just completed the year of work, blessing remains and supporting the workers there. We had done the 1st anniversary down at Ground Zero. A month or so later, I found out I was pregnant. I was ecstatic at the time. It was not a planned thing. I was going to be an older mother. I was thrilled. In some primitive way, I felt that this was my reward for being knee deep in death and in remains for the past year and several years before that as a hospice chaplain. I was thrilled. I felt that this little life was coming to me after being in the midst of loss of life.

On Martin Luther King Day, I was about 13 weeks pregnant. My kids were out of school. We all went to the doctor for a routine ultrasound. They were in the waiting room. They wanted to see the baby on the screen.

When the technician took me back to prep me, there was no heartbeat on the screen. It was very traumatic. My husband and kids were in the waiting room waiting to come in and I was looking at stillness on the screen. This propelled me into quite a tailspin. I felt like the rug had been pulled out from under me. I reverted to a very childish part of my faith that felt somehow I was punished or maybe there was no God. I really went into a moment of doubt. A week later I had to have a D&C. While I was laying on the table in the doctor's office, I just instinctively put my hands to my belly and I thought, *I have blessed so many remains. How can I let this little one go without offering a blessing?* I literally stopped her and put my hands on my belly and offered a blessing to the remains of a baby that I would never see. It took me years and years to come to terms with that loss even though I went on and became a hospice chaplain.

I think I was present to my patients and my families as best I could. But, part of me had gone kind of numb and shut down. It was writing about that experience that then led me to think about the experiences at Ground Zero and to think about interactions I had with patients and how much they had taught me about not just dying but about living. My experience with the miscarriage is not in the book because it was very raw at the time.

Those traumatic events can continue to teach us. I know it has made me a more empathetic person, especially when I hear about women who have had traumatic losses. Ultimately I am grateful, over more time, that I had that experience of life stirring within my body. Gratitude I think is the best healer and time and friends who did not tire of hearing me cry about that traumatic event.

Andrea: It makes me think about how things come into our lives because we are carrying grief for so many things. What it feels like to me is a connection to the stories you wrote about your experiences at Ground Zero. You still had to keep it together and you were embodying the grief. I was at Ground Zero a year later and I could feel the sorrow and the shock and loss. It was almost like the miscarriage was a way to process a lot of grief.

Andie: Yes, the blessing is really that to connect with another human being…First of all, sometimes the best way to help ourselves is to try to help someone else. Not to do it in an inauthentic way when we are not quite ready to. A lot of people, after they have lost a parent or a spouse or sibling immediately want to do volunteer work in hospice.   Sometimes we need to give ourselves time to grieve before throwing ourselves into that helper arena. When the time comes, I think it is very helpful to offer our hearts in love for another person.

That's, in a way, the story of the mustard seed in the beginning of my book, in the introduction. It is actually a Buddhist twist on the mustard seed, where a young mother who has lost her child comes to the foot of the Buddha and wants her life restored. He sends her into the surrounding town. If you can find one single family that has not known loss, bring me a mustard seed and I will restore your child's life to you. The mother goes into town and knocks on each door. She tells them, *I have lost a child and I am looking for a house that has not known loss.* Each time, the family would share their stories of loss because you cannot find a house that has not experienced the pain of death. Eventually she comes back to the Buddha, not with a mustard seed but with a heart of compassion.

So, hopefully that is what has happened to me, as I've gone into these very difficult areas. I have people who tease me and say, *what is wrong with you? You work with battered elderly, you work with mentally ill homeless people, you work with the dying. Are you some sort of martyr?* What is very hard to explain is that it is in those interactions that I most keenly feel the presence of the Divine. I can't quite explain that with the reasoning behind that. Somehow the sparks that fly when two people come to each other in some sort of honest vulnerability, that to me, is where God is most present.

Andrea: That is what I loved about the stories in your book. In each chapter, you take us into this moment of the microscopic connection with another human being in a
moment of life. And that is where the power of experiencing the Divine, experiencing who we are. I feel it is in those moments when I realize how I am alive. Have a heart to heart connection with someone, that is the power, no matter what is going on anywhere else. That moment is pure love.

Andie: When I think of someone like yourself, Andrea, who has experienced so much loss and has retained this joy and faith and openness to the Spirit, it is such a powerful witness. Because so many times, if someone doesn't know what you have experienced, they might say, *"well it is easy for you to feel this or that, what do you know?"* And if you begin to tell your tale…

I had an experience a couple of years ago with a woman who is now a friend, and sometimes that is how these friendships form. She is a very funny woman in my town. She had this horrendous time where her husband had pancreatic cancer at 45 years old and was failing. This is a man who had been in incredible shape, a real health nut. She was in the throes of this terrible time with him and this horrendous grief and she saw my daughter and I taking a walk. She said she looked at us and thought, *"How can they look so happy? They don't have a care in the world. Why is this happening to me when people can walk about like that?"* Little did she know I had been diagnosed with breast cancer. We sometimes look at each other and say, *"What would she or what would he know about pain? Nothing is wrong with them."*

When I was diagnosed and we began to talk, the thing I love about her is she told me this. *Yeah, I looked at you and didn't like you very much because you looked so cute walking with your daughter.* In the end, I was actually able to be with her husband in the last weeks of his life and to offer a blessing to him in their home when he died. That circle then came around and we have a wonderful friendship.

Your witness in the world as you tell your story is so inspiring to me and I know to so many people. I am in awe.

Andrea: Thank you. I do feel we are called to things that help us with healing. I was just wondering when you were saying you ended up giving a blessing to her husband while you were probably still in the process of healing cancer. What was the timing of your illness and his death?

Andie: I was undergoing treatment while he was still trying to undergo treatment himself. He lived for three years with pancreatic cancer which was longer than people expected with this kind of cancer. When he died, I had had four surgeries and had finished most of my chemotherapy and I had very, very short hair. My hair was just growing in. I did officiate his funeral service. It was the first time I did something in an official way without my wig or a scarf on. I was kind of vulnerable and I wanted to honor him and his journey by standing in front of a group of about 500 people with my little pixie hair, which was a challenge for me. It was also the gift that he gave me, to stand with him and stand in my own skin. Hopefully there was some sort of witness to courage.

Andrea: This is the perfect example. It was at a time when you could do that as part of your healing and it brought even more of a healing to you. I think this is a wonderful testimony of when to give and when to step into your faith, your belief to find those healing moments. Who would have thought that you would be leading the funeral and standing there in that vulnerability?

Andie: The thing that comes into my mind as I hear you talk, and I am thinking of anyone who is listening, is that the primary lesson I have learned from my own experiences and from the experiences that others have shared with me is that we really cannot live in fear. Life is too short to live in fear. Standing at his funeral, I could have been thinking that this could have been my funeral and someone else is officiating or I am just barely out of the jaws of this illness myself.

We don't have the time or the luxury in a sense to live in fear or if we do, it is not the wisest choice. Life is offering us opportunities for growth, for blessings, for joy at every turn.

Even in the midst of those difficult times. Even in the midst of a miscarriage. It is finding the wisdom to give ourselves space to grieve and honor the losses that break our hearts, and then trying to get to the point where we are not living in fear. And that's a challenge.

Andrea: And to find those moments when you do find the gifts. That's why I decided to be LIVE on the show on Thanksgiving and the night before Thanksgiving. To hold a space for the pain and the gifts that are underneath. If we are grieving a loss over the holidays, those can be some really tough days. There was someone who wrote on the chat line that she had just had a big break-up and her heart was breaking and she was trying to find the lesson. I said the first step is to feel the pain and as one human being can give another permission, I said, *"I give you permission to fully feel the pain right now. And to know that yes, there is a gift and there is a lesson and that will come. Be open to that when that comes but first feel the pain and honor the loss that that is the first step."*

Andie: The Buddhists would call that leaning into the sword. If we are willing to lean into the sword to feel the cut of that then we will at least not go into a place of numbing out. To be fully alive, it is to be willing to lean into the sword. To lean into the places that are causing us pain. In a way, it is lancing the boil.

Andrea: That's it. To go into that place of pain and it will shift.
 Can you share some of the blessings from Ground Zero? Would you share some of the stories?

Andie: Sure. For those of you who are more interested in some of the unexplainable, metaphysical aspects of being at Ground Zero, I think sometimes religious people are not sure
if they are allowed to believe in these things. One of the most profound things I experienced over the course of the time was that looking in the very beginning at what was initially that
huge pile. I literally felt like I could hear, in an audible way, the groans that were sort of emanating around me, a sort of Spiritual trauma that had happened there.

I think you said even later you could feel a resonance of that, the vibration of that, the remnants of that trauma. As the time went on, I felt like there was a gradual diminishing. There began to feel like some sort of restoration of peace there. There were in my mind, sort of spiritual entities, working hard to restore some sort of healing peace especially for those who were working so hard night and day. There was so much good that was happening there. We all did around 8 hour shifts at the morgue, so there was a 24-hour clergy presence at the morgue which was a little trailer that sat right on site. I might be following a rabbi, who followed a priest, who followed an Iman, who followed a nun. So, there was a continuous spiritual presence at the morgue; People of all faiths.

What I thought was so profound was the primary feeling. Again, this is a place that I would not look forward to going, but when you were there, it was very hard to leave because the feeling was of such unity and such hope among people who were standing in the middle of hell. And somehow, the human spirit response to this terrible event was not bitterness, as one might have expected, but rather was a complete affirmation of the holiness and the sanctity of life.

That was no more apparent to me than in a conversation I had with a young Port Authority Police Officer who was probably in his late twenties. This isn't in the book so I like to tell this story.

He was sharing with me one evening how he had been present, I think it was the night before, when they found the remains that were probably one of the hijackers. He couldn't elaborate. It was still a crime scene at that point. But it was pretty clear that they had found one of the hijackers. I was curious, I said, *"Did they desecrate him at all, was he spat on? How was he treated?"* Here were all of these police officers
 and fire personnel on site as a murderer's remains are discovered. He looked me square in the face and said, *"Absolutely not. We looked at these remains and said, This was someone's son. This maybe was someone's father or husband,"* and
they were treated with the same respect with which we would have treated any other remains. That really humbled me, Andrea. It really signaled to me the best of humanity standing in the midst of the worst of humanity in terms of what we can do to one another.

Andrea: The integrity that people were bringing. The honoring, the reverence of the space...

Andie: It's true. It's funny because being at Ground Zero, I am sure that not everyone was perfectly behaved. I am sure there were things happening that I wasn't aware of. Everyone with whom I was in contact and who I encountered were really becoming bigger than themselves in terms of their work. And then occasionally, when one of the little vehicles we called gators would have to go through the city because unfortunately, the way the roads were, sometimes a body would have to go briefly through a part of the street that was open to the public or kind of cut through. It's crazy. Sometimes a flag would be stolen off of the gator. So, there was still humanity there doing its thing.

On site there was almost this sense of humor and acceptance like, *yes, we're here doing this holy work, this difficult work and yet people are still people.* There was a very strange acceptance that we were in an impossibly odd position, something that had never really happened on American soil. The closest would be Pearl Harbor during World War II.

Andrea: There wasn't a handbook on how to behave. *Let's look at the past and decide to do it differently now.* It sounded like this was a brand new experience and each person had to make a choice as to how they were going to show up.

Andie: As you said, the people who were present on that day had to make choices. I had many service personnel tell me about the choices they had to make, if they happened to be there as a police officer, as a fireman, carrying people on gurneys, as the building was coming down. *Did they stay? Did they run? The thoughts of their family.* I had one policewoman tell me that she was there with her partner and when the building started coming down, she ran. She lost him in the smoke. She said, *"If I had gone back I knew I would have been killed and I have five children."* It turned out he also got out and if he had gone back he would have been killed. There is a choice. *Do I look for my partner or do I run?*

And the people who survived had to live with those choices. So many of them were looking to clergy like myself for some kind of forgiveness that they couldn't find within themselves for the choices that they had to make. That in many ways was one of the holiest parts of my work was to be there. In a way, as a spiritual stand-in for the Divine, for people looking for forgiveness, for choices that none of us should have to make in our lives.

Andrea: How did you keep a balance in your life during that time period? I am trying to think now. How long was it? Nine months, ten months of being a presence there?

Andie: My first shift there was Oct 2, 2001 and my last shift was probably in June 2002. What was that? About eight, nine months. And after June we were preparing for the anniversary and being present for those ceremonies. I would say it was about a nine-month period.

One of the things that helped me was having small children because when I came home, they really needed me to still be their Mom. And somehow the normalcy of packing lunches and wiping noses and hearing about their days and putting band-aids on knees and coloring pictures. Those sorts of normal things that signified that life needed to go on. There was no guilt for those whose lives were going on. We needed to live, really in order to honor the dead. None of those who perished wanted life to stop. Certainly for their loved ones who were so dramatically affected. So for me, finding the balance in a way was just drinking in the normalcy of my children and family life. I am a big animal fan, so I would spend time with my dogs, with my cats, take some walks on the beach and try to find some meditative space where I could re-center myself. But, it was still hard. I think I was a little more numb, than I would have liked to admit during that time, just to function.

Andrea: I wanted to ask that question because clearly this was an extraordinary situation that I hope we never ever see on the planet again, that kind of destruction and shock. And yet we do have nature and earthquakes and other things that happen. There are people who have someone with an illness that goes on for a long period of time and to find a way of balancing a little bit and the normalcy.

Andie: And again, for those of us who like to think of ourselves as compassionate people or as "givers" then sometimes there's a guilt about taking time for ourselves and that is so important. I have kind of learned that the hard way, too. We really cannot be fully present to others if we are not taking care of ourselves, at least not over the long haul. And as you said, if you have a loved one with a chronic illness or
you're in a job as a nurse or a social worker or special education teacher, some job that requires a lot of yourself emotionally then we really need to honor our own souls by nurturing them and taking time taking care of our bodies.
Feeding ourselves well. Spending time with friends. Those are things we shouldn't feel guilty about; honoring our own souls. If we are not honoring our own soul, then we can't really honor the souls of others. I really believe.

Andrea: It seems like it's hard to step away and feed our souls and yet, if you are not honoring your soul, what do you have left to give?

Andie: I think you can do it for a while. But, if you really are committed to the long haul, then start to develop techniques that work for you. What works for me might not work for someone else. One person might find it through exercising, or
running and that's their meditative space and others through music and somebody else through photography or someone else spending time with their pets or sitting in silence. It would be great if you could find something that resonates with your own Spirit.

It could be prayer, it could be reading inspirational text, the Bible, books, scriptures, whatever it is. I would just encourage, especially during these holiday times, to do things that are nurturing and restorative. Even for people who haven't had a recent loss, holidays also can be a very melancholy time. Writing is a wonderful thing, too. Journaling and writing and taking time to share our experiences, I'm a big fan of that.

Andrea: Just to create some space. Whether it's through writing or taking a walk to connect with nature or sitting and having a cup of tea and having a conversation with someone. Slowing down. To really look at what this season is about. How can we fully connect with other human Beings? In the long run, that is what is most important.

Andie: It doesn't always have to be a heavy conversation. It could be calling someone because we are thinking of them. We think of an old friend and we think of a loved one, and then we don't pick up the phone. Sometimes when that
person comes into our mind, I think it is a thought that is sent by the Divine to go ahead and act on it and pick up the phone. Chances are that person on the other end of the phone will say, *I was just thinking about you.*

One of the things I would like to encourage people to do, not only during the holidays, is to follow those impulses. I think sometimes Spirit is so close, just giving us these nudges. Our loved ones are so close just waving their hands in our faces saying, *"I'm right here."* The veil between us and what is that spiritual realm in the next world, is so thin but we are designed to be blocked from that because that is what faith is
 about. The Earth is our spiritual schoolhouse. We get those nudges, the Divine the spiritual realm is all around us and to
follow the impulses that lead us to connection to other people
and the Source of our life. Those probably are little pokes and prods that are sent in our conscious minds.

Andrea: Well, that is beautiful. A few minutes ago, I was going to let you know we were almost at the end and could you close with something. And that is just so beautiful. The way you were just talking about connecting.

Andie: The world feels like a very uncertain scary place at the moment. Those who pray and those who are spiritual people, sometimes I just shut my eyes and feel like we are all holding hands because we really need to hold this planet together. At the moment we have been given this beautiful home by the Divine to live in and it needs all of our prayers and all of our energies and all of our hopes for the future. That hope for the future will also help us through our grief.

As we make peace with our past, make peace with our losses, look towards the future as a place that is going to be a happy playground for the generations to come. We have a long way to go but we at least need to envision a peaceful planet in order to make it happen.

www.Revandrearaynor.com Andrea Raynor received her Master of Divinity from Harvard Divinity School. A United Methodist minister, she served as a chaplain to the morgue at Ground Zero after the September 11, 2001, terrorist attacks. Andrea has been a hospice chaplain since 1997, and is currently the Spiritual Counselor for Greenwich Hospital Home Hospice in Greenwich, CT.

Grief Transformation Show #16
Guest Andrea Raynor, Chaplain

December 6, 2010
http://tobtr.com/1369286

Chapter Five

Thanksgiving: Gratitude
By Andrea Hylen

Show originally aired on November 25, 2010

This radio show was originally aired on Thanksgiving 2010 in the United States.

I decided to host a LIVE show on Thanksgiving Eve and also tonight on Thanksgiving because throughout the years there have been times when I have spent holidays alone. I have also had years when I have been with friends and family and I have still felt lonely. Tonight, I felt that if there was even one person who needed to have someone speaking LIVE on Thanksgiving that I wanted to be here for an hour. I want you to know you are not alone. And I also know the recording will be here. So, if there is someone who listens in the middle of the night, I want you to know I understand and I am still here with you.

Every year is different and many times we feel a wide range of feelings during the whole season. Thanksgiving or another holiday can bring up feelings of grief. It doesn't matter if something happened today or something happened last week, or even ten or twenty years ago. If you are feeling the emotion of grief, then you are feeling the emotion of grief. It is not right or wrong. It just is. So, here we are.

I am going to open up the phone lines for anyone who would like to speak and share some gratitude this evening and the chat line is open, if anyone would like to post some words or feelings.

Connie, who lost a husband and son to suicide within six months of each other, sent a message for me to read to the listeners: *Andrea, if you'd like to pass along this message. It was so hard for me to get: we all deserve and can have happiness. It's ok to ask for Divine assistance; we are worthy, and prayers do get answered. Trust the messages, even if you don't understand them. Search your soul and things eventually become clear. Trust without judgment (then don't judge yourself if you find yourself lacking).*

Thank you, Connie.

Right before I started the radio show tonight, I saw two posts messages on Facebook:

One post: *This is the worst Thanksgiving ever. I hate this holiday.*

Another post: *I love Thanksgiving. It is the best holiday in the world.*

I was thinking about how two people could have such different perspectives on the same day. It made me think of several things that can help to remember on a holiday.

*First is expectations and whether or not you feel they have been met.

*Second is an ability to adapt to whatever is happening. To accept the present moment.

*Third is gratitude.

As you enter the holiday space, make conscious choices and notice your feelings moment by moment. The same conversation could seem humorous or hurtful. For instance, I could take it personally, I could remain neutral or I could react. Taking a breath or a pause or even excusing yourself from the table and going to the bathroom can create space for you to notice what you are feeling and it is good self-care to create some space before reacting.

One of the keys that has worked for me during this time of year is to find gratitude in everyday moments. I am not talking about when you are in the middle of a crisis or you just heard news about a loved one that puts you in the middle of grief or chaos. I am talking about every day simplicity. I woke up. I am breathing. I have a place to sleep. I have food. I feel love in my heart for this moment. I am here.

During times in our lives when we have challenges and difficult situations we can turn our attention to gratitude. One experience I had with my son, Cooper, many years ago was when I was 7 months pregnant with him. He was my 3rd child and during an ultrasound, the technician found an anomaly.

Something was wrong with his heart and he had an enlarged lung. There were some ideas about treatment and operations but no one knew what would happen in the next two months of growth in my uterus or what would happen when he was born.

For the rest of that day, I went through a wide range of emotions. *Why me, God? Haven't I been through enough already?* When we returned to the hospital for more testing and more clarity from the doctor, I switched into calm, focused attention like a researcher. I bounced back and forth between tears, despair, hope, despair, pep talks, and despair. The next day, I woke up with an inspiration. I decided to cross stitch angels. Throughout his life and sitting by his bed through every operation that is what I did. I cross-stitched angels. The activity of cross-stitching angels gave me a place to focus my attention, my prayers, my hopes and dreams, and feel gratitude.

There is so much power in consciously choosing gratitude. That decision and feeling and choice brings you into the present moment of what is happening. It helps you let go of the past and it holds you in the present. You don't know what the future is going to bring. The definition of gratitude is the state of being grateful, thankfulness, appreciation of the benefits received. When you choose gratitude in this moment, in the everyday moments, you can begin to see even more things to feel in gratitude. And when it is time, you will see the gifts.

My son had many operations. Every time he was in the hospital, I looked for little things. Gratitude is a path to joy in the midst of grief. I was grateful that my son was still alive in that moment. Gratitude didn't change that he had a heart defect. It didn't change that he needed an operation. It didn't give us any more information about how long he would be alive. But, it did bring joy into the midst of everything.

Cross-stitching was the action I took to keep me focused on gratitude. It helped me to see little things when my son had an operation and I would be in the hospital with him for two weeks. I would look around the intensive care unit to find things to be grateful for. Appreciating the person next to
 my son and praying for their recovery; Appreciating the

people who were sitting with their loved ones; Sharing a smile with someone across the room; Listening to someone else's story; A favorite nurse by the bedside who brought love and light to my son; Appreciating that there was a variety of food served in the cafeteria. Feeling gratitude for the sun shining and bringing natural light into my son's hospital bed. Appreciating the colors of the angel I was cross-stitching. Appreciating the love in my heart for my son and my daughters.

The attitude of gratitude carried over into other areas of my life and I began to discover even more things to fill my life with gratitude. I began to see the gifts. Gratitude helps us to release control, to flow with life and to be in the present moment.

In preparation for the show, I felt immersed in gratitude. It was present in everything I did and observed. I began this Thanksgiving Day by watching the Macy's Day Parade that was in New York City. I am living in California, in a new apartment and I do not have a television. I do not have living room furniture. To host this show, I am sitting on the floor with the computer in front of me on a chair. I am grateful that I have a computer and a telephone so I can host this show. I am grateful for the printer I use to print some notes that help me stay focused during the show tonight. I am grateful for the library that had resources for me to find books with quotes and inspiration about gratitude.

My desire this morning was that I wanted to watch the Macy's Day Parade. I could have been unhappy and focused on, *"I don't have a TV. Life sucks."* Staying in gratitude, I thought, *is there another way to watch the show?* I knew there might be a Live Stream that I could access through thecomputer. I couldn't find the link. I looked on Twitter and there it was! People were tweeting the links for each other. These are the everyday moments of making a choice in our lives. I could have been looking at how I didn't have a television instead of opening up to finding another way to see it.

And if I didn't have a way to see it at all, I could have felt the sadness and then switched my attention to what else I could do or be now. Feeling sadness and disappointment may have been part of the process but I wouldn't have to get lost by staying in that place. It is important to feel what you are feeling and to be real with that. This is where we begin to make choices about what is going on.

As it turned out, my oldest daughter, Mary, lives in NYC. She was cooking her first Thanksgiving turkey and we watched some of the parade together from different parts of the country.

One of the questions to ask yourself is, *"What is right in front of me that I can appreciate and enjoy?"*

I had a very quiet day today. As this show is airing now, it is 5pm here in California and I haven't eaten the vegetarian meal I prepared to eat with my youngest daughter, Hannah. She wasn't feeling well and we decided to wait until after the show to eat. I have a choice to feel gratitude right now. The food is here. We are going to eat later tonight. I am grateful that we have food. The simple fact is there are some people who don't have food. So, I could look at how I didn't have a big elaborate Thanksgiving dinner this year or I can look at the fact that I have food, that we are here together tonight on the radio show, and I am grateful to be alive.

I want to give everyone permission to feel whatever you are feeling and to think it is a good Thanksgiving or it is a lousy Thanksgiving and to know that there are points along the way where you can decide to choose gratitude.

I walked up to Priscilla's earlier today, my favorite coffee place in Toluca Lake, California. I am sure we all have a place like that or we could find a place like this. A coffee shop, a library, a community space where we can get to know the people who go there, too. Anyone who listens to more than one radio show will hear me talk about Priscilla's because it fills me with joy to walk over there and sit in the corner writing with a cup of hot coffee.

I walked there early this morning. The flavored coffee choice was Reindeer Caramel Crunch and I felt gratitude for that because I love that coffee and I feel in the holiday Spirit with it. As I walked to my table I saw someone with cupcakes. She was a stranger who I had never seen before. I stopped for a minute and appreciated the cupcakes. I made a comment that she must be meeting someone who is having a birthday. She told me no, she just brought them to share with a friend. We had a wonderful conversation about a passion in her life. She shared the story of how she went to college right after high school and after three semesters decided to quit so she could spend time looking at what really made her heart sing.

I was so grateful for this conversation. To hear a young woman who was taking the time at such a young age to determine what really makes her heart sing. It made MY heart sing. For the rest of the day, as I thought back to that conversation, I felt so happy. She is part of a younger generation of women who are really exploring what makes them happy and looking for ways to share their gifts in the world. Through her exploration, she discovered how much she loves to bake. She became a pastry chef. Today she gave me one of the cupcakes. Sweet potato, bourbon, apple pie filled with toasted marshmallow. YUM!

   I am sure that today, some of the listeners had some difficult or sad conversations with family members. In the midst of grief, you just have to feel that feeling. You don't need to take action. Feel it. Be with the feelings. Breathe.
The day my husband died in hospice there were hummingbirds in the garden. A group of us were sitting in the garden talking about him and having a moment of relief that he was finally free from the cancer and pain. The hummingbirds began dive bombing us and we began to laugh. The hummingbirds reminded us of my husband's sense of adventure and we decided that he must be in the hummingbird energy, playing with us and reminding us to be grateful for life. In the same moment of joy, there was also the feeling of loss. A "happy-sad" moment. It is important to honor the pain at the same time you feel the joy. Take the oxygen for yourself and feel all of the feelings. It is not always easy to see the gifts in the very beginning. Give it time.

A Few Quotes of Gratitude

Neale Donald Walsch: *On this day of your life, dear friend, I believe God wants you to know that gratitude in advance is the most powerful creative force in the universe. Most people do not know this, yet it is true. Expressing thankfulness in advance is the way of all Masters. So do not wait for a thing to happen and then give thanks. Give thanks before it happens, and watch energies swirl! To thank God before something occurs is an act of extraordinary faith. And that, of course, is where the power comes from. It's Thanksgiving Day in the U.S. Why not make it Thanksgiving Day in the hearts of people everywhere, all the time?*

D. Lightmoon: *Within life's most difficult challenges lie the seeds of our greatest gifts.*

A message from Author **Kater Leatherman** today said, *"Happy Thanks Living."*

That is one of the shifts I am noticing right now. People are looking for a deeper meaning to what is going on. For some of us, we had the same Thanksgiving that we had for years. Lots of people around the table with lots of food and for some of us we have had a totally different Thanksgiving this year where we stepped back to take a look at where we want to go.

Sara Ban Breathnach, Author of Simple Abundance 1995. An on-line gratitude journal link:
http://www.simpleabundance.com/gratitude.html

Stacy Robyn, creator of The Gratitude Experiment, 2005
http://www.Gogratitude.org

"Gratitude unlocks the fullness of life. It turns what we have into enough, and more. It turns denial into acceptance, chaos to order, confusion to clarity. It can turn a meal into a feast, a house into a home, a stranger into a friend. Gratitude makes sense of our past, brings peace for today and creates a vision for tomorrow." **-Melody Beattie**

Through a process of grieving the sudden loss of her teenage son and writing a book called Lessons of Love, Melody Beattie found her way through the pain to unlock and discover gratitude and the fullness of life.

Call-in Wisdom from Kater Leatherman:

Kater: Gratitude is the hearts memory. The more we are grateful for the more that will be given to us.

Andrea: I could think, *"How could I possibly feel grateful for anything when I have had this loss?"* There is something there. And I want to acknowledge that you may need to curl up in a ball on your bed and just sob. But, after that moment of deep pain, begin to look for gratitude in something.

Kater: Oprah has had a lot of shows about gratitude, but years ago she said on one of the shows, even if you are just grateful for the air you are breathing.

Andrea: It can shift the way you are feeling to feel the one thing. Even in the moments of sadness, you can find something to be grateful about. In that moment of gratitude, it can ease your pain.

Kater: It definitely shifts the energy. I appreciate the topic. I am enjoying sitting here listening. Hearing you talking about gratitude and hearing the reminders that are really so important.

Andrea: I am grateful for this moment, dear friend. It was wonderful to hear your voice. I have a story about the last few months of my husband's life and discovering gratitude.

Discovering Gratitude

During the last few months of my husband's life, I had the inspiration to plant 100 feet of roses in front of our house. My husband was dying of multiple myeloma cancer. We had exhausted all the possibilities of a recovery. His cancer was in the late stages when it was discovered and none of the treatments were working.

As I looked out at our yard one morning, the inspiration came to create a memorial to my husband while he was still alive. I defined it as a "barn raising." I asked friends to help us install a split rail fence. The dream was to finish it in a day. A group of about 40 friends came to install the fence, and move wheelbarrows of dirt and mulch. This would be the preparation for the garden. It was a beautiful day of a community coming together to celebrate a life while my husband was still alive. I did not tell him this was a memorial to him. I told him I wanted him to have something beautiful to look at and to know the fence was complete.

With the fence in place, I worked on the garden every day, digging holes and planting roses. Every day my husband walked to the garden and watched the progress I was making. He took time to look at nature, eat fruit off the trees and smell the roses.

Several years after my husband died, I decided to sell my house and move from Maryland to California. My daughter and I moved into an apartment instead of renting or buying a house. For the first time in five years, I didn't have a rose garden to tend. When a life partner dies, there are dreams that die with them. Our rose garden was one of the dreams that died.

One day, I was shopping at a grocery store and I saw a garden store with roses. I stopped and smelled about 20 varieties, finding roses that were very familiar to me. The next day I went for a walk and discovered a neighborhood with roses blooming and hanging over the fences. Just as people had stopped to smell the roses in my garden, I stopped and smelled the roses in my neighbor's yard.

I thought about how I had been feeling sad because I didn't have my own rose garden and then saw how that was only one way to look at it. I asked myself, *"Where do I get stuck in life because the picture doesn't look like the one I used to have? Where can I feel more gratitude for what is right here, right now?"*

When I opened my mind, I began to see roses everywhere. The roses along the street on my daily walk. Roses in the farmer's market. A woman giving me a rose when I went to church. Walking on a street I saw that it was named Rose Street. Now, I live in a world of roses and I have a beautiful memory of the rose garden I left behind for someone else to enjoy and tend. Switching my perspective from focusing on what I had lost and seeing that there were roses everywhere is finding gratitude in the moment of what you have now.

Sometimes we are so focused on what we have lost that we do not see what is beautiful right in front of us. Are there ways to let go of the old to see the new that can be met in a new way?

I had a dream when I was in high school to become an actress and a dancer on Broadway. I loved musicals. I loved tap dancing. There was a point when I decided to become a social worker and let go of being an actress. Years later, I realized I gave up a part of me and I wanted to reconnect and have a way to express. Did I have to be on a stage in order to have my needs met?

1. I started going to musicals or watching them on DVDs.
2. When I turned 50, I bought myself tap shoes.
3. I took classes where I got to dance with other people, too.

There are other ways of bringing joy into your life. Receive a daily message of gratitude. Make a decision to focus on gratitude every day. You will feel better instantly. Developing and nourishing a habit of gratitude. Find five things that you were grateful for at the end of the day and write it in a gratitude journal.

I still have moments daily or at least weekly when I feel lost. I reflect and ask myself questions. *Am I making the right choices? Is this leading me to something? What are the next steps to take in my life?* Finding resources to tap into to find a connection to a deeper place within yourself is a great support. So when you cannot find the gratitude within, you can connect with something else.

A wise, dear friend once told me to tend our sacred gardens. Tapping into gratitude is a sacred garden that is inside of you.

Prayer

I am going to end tonight with a little prayer. Take a deep breath. Let's create a personal, individual moment with ourselves.

Right now in this moment focus on your heart.
Feel that your heart is beating.
Your lungs are working.
Let's do a gratitude list together.
What is one thing you are grateful for today?
Pause and feel that.
Now, go into the second thing. Just knowing that we are holding a sacred space for these ideas to emerge.
Pause and feel that.
What is the third thing you can feel gratitude for today?
Pause and feel that.
What is the 4th thing?
Pause and feel that.
Now, think about the 5th thing.
Pause and feel that.
See how easy it is to find gratitude in your life.

My list tonight...

1. I am grateful I woke up this morning.
2. I am grateful that I can feel such a wide range of emotions.
3. I am grateful that my basic needs for having food and shelter are met.
4. I am grateful to have the opportunity to talk about grief transformation.
5. I am grateful for each listener who came to the call tonight, listened to the show recording and read this chapter.

Good night.

Grief Transformation Show #5
Thanksgiving: Gratitude

November 25, 2010
http://tobtr.com/1369275

Andrea Hylen

Chapter Six

Cell your Soul:
Owning and Clearing our Emotional Debris
Guest: Jeff Brown, Author of SoulShaping

Show originally aired on January 5, 2011

Introduction: SoulShaping with Author, Benevolent Warrior, Filmmaker, and Grounded Spiritualist, Jeff Brown

Before I share some information about Jeff and begin the Soulful conversation, I want to encourage you to do something tonight after the show:

Go to Jeff's website **www.soulshaping.com** And dive into the words, the images, the links, the videos and the pictures.

Andrea: Jeff, I have been talking with people about Grief Transformation on the show for over a month and we've covered a wide range of topics. But one of the topics I feel relates to everyone in the world right now is how we are all on a soul journey. We have moments when we think we are going to live life in a certain way. We've got a plan. Maybe somebody else had a plan for us. And things began to change.
     If you lose a loved one because they die, then you probably expect to go through a grieving period. But, if you have changes happen in your life, you are not necessarily going to understand this wide array of emotions that arrive and what to do with them. There is no path for that. There is no true space for that.

Jeff: Many of us move through our lives in a **Habitual Range of Emotion** which is that place in between vulnerability and rigidity or armour that we just grow comfortable with. And I think what happens is quite often our soul scriptures, the particular path we came into this life to walk and embody, are not congruent with the narrowness of that range, the Habitual Range of Emotion. Because that habitual range often develops out of defended-ness or conditioning or kind of a wide array of things that impact on us as organisms. For me my range was…I was really moved more in the direction of the armoured warrior for so much of my life. I was a highly emotional tantruming child in the early years and I now have really come to believe that is what kept me sane and able to move forward in my adult life. But, really fundamentally, especially in my adolescent years, and in my early twenties I was really tightly armoured. That was congruent on my path on one level and in another way was really incompatible with my Soul Scriptures which were to move in the direction of a more surrendered way of being.

So, when I first started to do this work, this uncovering of true path work in my late 20's. really what started to happen was I ran into conflict with my habitual range of emotion. My comfort zone or my discomfort zone, which was what it really was in so many ways. I didn't have an opening to a new wave of emotive possibility. So, for me for a long time I had to just lay on the couch and not move into activity. Activity was a wonderful way to save my life but it was also a way to avoid my feelings.

Even just lying on the couch and doing nothing brought up all kinds of feelings that I was holding internally, that I had no template to maneuver through. What happens for a lot of us is that's when we back-off, it is what is called a nervous breakdown.

There is always a possibility of seeing those emotions falling apart to a breakthrough to the next level of transformation on your journey. We are not really trained what to do with feelings we aren't familiar with and we retreat from the path before befriending those shadows. I think that is where a lot of people get stuck. A lot of people who come to my work are stuck in that place.

Andrea: I can really relate to that. Something came up for me when you were just saying that. I got married when I was 25 years old and I had all of these visions of the life we were going to live, thought I had found my partner for life and everything. And when the marriage started falling apart and I felt helpless to save it for 4-5 years, the words that I kept using to describe it to people were, *"He's refusing to grow"* and *"My soul is dying."* I was basically told to suck it up and this is the marriage I had and I had two small children. I literally felt that my soul was dying. I did leave the marriage but when I left I had to first get myself out and the image that I had was of a person on their hands and knees crawling out the door. That's how it felt. I felt that if I didn't get out of there I would literally die. Physically, I would have a death.

One of the things I really love about your work: I love the dictionary where you create words and phrases to what is happening. I wish I had the words then, years ago.

My question is: *Do you have anything to say about how we can listen to those calls before we get to that point of feeling like our soul is dying?*

Jeff: The school system needs to get involved in this process. The concept in the dictionary that I call Truth Aches. There are so many Truth Aches or symptoms that we are off path that we are not honoring the little voice of our intuition. The voice that knows the life we're here to live; life of Divine possibility.

We have so many very subtle and obvious cues but until we decide to spend some time in **Soulitude**, really spending time inside, getting to know our inner world, getting to know what things mean so if someone doesn't understand their desire to rent videos, for example. *To rent videos on a constantly addictive basis and it is connected to their desire to avoid something.* If they don't know themselves well enough to identify that connection, it becomes very, very difficult.

From the outside looking at it, someone may say that is not really true, not really addictive. I'm working really hard and that's the way that I turn my mind off. It's not always what it appears to be and the only one who can really decide what a Truth Ache is, what is a symptom, of being off path or ignoring Soul Scriptures and directionality is the individual. We are just not trained to think like this. Now, luckily, there are radio shows like this where we can begin to normalize and dialogue.

When I heard what I call Little Missy in the book, the little voice that knows, I had absolutely no idea who to talk to about that with in my 20's. Nobody in my world ever articulated anything like that to me. So, it became really like I was in a foreign land and trying to learn a new language. It took a long time to understand that that language was really intrinsic to my authentic Self and wasn't just a foreign invader trying to knock me off of the path of law. For a long time, the warrior I identified myself as, used to hear this pull from little missy, this inner dialogue, *"get off that path, your path is somewhere else."* It was vague and esoteric and really I saw that voice, the voice of really my authentic intuition, as my enemy.

Because that is what I was conditioned to believe. Anything that took me off the survivalist direction, like *"grin and bear it, never surrender, that's your husband, that's what it is, just deal with it,"* all of that stuff… *"You're lucky to have something, you're lucky to have a job, you're lucky to have a partner, you're lucky to have a roof over your head,"* because the generations before have a memory of not having many of those things. The voice of survival-ism became normalized and glorified and these more subtle voices were diminished.

I think we are now just at the very beginning of entering into an era on this planet where this idea of Divine purpose and the honoring of the intuitive self and the idea that we have Soul Scriptures inside of us, actual paths, directionality, something we are here to do or manifest in this lifetime. We are just at the very, very beginning of that. We need a tremendous amount of encouragement at this point just to begin to not push those voices away and to give them enough breath so that we become more acquainted with them.

Andrea: I love having the dialogue on a radio show where it can be shared. That's actually how this station started where Kathryn Yarborough and I were having conversations about Living on the Edge. Making choices even though we weren't certain where the money was going to come from and where is the next step. We've got the flashlight and we can only see one step. I think it is really important to have the conversations and share the uncertainty and messiness.
Jeff, I am at this point where I do write and share the vulnerability and my experiences are public but sometimes the journey can be so painful and so lonely that I am hesitant to encourage people to take the leap and live this life.

Jeff: Take the leap. We have to be careful with take the leap. Too many people have been encouraged by ungrounded spiritual models to take leaps without having their feet firmly imbedded on the ground. I call it **Ascending with Both Feet on the Ground.**

So, I couldn't have taken the leap without making sure that I had money in the bank and making sure that I took care of the bottom line so that when I explored those more nuanced, creative pathways I didn't have all pervading root chakra anxiety about money and survival. I think we have to hold it all together, what I call **Enrealment** in the book. It means that we honor the voice that's moving us in the direction of our truer path, at the same time we recognize that we still live in a practical landscape and that we are in Earthly form. We take the leap but we take the leap steadily and just recognize as we go that we have to stay connected to the Earth plane. Both because we have to survive but also because it's quite real. That was a hard adjustment for me because I was a forceful warrior that was always doing things quickly. So to understand that it was going to take me 15-20 years to go from semi-consciousness to slightly more advanced form of semi-consciousness where there's more gratification because I feel like I am more honoring of my path.

You know if you told me that in the beginning, I probably wouldn't have started. Because then I went in increments. So we make a leap of fate in the direction of those soul scriptures that lay inside of us our real callings, the archetypal pathways and transformations we're here to embody and the key lessons in relationships we're here to learn and grow through spiritually. At the same time, we recognize our connection to the Earth plane. To me that's it. And then you move slower.

I say growers are inchworms, I really believe that. We have peak experience moments, we have profound intense moments, but I think integration takes a long time before that can really become consolidated change so we just get it in our minds that this is a lifelong journey of transformation in the direction of our true path. From false path to true path and move like that and just move through those internal tunnels like that and deal with the world accordingly.

Too many people write to me that went the other way. They jumped. Like I'm born to be a writer so they sell their house, stick themselves in a room. They sit there for four years, nothing comes out of them and they've got no money, they've got no house and they just feel completely horrified by it. I am not sure that that is really the path to take for most of us.

Andrea: Yes, I understand that. I am a leaper and I really feel strongly guided when I'm leaping but it is usually based on a foundation of other things that were happening for years. There is a part of me that knew that if I totally ran out of money, I have such a strong base of community in Baltimore and I knew I could move from person to person, home to home and my presence would be welcomed there. It would be a continuation of my generosity in the past and allowing myself to be supported by others. But I think that is part of the individual exploration. Because sometimes it puts you into such overwhelming fear that you can't even see what the path might be or do you really feel such a heart calling to do it.

I would not say to everyone get rid of everything to follow a calling. I did clear out an 11-room house, kept what could fit into a 10 x 10 storage unit, sold a house, packed up a car and moved from Maryland to California. But, it was a year-long process, there was a strong soul calling and my teenage daughter who is seventeen had the same strong soul calling so we have had a year here of solitude and soul exploration that led to writing about Grief Transformation and the radio shows.

I don't think everyone has to separate from their life totally in a dramatic way. My dynamic was that from a very young age I felt that I had to merge with the people around me in order to help and support them. So for me, I had to go to an extreme. And it really took me 9-10 months before I could really feel the difference between, *Oh, that is that person's voice and this is me.* It just took me that amount of time.

Jeff: Got it. And in fairness, for some people, the extremes are really necessary, I really get that. I am not sure that is true for most people but a lot of people couldn't honour their callings if they were moving from house to house staying in people's environments. It wouldn't work for me, right? Even over the course of the autumn waiting for my new place to be ready and living somewhere else, I found it very difficult to write anything fresh or original. It really affected me in my consciousness.

I think it comes back to the individual knowing who they are and knowing what works for them and really knowing it. Not comparing their path to other paths. But doing all of that internal work to understand and to learn how to trust the nuances and the directionality that comes from within.

That is not to say not to dialogue with other people and to get support and not to get ideas from other people. But, at the same time to take it with a grain of salt. Nobody knows. Only soul knows the path it's here to walk. Any teacher who stands up there and tells someone they know what direction they're here to take is just lying or trying to sell books because I just don't believe it's possible.

Andrea: I think that's a message, too. We're moving away from that model. And if there is a teacher who says you've got to follow this and you've got to do these things to follow your path, I would run the other way.

Jeff: It's one thing to present tools and let people decide for themselves, if that tool works for them. But it's another thing to be dictatorial and dogmatic. We are moving away from Big Daddy knows best. We really are and I think that's really fantastic. Nothing makes me more satisfied in doing this work with people when we start an e-mail exchange with asking for an answer, as though I would know it, right? Then moving in the direction of them actually being empowered enough to realize that they know a whole lot more than they're giving themselves credit for. To me, that is just perfect.

Andrea: Yes, yes! And it's so exciting when the answer begins to emerge. It has to resonate within that field of energy that fits their Yes! That is their Truth in that moment!
Let's look at some of the other words in the SoulShaping Dictionary. **Nervous Breakthrough**. How about that?

Jeff: Let's begin by defining it.

Nervous Breakthrough: A profound (and courageous) emotional cleansing, a collapse of the false structures that have ruled our life, a breaking through to a more genuine state of consciousness. Often mischaracterized as a nervous breakdown. The key to the breakthrough is seeing the collapse all the way through to resolution.

For me, for example, after I walked away from law for the first time in my early 30's after I was called to the Bar in Ontario; I surrendered to this overwhelming soul-nami of old feelings. Old grief and anger that was really held deep within my system and armoured into my musculature and I just started crying and raging, not out in public, in my own
world in my therapeutic process. A tremendous amount of stuff came through me. It was really like a dissolution in many ways of the adaptive structures that I would have called Jeff. You know, that persona, whatever that was, was just falling apart. It was conscious. I think my ego was strong enough that it was actually choosing this. You know, I felt that there was a way in which I could have pulled out of it to an extent at any time and re-adapted to what I had to in the world.

But, I created space for it in my life. I didn't work very much, I was able to make enough money without devoting 5 or 6 days a week to it and I really got lost in that process. It was really clear to me at various points, Andrea, along the
way that if I stopped, there were midway points. If I just stopped, I was going to be kind of crazy. I mean, it was like I was going to have stirred up all of this material without

having it work its way through to any form of completion or cleansing. You know the process is a cleansing.

For whatever reason, of course, never all the way through, but enough of the way through, I was able to stay with that process until it just kind of organically stopped, at least at that point in time. Not that there haven't been others, but they were never as intense as that one. That's when I really got it that this whole shaming categorization of *oh, he had a breakdown or she had a breakdown* which we've heard about so much in society. So much of that is really a function…there's something courageous quite often; the fact that a person allows their real self to start to emerge in emotional terms. But, we're not conditioned and we're not set up in society to see those processes all the way through to transformation. So, it ends up being stigmatized, as opposed to being something that we champion and talk about as a fantastic clearing and re-clarification process.

Andrea: Did you find that once you went through that the first time that the next time that, because I am assuming…I'm relating to this from a personal point of view. I am thinking, *oh yeah, that one was the hardest and then, there was that next one and because I had survived the first one, I knew I would survive the next one.* Did you find that along the path?

Jeff: I think you get to learn the markers. It's like relationships beginning and ending. The first one is so horrifying. Eventually you've been through it and you know you'll bounce back and your heart will re-open. It's the same kind of process. You just become more familiar with the interior terrain. It doesn't seem as daunting anymore. The mountains don't seem as high to climb. Also, for me that first one was a pretty gigantic outpouring. The times after that, where I have created space for process, there just wasn't quite as much material to move through.

I think some of that, though I didn't at the time, has to do with how much releasing I did in my childhood. You know, how many tantrums I threw; how familiar I was with crying. It was so important to me to restore the organism of me, as a child, in this crazy house to release. It was like I was an animal. I moved like an animal. I moved through interior terrain like an animal. So I somehow had it in me that I was holding anger from the abuse in the environment and that I had to move it out of me.

Then, they took me to Clark Institute of Psychiatry in Toronto. They tested my I.Q. and they set me in with this pedophilic social worker to spend all kinds of time interacting with him and his weirdness. Ultimately, pulling myself away from that environment that was so much of my life being stigmatized in my early life. I was addicted to release. I absolutely did not want to hold onto my mother's stuff, my father's stuff or anybody else's stuff that wasn't mine. I really got it, you know?

In my 20's and even in my early 30's when that breakthrough happened for me, as daunting as it was, I wasn't holding a whole child's worth of material the way other people do. I think that really served me well; like these releases really serve those processes in two ways.

One, they create space inside for us to actually be comfortable and more at peace in our physical and emotional body. At the heart of those releases, and that is what **cell your soul** means for me, that *repressed emotions are unactualized spiritual lessons* and that the *emotional body is the karmic field where our soul's lessons are harvested.* So, through moving those feelings through to completion, not only did I create space inside for my true path to emerge and to live a more at peace life, but, additionally, I converted those experiences into the lessons that transformed my **soulular consciousness**. We grow through those experiences. That's how we change; through how we relate to emotional material in our patterns and issues.

There's so much wealth and fertility in that mind, if we are willing to really dig deep enough and spend enough time in there patiently working things through to completion.

Andrea: It is such a personalized path. It is so important to honor it. I am really feeling in this moment that some of the soul lessons and some of the things I have moved through are so different than what yours are. A different flavor.

Because I took on everyone's emotions and learned to navigate through *how to make everything better* in the household, instead of expressing things. Although I did do a lot of singing and dancing around the house and things like that to express. I didn't do anger, but I did things to try to move it out of the physical body.

When I think about some of my most powerful life lessons, the pieces that took me down to the core, it was learning that I could do or be something that I had no idea that I was capable of doing in a powerful way.

The moment that just popped into my head was when my third child was born with a congenital heart defect and he had his first open heart surgery. The doctor came into the room and told us he didn't think he would make it through the night. In that moment, something expanded in my heart in a way that I opened to unconditional love. The kind of love, I had no idea I was even capable of feeling or expressing. I sat by his bed and told him in that moment, with tears running down my face, that whatever he chose I was going to be there for him. I knew he was a soul. I knew he was here for something.

I experienced for the first time, unconditional love, absolute acceptance, understanding that even though there was pain I was going to be in that moment with him and I gave him permission. I told him, if he wanted to fight this, *I am here and I will be with you every step of the way and if you want to die and this is too much for you now, I will hold your hand until the last breath.* Within five minutes, his vital signs changed and he did choose to live for 19 months.

I think sometimes that is the stepping into this greater place of ourselves. Then, part of it is the release and part of it is, *I didn't even know I could hold that much.*

Jeff: I think that what happens quite often in the spiritual community is that we begin to define Divine purpose as finding some calling as though that is the only way your soul is going to grow and expand. You are born to be an artist so you become an artist and there you go.

Well, what is not discussed enough is the gifts associated with the shadow work. So for you, that experience, that very painful and difficult experience was an opportunity for you to embody yourself in a vaster consciousness and to grow in your spirituality, to grow in your relationship to reality which is really all spirituality is as far I'm concerned.

I wrote a lot about **JAB,** which is the **Jealousy, Abandonment and Betrayal trigger.** A real, deep abandonment wound that I carry in the bones of my being. It really plagued me in many ways in my journey. But, at the same time developing the capacity to hold the space for those feelings without turning to reactive behaviors in an effort to turn off that tap is one of the ways that I've matured in my consciousness. Therefore, I have become more able to live in reality in a more real and genuine way without escape hatches; without returning to my habitual range of linear emotion.

And that really for me, writing SoulShaping, honoring this call to write wherever this comes from in me, I feel in many ways, pales in comparison to the growth that has emanated from my burgeoning and developing willingness to work through challenging, emotional experiences; to hold the space for the shadow; to dance with the shadow; without jumping off the dance floor, right? And that's what you're talking about and unfortunately what happens is we're not taught or trained to do this. We're not supported enough in this. There's not enough of a soulpod for most of us. We need help doing this. Some people, often the most challenged people cannot afford the therapeutic process. The world needs to be set up a little differently or a lot differently so that people can be supported in moving in that direction and really so it doesn't just become us talking on our show about it. They have a real tangible experience of transforming their material into the grist of the soul mill that lives at its core.

Andrea: Your definition of **JAB- The Jealousy, Abandonment and Betrayal emotional trigger** reminds me of something I was talking about in the last week about grief. It was the thing that I think we miss when we have the loss of a loved one. We are focused on *"I miss that person,"* but part of what we're missing is the underlying emotion.

For one person, having a life partner die is going to bring up abandonment issues; for another person it might bring up inadequacy. There are underlying emotions that get so focused on the actual event of loss that we miss the underlying emotion that wants to be healed. The underlying pattern that's kind of stuck and that's one of the things that keeps cycling through whenever we miss a person.

Jeff: There's like this giant repression contract in the culture. Let's say that someone begins to open to the feelings below the grief. Are they encouraged in that or are they encouraged to grin and bear it? Are they handed a box of Kleenex when they start crying, allegedly because it's an act of kindness? But, really in effect, it dampens the flow of the movement of the grief.

I saw that so often in body centered psychology. People would be weeping and weeping and weeping and we'd hand them Kleenex. Rather than just getting beside them and putting our hand on their back we'd hand them Kleenex. And Kleenex was fantastic because they'd start wiping their nose and the physical effect was it blocked the flow of the release. It's really important to talk about how we deal with somebody else's material. How we support them in moving through it and really what it is reflecting back to us. If we are all party to this repression contract when somebody else is in that flowing
grief, what does it bring up in us that we haven't dealt with? Why do we need to find a way to tighten them up and focus them on the path and have them look forward and not look
back at all the rest of it? What is that about? Because what ends up happening and it is the **power of then**, the development of our consciousness stops at any point along the
path, when we stop moving through our processes. We're still back there. We can't be in the now because the now becomes a cerebral construct when the emotional body is still fourteen years ago.

I think the most important thing we can do in culture is create an environment where people move their emotions through in a timely manner before it gets so blocked up, repressed and congealed they can't even access it or it comes through as passive aggression. They don't even know where it came from; not only because they can then be clear and back, *present, fresh, innocent, authentic, in the moment,* they can keep growing as they go along. Before waiting for the latter years of their life, they start to unpack it.

Andrea: Jeff, I opened up the chat line and Monica has a question: "Going through a breakdown, what is your advice to make things better?"

My interpretation of the question: How do I move through this? Jeff, no one wants to feel.

Jeff: Your answer is a good one. Feel it. Create a space. This is one of the greatest challenges. People are in adaptive realities with families and responsibilities. They have a job. And again, in the culture, we don't create space for this. I think the first thing to do is to try to create some space in your daily and weekly life where you can really, really connect to those feelings and move those feelings without having to re-armor or readapt your personality and put them away kind of midstream. I think that is very challenging. And the other thing I think is important is to try to get therapeutic support for the process. Some people are able to do this work all alone in an isolation chamber. But, most people aren't. They don't know the terrain well enough and they need a really good therapist to help them through to the next place on their process. Those are the two things that come to mind for me.

Andrea: Yes, I absolutely believe in therapy and I have had great therapists. I also want to say, be willing to change therapists. Know yourself well enough that you've either completed a process with a person or something no longer feels in alignment.

Jeff: Therapists can usually only walk us down the path that they themselves have walked. I had an excellent first therapist. Very mind-y. Very capable and very well-trained. Very capable of helping me learn about basic fundamental concepts, like boundaries, slowing down and breathing. I didn't understand any of these things.

I remember when she introduced the term boundaries, the concept of boundaries, it was like something went off in my brain. It was like this radical shift having grown up in this boundary-less, invasive environment in my consciousness. Still to this day, I am just beginning to understand what it means to be a healthy boundaried person. But, then it reached a point where the cerebral nature of the therapist became frustrating for me. I wanted to go deeper into my body and do more body-centered psych work and talk just wasn't doing it. It was like I was just perpetuating my malaise in many ways. It took me a lot longer than it should have because I didn't get that you could leave your therapist.

To leave my therapist and to find a heart-centered therapist that really helped me to move to the next step on my journey. It's important to interview a therapist and sit down and really decide. They're not just doing you a favor, you're also doing them a favor. I mean it's an exchange. To really spend time with that therapist and getting to know whether or not on a body level you really feel you can trust them. It's really important.

Andrea: We have about 10-12 minutes left, I was thinking about the **Power of Then**, unless something else is coming up for you to talk about.

Jeff: No, let's talk about it. I'll read the definition.

The Power of Then: The effect the past has on our present consciousness, although the physical body travels forward chronologically, one's emotional consciousness always lingers at any point of departure. To move forward on the path, we have to go back and deal with the wounds and memories that obstruct us. We've got to be there then before we can be here now.

The Power of Now. Be Here Now. The whole now-ness trip. I remember sitting in this really cool, holotropic breath work with Stan Grof and Jack Kornfield was doing meditation. I can remember just trying to get into the now. Looking around at all of these Western people, caffeinated, armored, overly heady, surviving by their wits, surviving by my wits, thinking this seems kind of ridiculous. We're sitting on these cushions trying to get into the now and our bodies are completely back there. Our bodies are completely armoued, there's no fluidity in our breath. There's really no freshness in our emotive appreciation of the moment. All of that. Then, we would do these holotropic breathworks for hours; like hitting and pushing and heaving and spitting up and people channeling crazy things, and flying on magic carpets and moving aggression and everything. At the end of those breathworks, everybody looked like they were kind of here, like way more here. And I was way more here. I was more naturally meditative, rather than having to force it. Rather than having to work the now as a construct of a cerebral, mind-centered, paternalistic concept of nowness that comes through the mind. It came really up from my emotional body. I had to go down in order to go up.

 For me, I really got it. That it was really the most impactful thing in most of our lives was the then, was the past. And the thing that was preventing us from really knowing the now, in a really purified way, was our relationship to the past and that which hadn't moved through us from the past. Because whenever I was able to have those deep released processes, I felt almost immediately present.

 So, that's what the term really focuses on. I see so many people talking about now as a concept. Just like talking about all Oneness as a concept but not really having an emotive and felt experience of it.

Andrea: It brings up for me, your article about the soulpods and how important it is to surround ourselves with people who can understand that the process is going on.

The situation that just popped up is my middle daughter just graduated from college at Prescott Arizona. It was the first time all three of my daughters and myself were together this year. My one daughter is married and my ex-husband was there with his wife. So, it was quite the crew that was there.

Even with all of the growth I had had this year and feeling so much more connected to my body and the Earth and knowing who I am and even my middle daughter and I having so many conversations She is one of my soulpods and we have the language and know what's going on with each other and the process.

A couple of times things just came out of my mouth and I would stop for a minute and even she would say, *"what are talking about?"* I then said, *"I don't even know why I said that. I don't even feel that."*

But, it was the first time we were all there and I went into this automatic reflex of what I say when we're all together and I hadn't had the chance to clear it in a sense because I hadn't been around them. It was an old pattern.

Jeff: It was an old soul pattern. In terms of the whole soulpod concept is the more we can make an effort to find people who resonate with where we are at on our spiritual journey at different stages, the less likely we are to fall back into our habitual patterns relationally. Because then we get validated and reflected back and supported in this new shape, this new soul shape, this new way of being that we're beginning to embody.

For me that's very important. If all I was doing was spending time with the people I spent time with twenty years ago, I think it wouldn't take very long before I'd be right back to the same style of interacting.

When you start to spend time with people that reflect the next stage on your journey, you start to entrench a different style or form of interface, both with yourself and with others. Then, it becomes more difficult. It's still always possible. These grooves are so deep, particularly with family of origin, in your family and in your marital family. But soulpod becomes really important and experimenting with an entrenching, a new style of relating.

Andrea: I have a few paragraphs from your book SoulShaping. This one seems to relate to this: *We must have faith that we will survive that often-lonely space between old friends falling away and new ones showing their face. This faith is our buffer against the temptation to go back to the familiar. If we can hang tight and make conscious efforts to connect, the next pod will be walked in our direction when the moment is right. We call to them, they call to us, and our angels broker the deal...*

Question from the Chat Line: Someone named Spirit Divine wrote, *"several very dear people in my life who have passed in the last seven years and I'm trying to get past the losses and move on to find new people and continue my dreams. How do I completely clear that which is blocking me if I do not know what is blocking?"*

Jeff: I would say try to excavate the emotions; the deep, deep dark emotions. Create space for it. Do body-centered practices. Even things like OSHO's dynamic meditation or some of the bioenergetics work is fantastic at excavating, deep, dark emotional holdings and bringing them to the surface of consciousness. Talk therapy often isn't very effective at that. Quite often we really have to open the body and find the practice whether it's dance, yoga or bioenergetics that really excavates the material.

Breathwork was a very effective thing for me. Holotropic Breathwork is a form of breathwork developed by Stan Grof. This work for me was a direct access to emotions that in my waking consciousness I didn't have any idea how to get to.

Andrea: I agree. I do think there is a place for talk therapy and I know that you have recommended that, too. But I think some of this is so deep into our cellular bodies that finding those practices and having a regular practice is critical. So, when there is a wave of emotion that comes, you have a practice in place to support you.

I actually had a really powerful shift the other night, in the middle of the night on New Year's Eve. I was sound asleep. I woke up. I had a wave of emotion that might have been fear or anxiety. I felt the feeling, I took a deep breath, I imagined myself anchored to the earth and within seconds, out of my mouth came the words, *"I'm ready for a breakthrough now"* and I could feel a physical shift happen. I have a practice and it moved through me really quickly. I don't have a physical shift every time something like that happens, but you need a practice to work with emotions when they appear. Jeff, this has been a really rich conversation, I am so grateful you came on the show and were authentically you showing up here. I really appreciate that and being willing to be on this archived show for people to listen to.

A former criminal lawyer and psychotherapist, **Jeff Brown** *is the author of 5 popular books- Soulshaping: A Journey of Self-Creation, Ascending with Both Feet on the Ground, Love it Forward, An Uncommon Bond, & Spiritual Graffiti. He is also the owner of Enrealment Press and an online school, Soulshaping Institute.*

www.soulshaping.com
www.enrealment.com
www.soulshapinginstitute.com

Grief Transformation Show #42
Cell Your Soul: Owning and Clearing Our Emotional Debris with Jeff Brown

January 5, 2011
http://tobtr.com/1422820

Andrea Hylen

Chapter Seven

Discovering Gifts After a Loss or Change
Andrea Hylen

Show originally aired on December 17, 2010

One of the keys to grief transformation and living a deeper, richer life is to find a deeper meaning for a loss and for change. The death of a loved one, a divorce, the loss of a job or a home, the loss of a friendship or a physical illness in your own body or one that requires care for a loved one.

When we take the time to reflect and look for a deeper meaning, we can discover new things about ourselves and about the gifts within the sadness, the anger, the discomfort. We become able to feel it instead of pushing it away. Like going into a cave with a flashlight and be willing to see what you can see.

In the first few days after the death of my husband, I appreciated the hummingbirds that were in the garden at hospice. They seemed so full of joy right after he died. I appreciated the friends and family who came to say goodbye and to share memories. I appreciated the time to sit with my children and grieve knowing that that was the most important thing to be doing and being. Over time, layers began to dissolve until I saw the gifts in our relationship, the love without the petty details in life and letting those fall away.

When my son, Cooper, died I appreciated the moments of laughter during his nineteen months of life. I appreciated the moments when I had stopped everything to hold him and dance and sing and look into his eyes to see his soul. He taught me to live in the present and to embrace it. I appreciated the healing he brought to me. His presence taught me that I was a good mother and he opened me up to love
unconditionally. His illness, his surgeries, his birth, his death all opened my heart to love. He healed my broken heart from my first marriage and all of the pain I had from fighting my

first husband in court for custody of my older two daughters. Fighting against the system and the defense to prove I was a good mother even though I did not want to stay in my marriage. Cooper showed me that I was a good mother filled with love for her children. He taught me so many lessons in his nineteen months of life. He was a great teacher and I opened myself up to be his student.

When my first marriage ended, I was able to reflect on the gifts that appeared years later. I discovered my own personal power, moving from victimhood to powerful woman. I broke a family pattern of verbal abuse and staying in an alcoholic marriage. I discovered a strength I didn't know I had.

Everything has a gift in joy and sorrow. Sometimes the gift is seen immediately. Other times it takes years because the gift is buried under pain. But, there is always a gift. We just have to open our eyes and be willing to see it. Open your heart and let the gift appear.

Tonight I am going to share two stories about my deceased loved ones. One is about my grandmother and the other about my husband.

One of the ways I have honored my deceased loved ones and discovered gifts is to embrace the traits I admired most about them and make them my own.

My grandmother Jackie died in 1984, two months after my oldest daughter, Mary was born. Nana Jackie was pure love. As a child I thought of her as Mary Poppins, arriving in town with a suitcase of interesting jewelry, fur wraps and make-up. As a teenager, she arrived with words of *"think positive thoughts and your life will change"* just like Louise Hay, the author of **You Can Heal Your Life**. As a college student, I challenged her *"see everything as love"* words when I pointed to war and destruction and murder on the front page of the newspaper. She looked at me with more love in her
eyes. It didn't matter what I said or did, whenever I was in her presence, I felt like I was the most precious being on the planet. She adored me and shined her love and light, like liquid gold, all over me.

My grandparents lived in California during my childhood. My Dad worked for Pillsbury and every promotion meant we would move, as a family, to another part of the country. I lived in California, Minnesota, Virginia, Texas, back to Minnesota and finally Pennsylvania. My grandmother flew to our home every few years and as I grew older, she wrote letters filled with wisdom, hope and love.

She died when I was a 27-year old married woman with a two-month-old baby, living in Maryland. I woke up early the morning she died and knew something had happened. I could already feel her spirit with me before the phone rang with the news of her death. It was a surreal feeling of sadness. I could still feel her with me and could imagine that she was still alive in California.

At the age of 37, I got really sick. I was diagnosed with an autoimmune condition called polymiositis. My immune system was attacking my muscles and my body was physically weak. I followed the doctor's orders, researched alternative medicine and began an internal process of healing with a deeper spiritual connection. As I began to reflect on my life with journaling and meditation, my heart began to ache for my grandmother. I desperately wished for one more day with her. I wanted to talk with her about positive thinking and healing from the inside out. This would have been the perfect time to have a deep conversation with her. One day I read the letters she had written to me in my childhood and sobbed and sobbed as I read the letters out loud.

It was during my journey of healing that I began to talk with her spirit, to feel her with me and to hear her words. My aunt and my mother said that I was so much like my grandmother in her words and actions. That was the greatest compliment I could ever receive. I wanted to embrace the traits I admired so much and to live my life with her love and light radiating out to the world. She was my barometer of what it was like to be full of wisdom, love and leadership.

At the age of 53, I moved to southern California. First stop was Santa Barbara where a friend was going to provide foster care for my cats. My youngest daughter, Hannah and I needed some time to find a place to live. The closest town to Santa Barbara with a hotel that was pet friendly and affordable was in Buellton. It was an additional 30 minutes from Santa Barbara, a beautiful drive through windy roads, along the ocean and through the hills. I had reserved the hotel on-line and was following the directions. When we pulled into the town, I had a flashback memory and told Hannah that I had been here before. I didn't remember all of the details of this sleepy town, but I remembered Andersen's Restaurant and the split pea soup.

When I was 13, and lived in Minnesota, my younger sister, Joanne, and I flew to California to spend a few weeks with our grandparents, Jackie and Arthur. We flew to San Diego and drove to their home in San Jose. Along the way, driving up the coast, we toured and visited the San Diego Zoo, Disneyland, Knott's Berry Farm, and a little town called Solvang.

The trip in 1969 had been a dangling carrot for us to get all A's and B's on our report cards. When the final report cards came, I had a C in one of my classes. How could my parents tell my grandparents that the trip was cancelled? We didn't see them very often and the details and airline tickets were all set. My parents went to Plan B. I was required to write a report about my California trip. It was truly a blessing in disguise. On that trip, I took pictures, and collected brochures, pictures, ticket stubs, placemats from restaurants and even sugar packets. I learned to observe and record everything. I still have the scrapbook and report and have read it numerous times keeping the details and memories alive. It is a memory I cherish from my childhood.

When I arrived in Buellton with my cats, I knew the restaurant immediately. This was the same restaurant where I had saved sugar packets and a placemat for my scrapbook. This was the restaurant where I ate split pea soup with my grandparents and Joanne before entering the town of Solvang, a Danish town where we spent the night. My grandfather was born in Sweden and travelled to the United States when he was 10. This was a town where I learned more about my heritage. Forty years later the memory was vivid.

On this trip, Hannah and I ate split pea soup at Andersen's. I bought treats from the Danish bakery, took pictures, and walked through the town of Solvang, weaving new memories with the old.

Arriving back in California forty years later, I felt like my grandmother had rolled out the welcome mat. She was passing the baton to me and I would carry on the memory of her by radiating pure love to the world.

The next story is about my husband. Hurley had a huge booming laugh, the kind of laugh where the person throws their head backwards, opens their mouth and expands their chest to let it out. It makes me smile just to think of it. It was one of his greatest traits.

Hurley was a born explorer and adventurer. He was a skydiving jumpmaster, a falconer and a lover of roller coasters. When he was diagnosed with cancer, he was in the process of building an ultra-light airplane. He planned on learning to fly it when he finished building it. After the diagnosis, he lived for 10 more months and died with a few more unfinished adventures in the works.

A year after my husband's death, a friend invited me to go on a Shaklee cruise to Jamaica and Cancun and the Bahamas. Betsy and I both loved to travel and this was an incredible gift. When we arrived on the ship, Betsy and I were looking at the off shore excursion choices. We both jumped at the idea of going to the Mayan ruins and temples, shopping and lunch in the Bahamas and a variety of spa treatments on the days at sea. Then, Betsy found something she had always wanted to do, zip lining above the canopy of trees in Jamaica. Although not as extreme as skydiving, I could feel the palms of my hands begin to sweat and my stomach doing a flip-flop. My idea of adventure is long distance road trips, museums, nature walks, the ferris wheel, the merry-go-round and walks on the beach. I wasn't sure if I could do the zip lining because of the heights, but with Betsy's eagerness and the thought of my husband, I decided to go for it.

When my husband died, I didn't feel survivor's guilt for being the person who continued to live. But, I did feel a responsibility to live life fully, to add adventures to my life that he would never have the chance to do. I felt a responsibility to appreciate waking up and living each day.

In Jamaica, we were transported by bus to a location with zip line guides, and equipment. As I suited up in the harness and helmet, I felt my husband's spirit strapped in with me. Standing on the edge of the cliff, with the guide giving me words of encouragement and explaining how safe I was while connecting me to the zip line, I took a minute to stand there, to close my eyes and feel the deep connection with my husband. *"Okay, Hurley, let's go. This one is for you!"*

I jumped off the cliff to fly over the first riverbed squealing a scream of excitement and joy. For the next 45 minutes, we moved along the zip line landing on one platform after another. On the last zip line run, the longest one in the series of leaps, the entire line was above the tops of the trees. One of my passions is watching birds fly and soar. For the first time in my life, I felt like I was a bird flying over the tree tops. I wanted it to go on forever. My heart soared as I felt gratitude to have had the experience. Between the eagerness of Betsy and the responsibility I felt to live life fully, I had experienced one of the most powerful, fun moments of freedom in my lifetime.
    Someday I will do it again for the pure joy of the adventure and the gratitude for being alive. I will not waste one moment of the precious time I have here. I will embrace it all and live a life worth celebrating.

I encourage you to reflect on your life. To explore those deep, dark places and to bring that flashlight with you, to look and discover something new in the process of grieving. To embrace the things you love about someone, to discover hidden gifts in changes and loss and to live!

Grief Transformation Show #26
Discover Gifts after a Loss or Change

December 17, 2010
http://tobtr.com/1436200

Andrea Hylen

Chapter Eight

Stay Open: Spiritual and Self-Care Space
Guest: Carin Channing, Author

Show originally aired on November 27, 2010

Introduction: Carin Channing, LCSW, is a writer, musician and traveler devoted to the awakening of human consciousness.

Andrea: Carin and I met on Facebook during a time when we were each diving into a deeper silence within than we had ever experienced before. Tonight, we will attempt to put words to something that has no words. Silence. Moments of grieving that occur when you willingly step into the silence and let go of old stories, old roles, old pain and old expectations. When the calling to go within is greater than the calling to stay the same.

I am going to begin by giving you some context about why I asked Carin to come onto the show to have this conversation. I had an experience in 2009 when I felt *"an inner calling,"* to sell my house and release my personal belongings and life in Maryland including all of the roles I felt gave me value. I had lived in that community for 28 years. I moved to California and spent the last year listening to my inner voice. My youngest daughter Hannah, age 16, has been creating her own life in California, too.

All I knew was that I needed time to be in silence.

So, Carin, we're just going to have a conversation now and I am going to start it by asking, *"What led you to connect with this silence? Where did this journey begin for you?"*

Carin: I've been thinking about this today, Andrea, knowing we were going to talk about it tonight. I'm smiling though because I think the journey really started with something kind of loud and musical which was probably when I was in college and first started to go to Grateful Dead concerts. What happened during that time period for me was I just started seeing that there were other ways of living, other ways of knowing, outside of my standard "middle-class, pretty, white-bread" upbringing.

I really think that is where it started but it went on for quite some time before I actually got to a place where I started quieting myself down. It was the Dead shows and it was not long after that that I got turned on to a little book called, **Be Here Now**. Some friends of mine had discovered it on a road trip out to Colorado. They came back all starry-eyed and talking about this guy named Ram Dass. They had read this wonderful book. So, I decided to look into that, too. It was around that time period that a friend of mine taught me how to practice meditation. I jumped right into it because I couldn't fall to sleep at night. My mind was always going and going and going. I thought the meditation would somehow be a way to get some sleep. That was probably twenty years ago now. There's been a lot in between and since then.

Andrea: Would you talk a little bit about Ram Dass? Tell the listeners who Ram Dass is and about the **Be Here Now** material.

Carin: The book was originally published in 1971. The 40th anniversary is being released sometime soon and the publishing companies, *Harper One Publishing* decided to do a special writing project where seven writers were slowly working their way through the content of **Be Here Now** and then blogging about it. I was fortunate to be selected as one of those writers. So, I am now intimately acquainted with the bulk of the book.

When it first came out, the book was exposing a lot of Westerners to some Eastern Philosophies; some ancient teachings that we just hadn't seen here in this country certainly not on a large scale. The man called Ram Dass was born Richard Alpert and he was from a very successful Jewish
family on the East Coast. I have some things in common with him, coming from a successful Jewish very mind-oriented family. Myself included, we're all these neurotic Jews kind of gone wandering trying to find our way to calm our minds down. That's what Ram Dass had done.

There's more to the story but as a very successful man in his 30's, a Harvard psychology professor, he had gone off to India. While he was there he met a teacher who blew his mind, pretty much, and helped him see that there was more beyond the thoughts that were kind of running the show for him. That's what I was starting to learn while reading the book; there was more beyond the thoughts that were keeping me up at night.

Ram Dass and his Guru were like my spiritual father and grandfather; that's how I looked at those guys. I had the good fortune of traveling to India in 2001 and went to stay at one of the temples that is devoted to this teacher. Even though he died in 1973, there are still temples devoted to him in India.

At that time, I was still really, really in my mind. I remember being in this dirty, dusty ashram on the other side of the world and my thoughts were just going crazy. It's not like I got over there and I'm meditating and peaceful and yoga and we're all really chill.

I found I went all the way to the other side of the world and I was still there. Looking back, I realize, I still had quite a way to go.

Andrea: I love that because it is a journey. It's not like we are trying to get to some place which is one of the things I think about meditation. It being a journey of exploration. I am relating to this as, *I am going to study and then I'll be someplace,* or *I'm going to do meditation. Okay, now I'm going to go to India. Wait a minute I still have the chatter going on. When does that kick in to say I've arrived?*

It brings up the whole idea that I've been really looking at today. **The experience is the experience**. It is not really leading me to something. *I am having the experience right now.*

Carin: All vastness is in the moment that we're in right now. I don't know if it's a cultural thing. I don't know the why behind it. But, we are definitely culturally programmed to *"make it and get somewhere and achieve."* There's that and there's more. *I can be better. Improve, improve, improve. Round the next corner. One more meditation class. One more teacher.*

Andrea: And it takes us out of the present moment. It takes us out of the moment of what is actually happening right here. Because there's always this feeling of, *'I need to get over there.'* In truth, when you get over there, there's another over there to get to.

I'm 54 and I feel there has been this conditioning through my lifetime. In the past few years, I have been reflecting on, *why do we live our lives this way and why is that the only way to live my life? And why are people upset, if I want to live my life in a different way?*

And now, I am giving my adult daughter's permission to go ahead and live life the way they want to live it. I encourage them and ask, *"What's calling you? Why is that calling you?"* Or just explore it from that point of view.

People would ask me how my middle daughter was doing when she first moved to Arizona. I would say she's fantastic. The question would be *what is she doing?* I would say, *she's living life. She's finding ways of relating to who she is and discovering what she wants*. The response would be, *Huh? Well, what do you mean? Is she in school, does she have a job?*

I would say, *"I love the way she's consciously interacting with her boyfriend. She's exploring the food she's eating."* They were really basic things. I would say to her, *"I love that you are living your life. Don't look for something outside of yourself because this is it. Live your life."*

Carin: Andrea, I'm grinning over here. I know the people who are listening can't see me, but I'm just grinning. I had a conversation with another friend of mine who has been on a similar path to what I have been on for the last few years. We had a wonderful conversation recently about being asked, *"What are you up to? What have you been doing these days?"*

It seems like it would be easier to tell those things about your daughter than if someone would ask you the same questions directly. I'm sure you've had these kind of questions asked to you, also. Even at a friend's house for Thanksgiving. *So, what do you do?*

Maybe I am making an assumption, but I really don't feel that the people who are asking the question really want me to answer what's true for me: *"Well, I am standing right here with you and my feet are on the floor. I can feel a breeze on my left ear and this is really beautiful."*

You know, like that.

But, I'm seeing that maybe that's just some of my old stuff that we were talking about. Role playing and what's from our past and letting some of that stuff go. That may continue to be some of my own attachment to looking good or thinking that I need to coddle the person who is speaking to me. I'm not sure. But, I do find myself saying, *"Well, I do this for my job and then I have my column that I write."* It doesn't always feel authentic. I think that's part of what we're exploring, both of us, in these parts of our lives.

How do you go ahead and relate to other humans who might think that you're just really out there? Where is the middle ground communication that you can put into words?

Andrea: I felt like that when I first arrived in California. Most of the year before, I was getting rid of things in my home. As I was releasing, I would discover things. I had all of the tents and boxes of things for the Girl Scout community stored in my house, for instance. And as I started to find homes for those or release them or donate them and I didn't have any Girl Scout things left, I wondered. *Who am I, if I'm not a Girl Scout Leader?*

All of the releasing meant I was letting go of all of the that I identified with that I thought gave me value. When I finally sold my house and moved to California, I had cleared so much of who I thought I was and I was ready for answers. I arrived in California expecting I would have the answers to the next steps in my life.

I arrived, threw up my hands and said, "I'm here! Now what? I am ready for my assignment." And there was nothing. There were no answers. There was actually more clearing that I had to do. So, when people would ask me what I was doing or it looks like you are on a wonderful adventure, I felt at a loss of what to say.

First I would think, *hmmm…a wonderful adventure. I don't know what I'm doing here. I don't know how I'm feeling.* I didn't really feel adventurous at that point. I felt like I had to clear more. I had to have more silence. I had to just be with it, without trying to figure it out. So, when people would ask me what I was doing I would say, "I don't have words right now." After a while, I sent a letter to my Mom and Dad, my Aunt and Uncle, my sister, brother and a couple of close friends., and I said, *"I just need time to hear my voice again."*

To me that meant, I don't want to talk on the phone because I don't have words to share. You can find me on Facebook, you can send me an e-mail. I'm here, I'm okay, but I just need time.

One of my friends was frustrated with me because it has been almost a year. She said, *"Why didn't you tell me it was going to take so long?"* I said, *"Because I didn't know."* I still don't know. All I knew was that I had no words and I had to create space.

When my daughter and I stayed in Santa Monica, I took two walks on the beach every day whether it was rainy or sunny. Some days I would talk to the seagulls. I was grateful for all homeless population that lives right there because I fit right in with people talking to themselves, talking to the ocean. And I thought, yes, this is exactly where I need to be right now. Walking and talking to myself on the beach.

I would say out loud, *okay, I'm not sure what's next. Does anyone have any answers?"*

My point is I didn't have any answers. Even now I don't know why I am hosting 44 grief transformation radio shows other than I was divinely inspired to do that. So, now I have some answers for the question: "What are you doing today?" *I am preparing for the show and when the shows are over, I will let you know what I am guided to do next.* I don't have the whole picture. I only have this moment.

Carin: It does seem useful to say I'm working on this project, sort of a token thing. We're living in a different kind of paradigm and neither one is right or wrong. The structure where you get a job and things make sense and to a lot of our culture there's that and there isn't anything wrong with that. It's just different from how we're living. It's useful to have something to say that is satisfying to that side of things.

But, as I'm saying that, it's a little bit co-dependent, too. I'm thinking about my own family and that maybe they wouldn't be able to be with whatever I need to express.

I had a great experience recently when I was writing on the Be Here Now blog, my second to last entry there. By the way, if you're interested in reading some blog posts, you can find them at http://beherenownetwork.com/blog.

The second to the last one that I wrote, I realized throughout, I was writing about turning inward and becoming more and more of a hermit and I was becoming more comfortable with that. My second to last piece was really focused on that. Not long after putting that one out, I was talking with my Dad on the phone who was sort of questioning why he wasn't hearing from me a whole lot lately. I said, *well, Dad on my blog you can see that I'm not really talking to anybody right now.*

He said he doesn't really read them because it's not something he really relates to. I was reading something in Ram Dass's new book, **Be Love Now**. He said, *"If you're into bowling, you hang out with people who are into bowling."* So, I'm into this spiritual conversation and quieting and not knowing and things that appear do not have any direction. And my Dad is a CEO of a major hospital system; very different things than what we're into. He said that he doesn't usually read that stuff because it doesn't really click for him.

I looked at my blog piece and some of it would have been too out there and wouldn't have made any sense to him.
I took a couple of paragraphs out of that and it did make sense to the average reader explaining the quiet times and how I do
question whether I need to talk with my friends and family
about this. And I wondered, do I need to put out an apology or can I let you know, *hey man, this is just what's up for me right now;* similar to the letter you sent your family, Andrea.

So, I cut and pasted some of it in an e-mail to my Dad and he wrote me back that he could understand that and he was glad, he was happy. It felt like it really cleared some space for me because that relationship has kind of hung over me in more of a **should** than most of my other relationships. I have learned recently to just sort of ease off a relationship or what feels natural to me. But, my Dad wants to be in touch, he calls me once a week and I've struggled with what to actually say in conversations.

I felt really grateful that I got to use my writing which is my instrument. It's my craft to express myself, in a way that verbally, I wasn't really able to. He was able to really hear something here. Sometimes when we're in direct conversation with people we've known for all of our lives, like our family members, it's really easy to go into automatic roles and not really be able to speak from the heart, as easily. I have this expectation that the other person may not hear me or to take something from me that's not favorable or something. So, to be able to use writing and share that information, something like writing on the blog which is completely impersonal and not aimed at anyone in particular. Just saying, *here is my state of being right now.* It just turned out to be a terrific gift that I was able to share like that.

I think trying to have conversations with just anybody when you're out and about in the world and they want to know about this regular thing... *What do you do? Do you have a partner?* Just sort of average questions I think is probably part of why I am so quiet these days, too. I don't have answers for a lot of these things.

I'll give you another example. I was at a friend's house for Thanksgiving and it was just a beautiful day and everybody there was low key and interesting and warm and kind. We went around the table saying what we were grateful for and it was kind of a strange thing for me. I guess I had some judgment going on in my mind because it's not an unusual thing for me to be hanging out in gratitude.

I can tell when a real gratitude is happening for me and when I'm not in it. I also can tell when it's really coming from my heart or a *should* coming from my head. I should be thankful for this or that. Anyhow, I'm contemplating this as they go around the table and they get to me. Turns out I've been very moved by what some of the folks there were saying. When they got to me, I just wanted to sit there. I closed my eyes for a moment, felt my heart open and I had no words. I really didn't want to speak. I just wanted to be in that feeling of gratitude. But, I kind of brought myself back down and started speaking because I felt like it was something I was supposed to do in that moment to be part of the crowd or something like that. It was very interesting. I think it's just helping to establish what we're up to or maybe it's not even that. Maybe there's no explanation that needs to go around it. That's what I'm seeing now. We are where we are.

I think that people just go through phases where they need to be quiet.

Andrea: Well, it is a funny thing. What I value the most right now is silence and here I am on the radio talking for at least an hour every day and trying to put words to all of these different things. I know that a place where both of us have been channeling our words is into writing which is a very different way of being; sitting with words more than having an hour conversation.

Sometimes I will write a couple of words and I will just sit in the energy of those words. I don't feel that I have to do anything with them yet. I can just be with them. I might sit for 15-20 minutes and there might be paragraphs that come out of me or I might say that's it for now and walk away from it.

It's a very different place to be than coming on the radio and saying, well wait a minute, I don't hear anything, while we are sitting in silence now. Because that is what we feel called to do in the moment.

Back to Thanksgiving. This year on Thanksgiving, my daughter and I talked about how we wanted to celebrate it for a couple of weeks leading up to the day. We're new to California. I have very consciously stayed in this space of
silence. I go to a coffee shop once a day. People know me there. Some days I am chatty and other days I am quiet and writing in the corner.

My daughter decided she wanted to do a detox this week. She is almost 18 years old and is becoming more conscious about what she's putting into her body. So, I thought, okay; I am not really eating animal protein right now. My diet is more vegetarian now, too.

So, for the first time in 54 years I did not have turkey on Thanksgiving and I did not have the traditional meal that I have had for all of these years whether it was with one person or a crowd.

What I noticed on Thanksgiving was how I felt great about what we were cooking, a very simple vegetarian meal. It was delicious. But throughout the day I felt like something in my body that felt like discomfort. And this inner conflict of voices within me: *Oh, wait, I'm supposed to be eating turkey today. But, I don't really want to eat turkey today.* Voices and feelings that surfaced throughout the day.

In the experience of silence and listening to my own voice is finding where I have made changes and where there is a level of discomfort because there is an old habit kicking in. Whether my DNA is encoded, whether it is cellular memory or there is just a habit. Someone says, *"Happy Thanksgiving"* and I feel, Happy Thanksgiving, ding, where's the turkey?

So to go around the table and everyone is saying a gratitude and to find a way to express, that I don't have words right now. And to be able to say that I am actually feeling the gratitude in my heart with no other words. This is where I want to be. There's a bridge of Being with it and then letting people know what's going on internally.

I feel a responsibility, not to take everyone along with me, but to realize that some of what I'm doing is so different from anyone else in my family that I do feel some level of responsibility to communicate something.

Because no one has done anything wrong. My parents haven't done anything wrong. My sister and brother have not done anything wrong. My friends have not done anything wrong. I just have a stronger calling to spend this time with myself, with God, Spirit, whatever to describe this inner silence within me. I feel that so strongly, if I don't do this right now I feel like I would die.

Carin: My boyfriend says that everyone has their metal. He's really into heavy metal music. I'm not, but he says that my spiritual writing and my trip are like my metal. It's one of the ways I explained this stuff to my Dad. It's great because it shows how everybody's got this thing that they're into.

If I were to talk to some of my family members about God and Spirit. it just wouldn't connect and with others it would connect. When we can frame it, *every human is a unique individual expression*, that's just how it is. We can't help it. And like you said, you feel like you would die if you didn't do what you're doing now. We all have to live on what our path is, especially those of us who are living in a more intuitive way. It does not necessarily make sense on the outside but we can say, *"Hey, man, this is just my metal."* Like Ram Dass said, *if you're into bowling, this is my bowling.* My mom is really into politics. Andrew, my boyfriend says, that's just her metal.

I think it's a really nice equalizer. Sometimes in a spiritual community, and I think it's only fair to speak for myself, that sometimes I think that my way is the right way, not that it's that way for everyone. I don't think it is right for everyone to go live in a hole. I think some people want to be more social or be more outwardly focused. It's part of my own growth to get that there isn't even a right/wrong about that. That everyone is in the perfect natural place on their path and that waking up your consciousness is not necessarily better than going bowling. It just happens to be what I have to do because that is what I'm called towards. And to be a very successful businessperson is not any better than being one who lives on a wing and a prayer. None of the things are better than something else. It is just what we are called individually to do.

Andrea: That's one of the things I continue to remind myself. Part of pulling away and being different; I received different levels of support and there is a new dance. I have some wonderful friends who I have been friends with anywhere from ten to twenty years. Many of them said, *I send you blessings; I'm here; enjoy the journey; whatever you need.*

I had a friend who called me when it became legal for same sex marriage in DC. They are lesbians and have been together for, oh, my gosh, twenty years, I think or more. They live in Maryland. So, my friend called to tell me they were going to go to DC and get married and in May they were going to have a celebration. They wanted me to know about it.

There was no pressure about me flying back to Baltimore. They wanted to let me know about something exciting in their lives. I celebrated the fact that they got married in DC and they wanted to have a wedding a few months later. I was so happy for them. I said, *"I would love to be there and right now I am living one moment at a time."* I did not get any pressure about it. There was just this absolute beautiful moment of loving each other, sharing the celebration. And I have a number of friends who have really been holding this space for me to explore who I am and give me the space. And even though I don't know why I am here, how long I'm here. I don't have the answers. So, that's all cool.

On the other hand, I received an angry reaction from one of my friends. *How could I do this to her?* Over the last few weeks leading up to Thanksgiving, I feel that we have reached a level of acceptance with it and she's moving into her life and has released the need to have a hold on me. But, I'm feeling the attack energy still. I realized this week that that is part of my responsibility to heal. Whatever I need to do within myself to let go of those interactions where I was feeling the anger.

Because what I really do believe and the place I want to hold space is for everyone to follow their own path and whatever, that is fine. If someone wants to have the traditional Thanksgiving dinner year after year after year with the same people and the same food and that's what makes their heart sing, I want to say, *Go for it!* And for me, I need to take it one year at a time.

I have celebrated Thanksgiving with a variety of people and this year was very quiet. I felt that my calling was to hold a space on the radio for anyone who might need to hear a voice, this year. That's what I felt called to do. I feel great about the space I am in with it. I feel great about the meal and to me that's what it's about. Being able to follow my own inner calling and to accept what other people's callings are.

Carin: I expect that some of the backlash that comes up…Now I'm making this up because I don't really believe in whys or exploring too much in the whys of things because I think we end up going down a real mental road; When I am most interested in having the mind quiet.

I will say however, I think that people get challenged when they meet someone who is living moment to moment and is stepping outside of the normal way of doing things. Because in one part everyone has the same kind of desire within them to be really following their instinct and intuition and their path and not that many people do. It's usually really, really clouded over with obligations and fears being the primary thing. I think that it makes people nervous to be around people who do live on faith. Because they start to look at their own world and wonder, *am I really secure; am I really safe; what if I did really go and follow my heart, would I still be safe and secure?*

So, I think it is kind of a painful thing in other people sometimes, that can then show up as anger or hurt or *"you're offending me by being who you are kind of thing."* I suspect that that is part of what's coming up. And it ties in with something I was thinking about on our call tonight.

You were talking about having some kind of a responsibility to share what it is that you're up to. I think that we also could be planting seeds for people. Not that that is the primary goal. The primary goal is doing whatever your consciousness is telling you to do right now at this moment. At least for me and following the next thought and having the mind quiet.

But, it can have the added benefit of having radio shows like this and writing my column so that people can actually start to see it and can actually live this way. It's modeling. Part of how my column was born was that friends of mine would come to me as their self-care expert and they just really thought I had something really together, as far as
self-care goes. A big part of that was knowing when not to accept an invitation, you know. Even to socialize and go hang and do things if it sounded fun, but I knew for sure in my heart that that wasn't something I wanted to spend my time doing. It really is not hard for me to say no. So, you and I and folks, that we know, are living more intuitively. I think that even though there is some fearful backlash sometimes there's also a part of the population who really appreciates getting to look at someone doing this. I know I appreciate that about you, Andrea. I find you to be a wonderful model and I love hearing about the Jonas Brothers tour and I hope you're going to be talking more about that as these sessions go on.

It gives comfort to me, just to be reminded. Yes, we can live and be cared for and living in an intuitive way. You and I have to. We don't have a choice, I say that once you're on that path, it's what your path is and you best find a way to be cool with it.

It has the possibility of just having a wonderful curiosity. That's where I'm enjoying hanging out right now. I wonder how this is all going to work out. Because it is all working out. I think that is inspiring for people and scary. Both of those things, both inspiring and scary.

Andrea: It's funny because a lot of the modeling I do is on Facebook. I say, I'm writing again and today I had to curl up in a ball on the living room floor and sob. I would feel that kind of wave of pain coming so I just honored it, got on the floor, curled up in a ball in a way that said, *"Okay, I'm here, let 'er rip!"*

Once I finished sobbing, I went for a walk and there were words that came that I wanted to write; a whole other awareness that popped through. Modeling it and finding the balance. Making it visible so we can all learn together.

I had a situation happen in a coffee shop two weeks ago. There was a very nice gentleman who goes to my coffee shop and he was talking about something he was reading. In that moment, I felt a deep connection to what he was reading. I considered it a soul connection. I saw him. He saw me. We were talking about Gregg Braden's work and Fractal Time. It is kind of an unusual topic. But, there was a connection and I love talking about this material.

What it feels like in that kind of moment is a really intense love. He interpreted it as, *"let's go on a date."* Frankly, right now, I have made the decision that this is my year for me. I love weaving in and out of conversations with people, but I'm not interested in dating. The most important relationship I'm having this year is with me. I am really, really clear on that and I have plenty of time to find another person when that's where I want to be headed. Interesting, hmmm..beheaded (laughter) Taking my head off.

Carin: Yes, and that is where this conversation began is these old roles. We don't know who we are or where we are anymore. It is not a bad thing.

Andrea: I have had to grieve around the whole situation and feeling like I led him into a place where I wasn't clear. Maybe setting up boundaries in a different way. I have wanted to be kind but I have had to be very clear that I am not interested in a love relationship. Dating, life partner or anything like that and he has been persistent.

Have you found moments of going into silence where there are moments of grieving or letting go of parts of yourself?

Carin: I look at how I have known myself for a pretty long time to be a community person. I live in Texas now and I was like this when I lived in Ohio and when I lived in California. I have had lots and lots of people I've known and wonderful friends and terrific communities; a wonderful gift I learned from my Mom. She always had great, great long term groups of friends.

I realized last winter I had a bunch of people over and had kind of an orphan's Christmas potluck and I thought, *"Oh look I've really learned this thing about having wonderful friends and community around me."*
Well, I didn't know at that time that as the year went on I would really be retreating from all of that. I don't really feel the loss of it because I feel so complete, in general. I do need to work out a tiny bit of guilt feeling, which is not productive. Just something for me to work on there. And like you were saying about finding ways of expressing that in community because I don't want people to feel they have done anything wrong.

I don't miss the relationships. I am very interested in talking with people who are into my type of bowling and really not into other types of conversations now. It's not exactly that I have been grieving the loss, it's more that I have grappled with letting them down easy. Saying that I might be back around again and I might not be and allowing myself to keep on shifting. I really feel that my community has respect for that and so I think it's working out okay.

Andrea: I am a huge community person. So, thank you, God for Facebook, because it provides a place for me to check-in to be a part of a community on my own terms when I want to connect and then to detach and find the flow.

One of the things I have seen this year is the roles that I have played in my family for so many years. Deciding where I will play and where I won't play anymore. And I really got to a point this year where I saw how I put many things on hold for myself because I wanted to be in community with my family. And now I have said, the next 54 years are for myself. So, that means there is even more consciousness of every action. I called some of my family members to say Happy Thanksgiving because I wanted the connection. I love them. But at each step, I ask myself, *do I want to do that, do I not want to do that? How do I want to be in relationship here?* And then they get to make choices, too.

My parents decided to do something brand new this year and they weren't home when I called. So, I left the message on the answering machine. Then, I got to deal with the feelings of, oh, my gosh, they're not there. Well, good for them, they followed their heart. Like going back and forth with how to be in this new space.

Recently, I saw a movie called Ghetto Physics. One of the questions was to ask yourself, *"Who or what informs your choices."*

How are you deciding what to do, how to be? Is that based on something from your past? Is that based on what your heart tells you? Then wondering, is this the track I want to be on in my life or even looking at how I got on this track. I want to switch tracks right now and I am taking the time to explore that.

That is part of the whole year of silence. And it might be two years, it might be forever or I may find a way to weave back into my community in a more active role. I am just honoring what is. I said a year just to give it some structure.

So, you're feeling that, too?

Carin: I have wondered that, too. Long term plans don't really make a lot of sense to me. I just ask the Universe to guide how things are going to go and let them arise for me and then I check my intuition moment to moment because living any other way doesn't make any sense to me anymore. But, I do wonder, am I going to come back around or not. I don't even really have a strong sense of what "I" even means. We were talking about where this path started that seems like a very different person from me all those years ago and even where I was five years ago and even where I was a year ago. I think we're changing really rapidly which is part of the reason that we need to be able to tune in, get still, go into the emptiness and the space because that's what never changes.
The only thing that's changing is what's on the outside here.

Andrea: Someone posted on the chat line that they grieve the loss of a friend. They said, *"He connected to me. I connected back to his secret and he deeply withdrew to the point of not being able to connect. Lost another friend when I had to make him realize what we had made our initial friendship had died, so I had grown past it."*

I think that is one of the pieces of this, too. I was talking with a friend the other day and we are really in sync with doing some projects together. And when we get together
there's this aliveness. But, one of the things we've agreed is to follow the energy of it. I always say follow the bouncing ball and if the aliveness takes us in different directions then we honor that, too. There's an agreement up front of, *I'm here now and let's talk about it, if it switches for either of us. And see where that goes.*

Carin: I love that. I absolutely love that.

Andrea: So, having conscious relationships. If a relationship doesn't go that way, a harder ending or switching over. But, I'm certainly entering into relationships with more consciousness.

Carin: It's brilliant. I think when you are needing the space and the quiet that you do need right now. It is a brilliant way to allow people to move into your life, just letting them know how it is for you. I appreciate that.

Andrea: I want to thank you so much for coming on the show tonight to put words to things that don't have words. Even to let the audience know that there is a stirring going on for many people who are feeling called to silence.

How would you like to end this conversation for right now? What would you like to say?

Carin: When you ask that question, I find myself similar to sitting at the Thanksgiving table. Just getting still and feeling my body, sitting here on the couch. Everything we need to know as individuals is right there within us. It is in the silence or a very mind based society. If these words are unfamiliar to you, listeners, please come by my website and maybe there will be something that might make a little more sense to you. The website is a Dear Abby-style spiritual and self-care support space. I am hopeful that in our conversation here
tonight, Andrea, there will be some connections for some folks who may be experiencing a similar awkwardness or
discomfort with old ways of being and they could use some support just knowing *hey, quieting down and getting into your own tune, it's a beautiful generous thing.* We support you and I thank you so much for having the conversation with me, Andrea.

Andrea: Thank you for coming. This is really why I wanted to have conversations like this is to let people know that this is happening, that there is this stirring that is happening within and there are whole communities of people and individuals around here who are feeling this deeper calling to go into silence and to look at what path we're on and to ask questions or to just even be in the silence. I appreciate you.

Carin Channing *is a hands-on authority in rest and creativity encouragement. She envisions bringing simple, introspective creativity to every person on the planet. She is the author of the book 365 Days of Doodling (Discovering the Joys of Being Creative Every Day and for families: Doodle Book Junior – 101 Creative Prompts for Kids.*

http://doodleoutreach.com/

**Grief Transformation Show #7
Stay Open: Spiritual and Self-Care Space**

November 27, 2010
http://tobtr.com/1369276

Andrea Hylen

Chapter Nine

Thanksgiving Eve: Remembering
Andrea Hylen

Show originally aired on November 24, 2010

Tonight's show is about remembering: Happy times, sad times, honoring people who have died, honoring people who are living, honoring the path you have walked, are walking, and will walk.

One of the reasons I wanted to do this show tonight is because over the holiday season there are moments of sadness and grieving mixed in with the celebrations. Some of our greatest losses happened during the holidays. Many of us are also grieving the death or ending of a relationship for the first time during this holiday season. So, during this time when the emphasis is on get-togethers and parties and presents and food, I want to encourage you to be gentle with yourself and to know that I am here holding you, as a voice of love in the dark.

I have spent holidays alone. When it is your choice it is one thing, but when circumstances in your life mean that you can't be with people you would like to be with or a recent loss has changed everything in your life, it can be a very lonely time. I thought if there was one person who needed to hear a friendly voice reaching out tonight then it is worth the time to show up here. I want you to know I understand. I understand the loneliness. I understand that even if you are listening to this while you make pumpkin pie and sweet potatoes, you may be feeling a mixture of feelings.

There may even be moments when you are having a fantastic time. It's the night before Thanksgiving, you're cooking and then there's something in the background that happens. A song is playing or there is a smell of a certain food and you have a wave of sadness or grief. You may be cooking your grandmother's sweet potato recipe and you miss her. It's natural and it's okay to have feelings of sadness in the middle of a great day. It is normal, we just don't always talk about it. My wish for everyone is that you will learn to dance with all of the feelings and to give yourself permission to feel whatever feelings are showing up, whenever they show up.

So, here we are the night before Thanksgiving. I have been thinking about Thanksgiving all day and some of the memories associated with it. Here are some of my personal Thanksgiving memories. I hope they stir some memories and healing for you, too.

A quiet dinner for two memory popped up today. It was when my first husband and I were expecting the birth of our first baby, Mary. I was 8 ½ months pregnant and driving two hours to Pennsylvania would mean I would be too far from the hospital if I went into early labor. And with holiday traffic, we did not want to risk being that far from our home and medical care.

It was the first time I cooked the traditional meal of turkey and mashed potatoes and stuffing and sweet potatoes and pumpkin pie. I am sure I made stuffed baked potatoes because that was my mother-in-law's specialty and we didn't want to miss eating them! It was a sweet dinner celebration with football games and Christmas music playing in the background, and excitement stirring in my belly of what was to come with the birth of our first child.

I have always loved cooking Thanksgiving dinner. The focus is on food and connection with people. Gratitude. Tradition. Love. One year, I wanted to pour so much love into the meal that I made way too much food. This was the first Thanksgiving after my second husband's death. He died in July. We had friends over to celebrate and eat on this November holiday. I made so many side dishes that I forgot to put three of them on the table. The table was full and felt incredibly abundant and crowded. Reflecting back now, I know I was trying to fill up the table with food and people in the hope we wouldn't really feel what was missing. My husband's presence.

Even though my husband was 5'7" and a thin man, he could eat three times as much as anyone else at the table. I kept cooking and cooking as I thought about what he would like to eat. I wasn't thinking about the amount of food I had cooked and I hadn't adjusted to him not being there for the meal. Looking back now I can see the gluttony, the sadness, the laughter and the love that was at the table. So many feelings and so hard to experience the first Thanksgiving without the presence of a dear loved one.

One of my favorite Thanksgivings was in 2007. My youngest daughter Hannah and I drove from Maryland to Florida to spend the holiday with my parents and my sister and her family. It had been a long time since we had Thanksgiving together. It was a fun day. My nieces and nephews were there and we hung out in the kitchen and talked and laughed. When the turkey took longer to cook than my mother thought, it didn't matter. We all really enjoyed each other's company. It was spontaneous and fun and I treasure that year.

The year I separated from my first husband was a really hard year. I was numb with pain. I can feel the sadness surfacing even talking about it. As human beings, whenever we think about the past we can still feel the feelings whether there is joy or pain.

My little girls, who were two and three, spent that holiday with their Dad. I can remember going to Pennsylvania to spend the holiday with my family. I didn't really feel like I could get support there but my sister was in town with her family and I wanted to put on a brave face. No one was supportive of the divorce. I can remember driving home the next night and coming down with the flu for three days. It was such an emotional time, I got physically ill.

After that year, I hosted Thanksgiving at my home and I started a habit of asking people at work where they were going for Thanksgiving and inviting them to my home. There were a few people who came one year because there was a blizzard and they couldn't get home to their families. I added crafts and an international, cultural flair where we learned about a different country and the holiday traditions. Taking charge of a holiday by opening your heart and your home can inspire a new tradition in wonderful, creative ways. The sadness of the past can inspire new, joy-filled ideas.

The first Thanksgiving at my daughter Elizabeth's home was special. I had to let go of planning and taking control of shopping and cooking. I was trying to convince her that shopping the day before Thanksgiving was a terrible idea and we needed to shop on Monday not Wednesday. When I finally let go and followed her lead, we had a blast shopping the day before Thanksgiving in Whole Foods. Elizabeth was in charge of the list and five of us were sent into different aisles looking for food. It was like a scavenger hunt. Someone would discover samples in one aisle, find the rest of us and take us to the spot to eat samples together. It was fantastic! I highly encourage you to let go when you go to someone's house and just enjoy the celebration. Let them organize it and be in charge.

This year is a quiet year. Hannah, my youngest daughter and I are in California. I stopped eating chicken, turkey, beef and pork about six months ago and she is doing a detox with vegetables and juice. I looked through her detox book and found a vegetable soup for
lunch and a rainbow salad for dinner. I am filled with gratitude. It doesn't really matter where I am for
Thanksgiving. This year, I feel really grateful to have a place to live, an opportunity to host 44 radio shows about grief transformation, and a refrigerator full of fresh vegetables. I feel grateful that tomorrow morning I can walk up to Priscilla's, my favorite coffee shop, see the staff
and meet some new people. I am also grateful my cats are living with me again.

This next story is about Halloween, a day that has a lot of meaning for me and this year was filled with lots of feelings. I am sharing it as an example of what to do with unexpected feelings of grief and sadness. How to honor the feelings and also transform them to joy.

I woke up on Halloween morning with a heavy heart and waves of sadness. I lay in bed, took a deep breath and scanned my mind to see if it would give me a clue as to why I felt this way.

Halloween is my favorite holiday. I knew that something had to be stirring within me because I felt so sad. Instead of pushing it away, telling myself to get over it, I did a variety of things to stay with the feelings and allow awareness, with an opportunity for healing, to arise.

I took a shower and imagined the water clearing the way for me to understand, feel and heal. Meditated for 15 minutes emptying my mind of all thoughts. Walked to the coffee shop. Talked with a few people. Connected with social media on the computer. Walked home. I continued to connect with my heart, breathe, look at nature and stay open throughout the morning exploration of feelings.
I finally uncovered the root of the sadness. I was feeling the loss of a community. Halloween, Thanksgiving, and Christmas are community holidays. I have made choices in the last year to disconnect more from my family and friend community so I could hear my own voice again. I made the choice to move to California. I made the choice to spend more time alone listening to my inner voice. I made the conscious decision to go to the Agape Spiritual Center in Los Angeles and to limit community activities for now. I did not want to move from one community to fill myself up with another. It would have been a distraction when I first arrived. I wanted to empty before filling myself up again. After nine months of minimal connection, I was feeling the loss and I was aware of feeling like an empty vessel. I am beginning to hear my inner voice in the emptiness.

Here were some of the memories that surfaced on Halloween that brought up feelings of grief:

1. I married my first husband on Halloween 29 years ago. We have been divorced for 20 years now. I am happy we divorced and sad that our love and dreams died. Both are true.

2. First Halloween since we moved from Maryland to California.

3. First Halloween without young kids to interact with on Halloween.

4. A friend starting an Artfull Spiritual Service and potluck gathering in Maryland today. I am missing being a part of a community where I know people and they know me.

5. A store, Mystickal Voyage, was closing in Maryland. Another place I used to gather with community. I am not there to say goodbye in person.

Endings. Waves of sadness. I was grieving the loss of a connection to a community.

But something was changing as I became aware of this loss. I began to look at the new that is emerging. My daughter and I were invited to a community gathering. Organized by a group of women called the LaLas. They are a group of women who have come to Los Angeles with their children who are in the entertainment industry. They left their communities behind to support the dreams of their children. They had a potluck and went trick or treating in the neighborhood surrounded by Warner Brothers Studios in Toluca Lake, California. To bring you into the image: Think actors, set designers, make-up artists and elaborate displays. It was like being on a movie set. Incredible creativity and expression!

I met new people today. I shared my voice. I walked through the neighborhood for hours looking at the decorations, laughing, joining in with the community. This was an opportunity. I felt the sadness and released it to experience the present moment.

A new beginning. New memories. My heart is beginning to heal.

I have one last memory to share with you tonight.

Our loved ones live on in so many ways. Have you noticed that, too? It doesn't matter how long it has been since someone died. Five years after the death of my husband, I still think of him daily. Moments appear that bring waves of sadness and memories of joy. And the most important experience of all, a knowing that he is always near.

I woke up this morning and walked into the kitchen to make breakfast. Last night, I left a pan of dinner on the stove for my daughter who would be returning home from work after I was in bed asleep. As I picked up the pan to wash it with a few other dishes, I saw it. One ravioli and one carrot. She had eaten everything except for one ravioli and one carrot.

Standing in the kitchen, staring at the ravioli, I had a wave of remembrance. A slow smile parted my lips and I wondered if this was in her DNA. She was only 12 years old when her father died. I don't think she could have remembered this habit of his. It couldn't have been environmental. It had to be encoded in her DNA.

My husband had been a great "leftover food" eater. He was self-employed with a used car lot and auto mechanic shop less than one mile from our home. He worked a variety of hours, sometimes going to work early in the morning to open the shop, or staying late at night to complete a car sale or work on a car. Hurley, my husband, would pop home in the afternoon for a bite to eat. Many times I would see him standing in front of the refrigerator looking for the oldest leftovers, the ones that needed to be eaten before they spoiled. I would guide him to the plastic containers of different shapes and sizes and choices. Then, he would grab a fork from the drawer to mix casseroles and side dishes and eat the food cold. Standing in the kitchen, he would tell me the latest stories from work, laughing between forkfuls of the leftover concoction.

On the nights when he worked late and the rest of us were already tucked in bed, he would eat the leftovers and always leave a few bites in each container. A few bites of lasagna, a piece of cake, one ravioli, one carrot. One day, I asked him why he left one bite of food in each container. I asked partly out of curiosity and partly out of annoyance because I was left to clean it up! So, I gently asked, "Why do you leave one or two bites of food in the leftover containers?" He replied that he left it for me. As he ate the food late at night, he thought I might have gone to bed with thoughts of eating the food the next day. It was an act of kindness. He thought I might have wanted the last piece of cake and he didn't want me to be disappointed when I looked in the refrigerator and it was gone.

Today as I stood in the kitchen, I ate the last piece of ravioli and the last carrot, as if it had been saved just for me. I thought about the little moments of random kindness that are always surrounding me. It reminded me to pay attention and notice more. It is the simple moments of love and kindness that we remember. A touch of the hand, a kind word, a smile, and one ravioli left in a pan.

So, on this Eve of Thanksgiving, I thank you for being here and for listening. I hope that it brought you some comfort and helped you to remember and feel your own "happy-sad" memories.

Grief Transformation Radio Show #4
Thanksgiving Eve: Remembering

November 24, 2010
http://tobtr.com/1369273

Chapter Ten

The Transformative Power of Love and Music
Guest: Alan Peterson

Show originally aired on December 2, 2010

Introduction: Alan is a New Thought singer/songwriter, a former member of the Living Enrichment music team and a former music director at both Whole Life Church, Beaverton Unity in Oregon from where he recently relocated to the Baltimore Maryland area. Alan has released 3 solo CDs "World In Love", Music Of The Heart" and "Circle Of Love as well as a live CD with his former band Harmonic Convergence. www.alanpetersonmusic.com

Andrea: I met Alan on Facebook in the spring of 2009 when I was in the process of emotionally releasing my house and clearing all of the stuff out of the house that I had lived in with my husband who had died a few years earlier. I was ready to release the house but lots of tears came with that process. I was posting songs on Facebook and sharing with people that I was grieving and Alan shared the words of a song he wrote called, **At Any Given Moment.** I have never had a conversation with Alan in real life. So, it feels so fun to be on the radio with you tonight. So, thank you, thank you, thank you.

Alan, let's get right into the conversation. I have so many questions to ask you and I am so curious about so many things. Let's begin with…*Where did your love for music begin?*

Alan: Well, I remember as a young child, my older brother was into the Kingston Trio. I would listen to his records and we would go to concerts and see them live. The live concert was the most impressive to me. That's when I first started really listening to music. That was in the late 50's. Then, as I got a little older and developed my own tastes a little bit more, I got into the rock 'n roll era. But it was really back then, when I discovered radio, 45's and that sort of stuff, that I already knew that there was something so special about music.

My parents had a baby grand piano that I would play. No one really considered it playing, I wasn't a child prodigy like Elton John, or anything like that, but I enjoyed making sounds on it. I wouldn't bang on it, but, it might have been a good meditation thing that I was doing on it. I would just sit there for hours and let the sound of the piano carry me away. And I still do that today. When I was a music director at Beaverton Unity, they had a baby grand piano and I would go there hours early just to play a piano like that. I'm a guitar player from the 60's but piano is something that is more special to me, more real, and it just sent shock waves through me when I played.

Sometimes there is a little voice that says that I'm not good enough or whatever that might be. But, when I sit down to play, I just let go and it all comes flooding to me and I know from way back then that I was connected in a way. It was a long journey to get here and a lot of different twists and turns on the road to get to where I am now but it all started back then when I was just listening to my brother's music.

Andrea: How many brothers do you have?

Alan: Two. The one who was into the Kingston Trio was twelve years older than I was so I was fairly young. Like I said, it was the same thing as going to a musical and seeing people singing on stage for the first time and feeling that power. Feeling the power of live music.

Andrea: I think one of the ways we connected on Facebook was that I was about to go on this road trip and follow the Jonas Brothers. It's not exactly the same type of music but just the power that I had found for two years, taking my daughter to see this particular band in concert. There was so much healing that was happening in my heart. I can really feel as you talk about music, there's this energy that comes from you with your heart opening. Just hearing you say the words *baby grand piano,* I can really feel that passion and that love there.

Do you play the piano on any of your CDs?

Alan: Most of them I do not. I have been singing or playing the guitar. The next one I'm going to record and play the piano myself. I have a good friend who is a virtuoso named Daniel Crothers. He played most of the instruments which are keyboard instruments on that CD. So, when I'm recording, I let a real virtuoso do that because they have much more expertise than I do. But, I'm getting around to feeling a little more confident in myself so I think this next time, I will let my fingers do the walking.

Andrea: I love it! I really think of you as being a guitar player. I know that Daniel Crothers has a Youtube channel where I have seen you playing guitar and listened to your music. I have really loved it, from watching you in person on Youtube. I haven't actually seen you play in person. I lived in Baltimore for 28 years and just moved across the country to California. And you left Oregon to move to Baltimore.

Alan: Actually, I waved to you in Colorado.

Andrea: I know that at some point our paths will cross in person. When did you first start playing guitar?

Alan: My father bought me a guitar sometime in early grade school because I was enamoured with folk music at that time. I struggled with it. It wasn't a very good guitar. If I may say to all of those prospective parents and prospective guitar buyers make sure you have a guitar that's playable; the strings are close to the frets so you can actually play the thing. That's the hardest thing for beginners to get because the strings do hurt your fingers for a little while. If the strings are like an inch away it takes a long time to get there. I started playing. Then, I took a few lessons. I kind of dabbled here and there and jammed with a few people. But I didn't do too much with it. Just had fun like a lot of people did back then.

Andrea: I always tell people that you are a singer/songwriter. When did you write your first song?

Alan: I don't remember the very first song that I wrote but mostly it was back in the 60's. I was a political, anti-war, peace activist back in the early Simon and Garfunkel days. Everyone was trying to write Bob Dylan. I did okay with it in a simple way. I've learned on my own that just letting go and just writing without a true intention, that's when the love comes through in my heart and my writing. I do a lot better than trying to write one piece and finding music that fits. I kind of switched from the protest thing to a little bit more of what is in my heart, which is Spirit and love and transforming people's lives as well.

Andrea: Was there a time in your life where music started to be something that was a support with either healing or helping you through a challenging time? Did you have that connection with music?

Alan: I believe that I did. As a teenager, most people have some trouble or anxiety. Mine was just more a feeling of being alone and feeling isolated. Going through that and having music helped me to find connections and find a connection to myself. In later years, a lot of the stuff I was feeling actually still resonates with me. A lot of Beatles and love, that's my theme and I'm sticking to it. I guess I was a bit of a love child in a way and a bit of a peacemaker in those days and I believe, that still resonates with my heart. Those kinds of songs helped me through the dark days of becoming a person. Coming from a child to an adult and realizing that it's okay to be a child even if you are an adult. That's sort of my philosophy, too. Not to be a kid, but, to let that inner child shout, not suppress it, and I think that goes back to their era. Call it freedom and a loving existence and I still cherish those days a lot.

Andrea: I really connect with that, Alan. I have three adult daughters. They know when a song comes on the radio or a song I'm playing in the car, they always know if it's a song from my childhood because I automatically put my right hand to my ear like I'm holding a transistor radio. I know that I had some sort of ear thing with it but I really liked just holding it up to my ear and dancing with it. They imitate me and they know the songs and will sometimes hold their hands to their ears, too.

The songs from that era, and for me it was probably late 60's, early 70's when I was listening to them. I would be in the backyard, in a bikini, listening to the transistor radio hoping some cute boy would come by to see me, probably. That was connected to the music, too. That music just opened up my heart. And it was such a lifeline during those times of not being sure of myself.

They were confusing times in the world, too.

Alan: Music was transforming at the time, too, along with the rest of us. Music grew up with us. That's why each day something new was happening in the music world. It wasn't like someone was just writing a song, or following a formula for a song. There was a lot of experimentation in music. That's part of it. It was all new; it was all brand new. I'm not going to complain about the music today because there's a lot of great music. But, back then, it seemed like there was something new coming out every day. Not just a song, but a new sound; a new way to express and there was a lot of expression of love and freedom. There was the civil rights movement, women's rights movement and beginning of the gay rights movement. All those things were founded back then. It was a time to discover yourself and music was at the forefront of that.

Andrea: I think it encouraged playfulness. It encouraged out of the box thinking and creativity. In some ways, it was preparing us for other times in our lives when we were going to have to expand and think differently. I can remember, and
this really shows how music was transforming at that time. I wanted a Beatles album so badly, for Christmas. I think I was 12 or 13 years old and I asked my Mom and that was all I wanted for Christmas was a Beatles album. She was so proud of herself when she gave me an album, but it was a symphony orchestra playing the Beatles music. I can tell you, at the age of 12 or 13, I was crushed by that. But, to her, I wanted the Beatles music and why wouldn't I want to listen to the symphony orchestra playing it? Now as an adult, when I look back at that time, the fact that the symphony orchestra had actually recorded the music of the Beatles was showing how this new music was so popular and some of the more traditional orchestras were trying to adapt the music to a variety of instruments.

That was such an amazing time.

I can look at times in my life when I would be low or I would be going through some sort of a change. I talk about grief transformation as any time there is a loss, a sadness, a disappointment or there's change. You know, we can decide to make a change in our life. It can be something we want. We can decide we want to move but in order to make that move we have to let go of something and that carries a level of sadness with it. I have just found that music has carried me through so many different times in my life as a lifeline. Do you have any examples of when that has ever happened to you?

Alan: I think you're right on. I actually have a song called, *Music of the Heart* that talks about that. Just the highs but it also can be the lows. It helps you define those things. It helps you remember how things are. For example, for me just recently, prior to my coming to Baltimore, I discovered a band called, *Here to Here*. They are out of Florida originally. They just finished traveling the country for 10 months. I think they
are in California now. They have a song called, *Your Dreams*. The words are, *"Your dreams brought you here, where will you be tomorrow."* It's a powerful, powerful song and described the transformation that was occurring with me. I was going through a full transformation in Oregon. Living there for 59 years and basically leaving everything behind to pursue my dream of music. And to have a song like that come into my life inspired me to dream, to believe in myself, to believe in my dreams, follow my heart, follow my path, my passion; To follow the things I believed in for a long time.

As John Lennon's song says, *"Life passes you as you're busy making other plans,"* and that happens to the best of us. And so to have a song like that…I actually have a song called, *Follow Your Dreams, Follow Your Heart*, it's the same type of a thing to remember. To remember where you've come from and who you are. Listen to the child inside of you. Believe in yourself. Believe that your dreams are important. It's not just kid stuff.

So, for me to leave Oregon after living there for 59 years, and never moving anywhere outside of the state and moving to Baltimore, a place where I'd never been before to live and to pursue my dreams; to pursue my goals and aspirations was a big step. My music and this song really had a lot to do with it.

I have been greatly inspired by music in all these things. The Beatles. *All you need is love.* That was John Lennon's anthem to the world and along with *Imagine.* Those two songs alone defined a generation and defined my life. *All you do need is love. All you do need is love.* And if you can imagine, then you can build dreams and build a life that you want to build. I think it's easier for some folks than others. Some people have a lot of hardships going on. I understand all that but never stop believing, never stop dreaming and never stop imagining. Without love in your heart, you're never going to get anywhere.

First thing to do is you've got to love yourself. Love yourself first and then you'll be able to love other folks, other beings, other creatures and go out into the world and spread that love. It may sound a little 60ish but I believe it. I believe it still and I will believe it until I move on to the next level.

Andrea: Well, I'm definitely sold on that and I know that for a long time I heard the words *love yourself first* and I thought I knew what that was. And now I know it more. *Checking in with myself throughout the day. Does this support me? Am I choosing me?*

Even things like…it's a hard thing to describe unless you've had the experience because giving is important in the world. Okay, maybe this is the way to describe it for me.

I went through a period where I had an autoimmune condition. My immune system was attacking my muscles. Part of what was going on for me was I was putting other people ahead of me all the time. It had created a situation of being totally out of balance. I ended up in the hospital after a period of putting other people first and not being able to say, *No.* I created my best friend, "Andrea." If people would ask if I would do something for them or if I could be someplace, I would say, *I made a commitment to a friend of mine, I'll call you back.* And I would take a minute to check in with myself. *What do I need? How am I feeling right now?* Because if you don't start with self-love and self-care you will get sick, there is nothing left to give to anyone. So, thank you for bringing that present. Love yourself first. If people can understand that, love yourself first. Because then that love within you grows so much that you can radiate it out.

Do you see that? Do you feel that?

Alan: I agree. That is part of my scenario, too. In the past, I believe that I lost myself in helping others before I helped myself. And again, that's not a greedy thing and it's not about running to the front of the line, it's just treating yourself, what's in the highest good for yourself and others, not just what's in the highest good of others.

It's extremely important. I've done a lot of posting on Facebook myself and a lot of it is about loving yourself. If you don't love yourself then it's hard to love anybody else because you're basically dying inside. At least that's what I was doing. I was doing so much for other people, I always put myself second and then your dreams start to wither. And you start getting old that way. Age creeps up on you. Rather than saying, my dream is just as important as anybody else's. I follow my heart and if I do my dream I can help other people more as a powerful individual living in the moment of my dream to help them.

Rather than running around, hmmm, I'm not feeling that good because I'm not doing my stuff. So, you're not having much power and you're not believing in your power or stepping into your power. With your power, you can help more people, you can love more people. You can love longer. You can love stronger. Love, love, love. I do believe that with all my heart.

Andrea: When you come from a place of self-love first, people can feel the love more than when you're just giving, giving, giving. When you are depleted and you haven't started with self-love, it actually doesn't even feel good. I have had people give me gifts and it seems like a very generous thing and it just feels like yuck. Because the energy is ungrounded, they haven't stared with themselves first.

I have a question for you.

Everything about you is love. Your songs are about love. Your Facebook messages are about love. And whenever I think of you, Alan, I think, he is on a mission of spreading the word Love. It is not just that it's important to you. It seems like you're on a mission.

I am wondering where that started. Is that true?

Alan: I am on a mission.

I can go back into a little bit of my history of where it started. After high school and a little bit of this and a little of that, I've done a lot of different things. One thing I did was go to law school. I am an attorney. I practiced law for about four years and realized that wasn't for me. That wasn't my style;
that wasn't loving enough, too much cut throat. Then, I got involved with New Thought at the Living Mission Center and Unity and listened to the message of, *"Follow your heart. Follow your dreams."* So, at that point in time that's when I decided.
My dream has always been music. I'd had that thought in the back of my mind. *Ah, that's what kids do and whatever. Okay, if I'm going to be going to these churches and doing these things, I'm going to follow what they say to do.*

So, it was at that point in time that I actually took out my guitar and really started to play. And what I did was, I kind of did this backwards, I wrote the music.

World in Love was my first album. I wrote the music, recorded it and burned CDs and then had to figure out how to play it. I had never really played in public much before.
The point is, during the writing of that album and ever since, I basically just allow Spirit to write the music for me. And what comes out is love. No matter how I slice it, it's a love song. It may be a love song, *I love you,* but there's also some Spirit involved in that. 90% of the music is all about the inner voice of Spirit. Like the song you like, **At Any Given Moment**. *"You can Hear the Voice, calling your name as a child."*

It's the inner voice that calls each of us. Some people might not think it is Spirit, that it's just me talking to myself. You listen a little closer. You'll hear that it's love calling you to be all that you can be. And so, as the music is written through me, I basically sit with pen and paper and change a word here and there. It's written through me in a flow.

As I've been doing that, the mission has become more and more clear. I just know it is my mission in life to spread the word of love, to continue on where many wonderful songwriters have gone before, including John Lennon who I consider a hero. To help people realize that love is the answer.

I have a song called **Love is the Answer** and I go through this long process of saying these things. And then, I say, now, go out and play. Do not take yourself so seriously. Go out and play.

Andrea: Actually, my business is called Live a Life Worth Celebrating. At different times in my life, I have thought, *what are we doing here? Where are we trying to get to? Or what are we accumulating?* It is wanting that heart connection.

When I gave the Eulogy after my husband died, he had prepared a resume about six months before he died because he was thinking about getting a part time job to learn something and he decided to sit down and write a resume. There were things on there I had no idea he had ever done. When I looked at it and I was able to deliver a eulogy about him, all I could think was just live. That's what it is. Stay connected to your heart and live your life. So, that at any point when you're looking back, you can say, *okay maybe everything didn't go the way I wanted to exactly but what a rich life. I've lived every day, instead of waiting for something to happen.*

Alan: I try to post something on Facebook every day. Today my post was: *"If it were to all end tomorrow, would you be satisfied?"* When I left the Portland, Oregon area and I still say this to anyone who will listen today. My belief is: I don't want to be on my death bed saying I wish I did that, I wish I did this. I wish I had done that. I was called to come here. I met a woman named Elizabeth St. Germain. We are putting together some of my music and some of her spiritual exercises and kinds of things. Putting some classes together. Putting some seminars together. To go out and bring the message to the people. The main reason to do this is to help people. Not to make money. Not to be famous. Not to be a rock star. None of that kind of stuff. It's to help people. To help people to realize who they really are. That's all. Realize who you are and where you've come from. To remember that you are Spirit. To remember that you are love. You are loved and you are love both. Just with those simple words alone, it helps a lot of people.

I know with some of my songs, people tell me they get a lot of inspiration from that. It's not a high, holy roller kind of music. It's more, *"You are loved. You are light,"* kind of thing. Let your light shine. Let your love light shine. I say that in a lot of songs because it is exactly true. You are love, now let it shine and go out and play. Go out and be love.

That's what I was telling you when I first talked to you on Facebook. I was saying similar words to that. Just because you seemed to need that. I wasn't trying to sell you anything. I was just trying to say, *Love yourself. Love Yourself. You are beautiful.*

Andrea: When we started to chat on Facebook, I was releasing things in my house. Part of posting was to be real with what's going on. I don't talk about every single detail that's going on in my life on Facebook. But, I do believe there is an opportunity to share things with people in a way that is meaningful. I posted things like, *"I woke up with a lot of sadness this morning."* It had been almost four years since my husband died at that time. And I just wanted to be real with it. I wanted to let people know I woke up this morning with sadness and this was the music I was playing. Almost like I was on a radio show and sending it out to my listeners and saying, *here's the music.* Then, people would respond and they would share their own stories and there would be people like you who would reach out and say, *I'm right here with you.* Or say, *it's all love.* And you had those words and they were beautiful and precious.

Actually, I was selling my house and I was going to go on a trip with my daughter thinking we were going to be mortgage free for the summer. And before we found a place to live, we could go on this concert tour and follow the Jonas Brothers and create a great memory. And then the contract on my house fell through right before we were going. We had everything planned. We were living in a house with a couple of pieces of furniture. We had one bed. My daughter was on an air mattress. We had no other furniture. The little bit of stuff we had left was in a storage unit and I was thinking, *now what? Do I stay here or do I leap?* And you were one of a handful of people who told me to follow my heart and to just trust that the answer was within me. I am eternally grateful because I had an amazing adventure. I am writing about that journey of following my heart.

Alan, can you share with people what started to **wake up** in you, when you knew that it was time to leave Oregon. I think it is a real gift to give people some words to describe
this. What it looks like to make a decision to leave. Or things you had to let go of. What was changing in your life?

Alan: First of all, I had this deep calling to play music for a long time. It was always there. But, life was happening while I was busy making other plans. Days and years and months go by. Not for bad things, for good things. For family. For kids. For things like that. But, I got to a point where I thought, *I'm getting to a point in my life where I either have to put up or shut up. Live like you are dying.* (Tim McGraw's song) So, I felt the need to go. I was going to kind of do what you did. Grab a van and throw anyone in who wanted to go with me and travel the country. No one wanted to go. Everyone was afraid to go. Then life happens. My kids got old enough. They were out of school. I thought, *I have to go. I just have to go.* And last year, I knew I had to go. I had plans to go. Everything was holding me back. Life was busy making other plans.

    I finally decided for myself that I had to do this for myself. I tried to explain it to everybody. I got my stuff together and there was a shift in me when I decided I had to do it for myself. There was a shift in me and before that I did feel like I was dying. I did feel like I was curling up in a fetal position and saying, *I'm too old. I can't do this because of that. There's not enough money. I can't do this because of that. If I do this, people are going to laugh at me. They're going to think I'm stupid. And I was just slowly curling up, curling up. And dying.*

    But, something inside of me, pulled me out of it. I think part of it is my relationship with Elizabeth. And I decided to believe in myself. Maybe it was a little bit of faith. But it was me getting out there and encouraging other people. I helped quite a number of people saying, *"You can do this. You deserve this. You deserve to be happy. Happiness is not just for everybody else. Happiness is for you and me."* And in my life, Alan's life, I deserve joy in my life. Just as you do. Just as everybody does. So, what brings you joy?

    What brings me joy? What would bring me joy is to pursue my dreams no matter how old I am. No matter if I fall on my face. To pursue it. To say I've done it. If my music doesn't go anywhere, that doesn't matter to me. It was the point of taking a step, taking a leap of faith to go out and do
this kind of thing. So, I had a shift inside of me and all of a sudden I felt stronger. I felt taller. I was losing weight. Things were going on in my body. And I believe that Spirit was directing me to this point to the demarcation line.

Now you need to go. Now you finally need to step out. After all that is said and done, it's time to go and follow your heart. Believe in yourself. Believe in the joy of life. What brings you joy? As long as you're not hurting other people in a physically bad way and you've done your best to settle all the scores. Then, it's time to go. It's time to go on your own or with somebody else. It's time to do it.

Andrea: Did you feel that you had support from anywhere in your life?

Alan: Actually, when I decided to go, a lot of my friends that I left behind said to me, *Man, you've got guts. I wish I could do that. I wish I could go there with you. I wish I could do what you're doing.* Most people said that to me.

Some people said, *What are going to gain? What do you expect to get out of it?* I said, *I expect to get the satisfaction out of doing something.* They said, *No, no, no. What are you going to get? Money, fame?* I said, *No. That may or may not occur.*

The main thing that will occur is I will have gone for it. I have taken a leap of faith, just like you, Andrea. Just like the Jonas Brothers kind of thing. I have stuck myself out there.

I believe in myself. I believe in my dream. Whatever that means, however that looks as I walk down the path of life. If I don't try it, I'm back to curling up in a ball and dying because I'm not following my passion. I'm not following my heart. I 'm not living in love.

Andrea: It feels like this throwback to the time period we were talking about. I don't like to put everything back into the 60's because I think that there is some judgment about the 60's and what that really was about. So, I'm careful to compare. To me, that time period was about waking up and it was about becoming creative and transforming and opening to new possibilities. Michael Bernard Beckwith, the spiritual leader at the Agape International Spiritual Center here in Los Angeles, is always talking about infinite possibilities. That we get onto this track in life. I am on the track and I go from point A to point B to Point C and that's it. We have forgotten about this whole idea of being here for a journey where we get to discover things about ourselves and we are in relationship with people. We're in relationship with music, with nature, with ideas and that the traditional way of living is to follow this track until you die.

There have been other things stirring in me. To live, to experience life, to push against that boundary and get off the track and find ways of doing that. I think the more we follow that calling, that calling of Spirit, the more people will follow Spirit. However, they want to connect to Spirit, God, nature and whatever the words are for them. We are being called to connect with ourselves and open to greater parts of ourselves.

Sometimes it makes no logical sense at all. I get that. So, to answer a question of *what is the gain* becomes *I am living my life. I am following this inner calling.*

Can you put words to what it feels like to have that direction from Spirit? I know I'm putting you on the spot with this question. It has been a question I've been exploring with several people recently.

How do you put words to things that have no words, to help people understand this?

Alan: Shortly after I got here in Baltimore, Elizabeth and I went to a beach in Delaware. We were sitting at an outside café having something to eat. As I turned to my left and looked across the ocean, the moon was rising, a great, big orange to pink moon. I stood up and I said *I have to get out of here*. Most people in the restaurant looked at me like I was crazy. And I said, *Look at that moon. I have to get out of here.* I wanted to go down to the beach. I wanted to experience this moon.

There was a gentlemen sitting at the table next to us and he said, *I'm not in love. I don't need no blankity-blank moon.* We got up and left and went down to the shore and sat and watched the moon. The moon rose in all its glory. But, the point was the man. The man was an angel to me. I think of that man every single day who didn't see the love or the Spirit in the moment. He needed something else to spark the beauty of life rather than finding it in himself. Maybe what I should have said was *take my hand and I'll take you down to the beach with me.* Although, he probably would have hit me.

But, the point is, he has been an inspiration to me, in his own negative way, saying *I don't need that because I don't have something else to draw me to it.* I want to say, just go do it. Just go find it. It's right there. It's right down there at the beach. *Just come down to the beach and sit down and feel the beauty of it all. The portrait of life, the portrait of the earth, the moon, the ocean, all those things.* Those things are what give me inspiration. Gets my heart pumping; gets my juices pumping; everything flowing. Then, in my own case, if I can sit down with a piano or a guitar and let that flow through me, that's when miracles happen.

Andrea: Being in the moment with the love that is already within you. That's how I think of it. When you saw the moon, there is already the love that is awakened within you that calls you to those moments.

Alan: For me, from that spot, I choose to love each day, as a new love, a new day. Every day is a new love. So, if I love you today and I love you tomorrow, it's not the old love from yesterday. It is a brand new love; a brand new love with all of the excitements, all the good stuff that comes with it. Choose to live life that way instead of that old thing, *been doing that for years, blah, blah, blah.* I have to look at each day, each moment with new eyes, new love with new exuberance. Like Tim McGraw's song, *Live like you were dying.* Live like tomorrow is your last day because it might be. And you might inspire other people to feel that same way.

If we all believed that, if we all believed that tomorrow might be our last day, we would all act differently towards each other, towards the Earth, towards other creatures. We would all sit down to write the great symphony, the great model, the great inspiration that's in our life. Write that down, to tell our kids we love them. All those things would happen now and then what. Then, you could do something else. Then there would be something else to write, something else to create, something else to believe in that would all be based on the feeling you have for yourself, for the family, for the world, for the moon.

Andrea: I have heard people say, *what would you do if this were the last day of your life?* Many times I have heard people say, *I would pick up the phone and call my kids or another person.* My feeling is, if you're not living every day that way, being current in your relationships… And I am very lucky, I do have a great relationship with my daughters but I'm current with it. Sometimes I won't talk with them for a month or so, although we do have Facebook and stay connected there, too. If I knew I only had one day I would do what I was going to do anyway on that day. Live your life that way all the time so you are caught up on your relationships. You are complete.

    This year I have stepped back from my family, so I have had fewer phone conversations. I took the year to hear my own voice. But, I was already current with them. We have had so many incredible life experiences. If I found out that today was my last day, I wouldn't feel like I had to call them. I
have already lived life with them. Be current, not that you had one more word to say to end. That's what it makes me think of when you share those moments. *Right now, this is it, there's the moon. Go enjoy it!*

Alan: *Go be in love. Be in love. Go love yourself. Love the world. Go take care of the things you need to take care of. Call your parents. Call your friends.* I totally agree with that. I totally believe that. It is not only a shift in doing stuff. It shifts you.

Andrea: Alan, we are at the end of the show now. Is there anything you want to say to people? Any last thoughts?

Alan: Here is a quote I wrote on Facebook a few days ago:
Remember to love. If you doubt, remember to love. If you fear, remember to love. If you're angry, remember to love. If you think you are alone, remember to love. If you lose your way, remember to love. Remember to love others. Remember to love Spirit. Remember to love yourself. Remember to love and you will be loved.

Musician, songwriter, speaker & coach **Alan Peterson** uses the transformative power of music and lyrics, to uncover the truths that lay deep within the heart. Alan's playful, positive and sometimes rebellious approach provides a soundtrack to the soul, facilitating an experience that empowers audiences to create deeper, more meaningful and joyous lives. www.alanpetersonmusic.com

Grief Transformation Show #12
The Transformative Power of Love and Music

December 2, 2010
http://tobtr.com/1369281

Chapter Eleven

Peace on Earth and Inner Peace
Andrea Hylen

Show originally aired on December 24, 2010

A few nights ago, we experienced the darkest night of the year in the northern hemisphere; the winter solstice and a lunar eclipse that happened a few days ago. This was worldwide news with the potential of 1.5 billion people being able to see the eclipse.

It brought to my mind the thought of being in the darkest times of our lives and the opportunity to discover rich places in this time of darkness. Think about words you could use during this time of dark. Words like stillness, silence, and the muddy pool of the river where all life grows in the dark.

I am going to ask you to hang in here with me, while I step into the darkness of life on planet Earth. I promise that on the show tonight, I will take you into a place of hope, peace and transformation. I'm not going to leave you in this place of darkness. We are going to experience moving through this together.

If you have a candle, light it to create a sacred space for yourself. As we journey through this discussion it can be a time to discover something within you; a time to discover a deeper place within you. I encourage you to do that. I have a candle lit creating a space right along with you.

This year I have been on a deeper self-discovery of personal grief transformation. Grieving has been a part of many of my life experiences over the last 50 years. I had a brother who died in 1961 from SIDS (Sudden Infant Death Syndrome), a son who died in 1993, from a 4th stage neuro-blastoma cancer and a husband who died from multiple myeloma cancer in 2005. Each experience led me to a deeper understanding of myself in relationship to others. Each of them, my brother, my son, my husband, taught me something that I could not have learned any other way than through loving them with my heart and soul in life and death. It has been a personal journey that I have shared more and more this year through writing and speaking and through the grief transformation shows.

In sharing my experiences this year, I have also discovered something else.

There is a wave of grief circling the earth. Some of it is obvious, like when we are grieving the loss of loved ones. But some of it is the grief of loss and change. Loss of jobs, lifestyle, dreams, education, our financial system, government, world-wide hunger, earthquakes, many earth changes, oil spills and more. It feels like the waves of loss and grief have increased in frequency since 9/11 (Sept 11, 2001). We have arrived at a place where the world and each of us are in desperate need of healing on all levels.

When I talk with people about grief and I listen, the universal description I hear is the amount of grief that continues to come into each person's life has increased. The waves of grief are so persistent it is hard to catch your breath. It is one of the reasons I believe it is important to have more discussions about it. I am talking about this to let you know you are not alone. It is happening to everyone, everywhere. If you don't have your own personal loss, disappointment or challenge you have a friend, a family member or neighbor who is experiencing a loss.

We see foreclosure signs and store closings. We see it in newspapers and news shows. We can even see it in dramas and sitcoms on television, or headlines on internet sites on the computer. Even if you decide to avoid the news, it will show up somewhere. On Facebook or on the headline of a magazine as you stand in the check-out at the grocery store.

A year ago, my daughter and I arrived back home after being on the road for two months. The day after we arrived, I drove over to the local coffee shop. My daughter and I went to some Jonas Brothers concerts and I had a special souvenir for
the daughter of one of the employees. When I pulled up to the coffee shop, I wondered why the parking lot was empty. I got

out of the car, walked up to the door and saw the Closed Sign. The store had closed while we were out of town. I walked back to the car, climbed in and put my head down on the steering wheel and sobbed I didn't get to say good-bye to anyone. These were people who had been a part of my life, my travels, the ups and downs of my husband's illness and death. This was a place where I shared in community and out of the blue, the store, the employees, the people who gathered and shared in a community gathering were gone. It may have seemed like a little thing but to me in this moment it felt like the death of something special. I was feeling a wave of grief that was real and connected to change.

The first step in grieving is to have the awareness that you are grieving. If you ignore it or sweep it under the carpet, it will appear in other ways. It can appear as illness, as irritation, as impatience, as stress, as depression, as anger or rage or sobbing without really knowing what the emotions are connected to.

Think about this for a moment. What is dying around you? It could be a loved one and it could be parts of your community and other things that represent death. Opening to the feelings is part of the journey we are on together. Don't rush it. **Pause and let an idea bubble up.**

So, here we are. We're in the dark, and in the midst of the pain and despair, we have to begin to think in creative, innovative ways. How are we going to survive in this pain and bring in a creative flow of new ideas, new ways of being in the world? We are living on the edge of the greatest change that has ever happened in the world.

Let's begin here:

First, take a deep breath.

Then, begin to open to new thoughts of: Simplicity. New priorities. Support. Collaboration. Simple pleasures. New discoveries. Joy in the midst of chaos. Ask yourself, what do I need to change in my life? What do I need to let go of and release? What support do I need to do that?

Here is a list of ideas where we can all begin to shine a light.

1. Grieve what is lost. Start there. Turn on the music. Open the floodgates of sadness and despair and pour your heart out to another person. Feel what you are feeling.

2. Let go of the attachment to the life you thought you were meant to live. If you have to do things to control and hold on tight to keep everything together, it is time to let it go. Think new thoughts.

3. Dream new dreams. Open your heart to new possibilities.

4. Bring in more wonder and curiosity. If you can't open to that easily, find a way to tap into the part of you that is childlike that had wonder and curiosity. Go to a toy store or playground. Swing on the swings. Buy some bubbles or another childhood toy.

5. Listen to music from your teen years or another time when you felt an inner freedom. Get up and dance!

6. Bring compassion and patience into every situation: When someone does something with anger, frustration, or rudeness like cutting in front of you in line or in traffic, imagine that there is something else going on in their lives. Let go of the judgment and send them love. You can be the one to shift your perception, to send love, to open your heart to see the God-self in the person underneath the current, out of control behavior.

7. Connect with nature. Really look at how nature changes right before your eyes every day. This is another way to evoke wonderment. Pick a tree in your neighborhood and watch with wonder how that tree changes throughout the year, day by day.

8. Before going to bed at night, close your eyes, put your hands on your heart and feel love. If it feels like so much is going on that you can't feel the love, ask the angels or for
Spirit to fill you with love. Tap into a time when you felt love. Pretend and act as if, until you can feel it on your own. As you feel the love, send it to yourself, your loved ones and imagine that you are a beam of love radiating out to the world.

9. Before you leave the house, imagine that you can fill yourself with love. Love is FREE! As you walk or drive your car, imagine that everywhere you go you are leaving a path of love.

10. Learn to witness another person's pain without trying to fix them. Each of us has a path to walk in this lifetime. On the pathway, there are experiences for us, each of us, to feel joy and sadness. Believe in each person's ability to learn and grow from their own life experiences.

11. Give someone a hug. Look for moments throughout the day to reach out to someone and give a hug.

12. Trust that we will survive and thrive. Look for the good that surrounds you in everyday moments. Look for the miracles of life.

There have been several key things I have used to change the energy in my life this year and to find moments of relief and even joy:

1. Slow down and Breathe: In a long line at the grocery store? Close your eyes, take some deep breaths and remind yourself that in this moment, all is well.

2. Develop a practice that helps you stay connected to your heart: Meditation, Tai Chi, Yoga are some examples.

3. Simplify: Re-evaluate where you spend time, money and emotions and pick the most important. Let the rest go. Look for ways to fill yourself before you connect to help others.

4. Feel gratitude: Go even deeper into this practice for yourself this year. Before you get out of bed in the morning, think about one thing that fills you with gratitude. I may have a song playing in my head and I look at what may be communicating a message of gratitude.

5. Look people in the eye: Take the time to look at people and see them. Connect with the person inside. It makes my heart

soar even to think about that. Take the time to really look at someone, like the person who is handing you the receipt at the grocery store. Take a minute to really see the person.

As you practice this, add more things to the list as you experience your own ways of dancing with the waves of change. It will help you let go of old behaviors that deplete your energy and replace negativity with positivity.

This is a story I wrote about a powerful, personal experience of peace.

Oklahoma City: An Experience of How a Disaster Was Turned into a Demonstration of Peace on Earth

For several years I had an overwhelming desire to travel from Maryland to Oklahoma City. I wanted to go to the city because I read about a peace memorial that was built there after the tragedy of a bombing at a government building that happened in April 1995, killing children, women and men. On the day of the bombing, I watched the news reports and I prayed along with the rest of the world as we watched in disbelief. There was something about the site and the re-building that made me want to be there in person. A road trip I took with one of my daughters finally led me to the peace memorial. After spending a full day there in 2008, these are the words I wrote that evening in my journal:

Words seem so inadequate on this day.
    By spending the morning and the evening at the Oklahoma City Memorial, I feel that my life has been touched in a profound way. I sit here staring at the blank page feeling the stillness, not knowing how to capture this experience in words.

A field of empty chairs represents the lives lost on April 19, 1995. My heart felt like it was bursting open when I first entered the Memorial. Tears ran down my cheeks, as I opened to the emotion. I felt like my heart was bursting with love and gratitude. Love and gratitude? This took me by surprise. I thought I would be feeling grief and loss and sadness. I found out later that the entrance we walked through was the Door of Hope. And that is what I felt. I felt the love and the hope.

Through the tragedy of loss, the powerful emotions of forgiveness, healing, hope and love have arisen here. Beginning with the people who responded to help immediately, to those who came from afar, to the words of love from children, this is an example of the hope and beauty that is arising on the planet.

The people of Oklahoma City have risen from the ashes and chosen peace. They are an example of peace on Earth as we each make conscious choices for inner peace.

In a museum space at the memorial, an educator reached out to me and shared the peace that has been birthed here. Conflict resolution classes in schools; Cards and artwork from children, like the tile that reads, "The world cares." Sharing tools of peace with the children.

Every night when the sun goes down, the lights below each chair shine brighter and brighter. As the darkness spreads throughout the city, I see the moon at the highest point in the sky. There is stillness. The chairs that represent loss are transformed and emerge into brilliant candles of hope and light.

I see in this moment it is in the greatest times of darkness that we become the brightest lights.

One of the gifts of grieving change, loss and disappointment is we can begin to look deep within ourselves to discover new awakenings, new ways of expressing who we are and we can take charge of the grief to lead us onto new paths. That is what the people in Oklahoma City did. They felt the feelings and they took charge of their grief to lead them onto new paths. They introduced conflict resolution, to bring peace into the schools and to look at where they could make a difference to bring in more light so this would never happen again.   When we can look deep within ourselves and discover new awakenings of expressing who we are, we heal. This is where we begin to see the gifts within the grief. This is where we begin to heal and transform and learn the lessons our soul is crying out to experience.

This next reading is a part of my journey to become a Minister of Spiritual Peacemaking. It is an example of how to discover inner peace with yourself.

On the weekend of my husband's memorial service, a flyer arrived in the mail. It was from a friend of mine who had moved from Maryland to California. She was organizing a retreat in Santa Barbara for December, five months from now. Before I saw my friend's name as the creator of the retreat, I saw the words Evolutionary Women Retreat.

Evolutionary Women. I didn't know what an Evolutionary Woman was but I knew I wanted to be one. A few days after the memorial service for my husband, I made the commitment to fly to California and attend the retreat in five months. I spent time reading spiritual books written by powerful women as a preparation. I knew that Barbara Marx Hubbard, a futurist would be one of the speakers. She would talk about Conscious Evolution. I watched DVDs to learn more about Conscious Evolution.

The retreat was powerful and life changing. I learned that I am an Evolutionary Woman. The choices and decisions I have been making all of my life are helping me, my family and the planet to evolve. On the plane ride home, I began to wonder and pray about what I was going to do with this new discovery.

In January, I started to wake up at 3am every morning. Wide awake, my soul was craving reading and studying. The feeling was so intense I felt like I was starving and would die if I didn't wake up and study. I craved books and knowledge and understanding. Every morning I woke up, lit candles in the living room, brewed a cup of tea, turned on the woodstove and eagerly opened the current book.

For two months, I read books on a variety of topics of different types of spirituality and religion. I read books about fairies in the garden, animal spirits, shamanism, Huna rituals from Hawaii, Violet Flame healing and books about different hands on healing modalities. It continued for another month on topics from shapeshifting to the Course in Miracles to Power vs Force and conscious evolution. I underlined the words and took notes. It felt like I was studying in preparation for something.

One morning after two months of doing this, I woke at 2am with an urgency to get on the internet and search for a program to study, a deeper spiritual program. I felt like I was shot out of a canon with the feeling of "Do it now!" I hopped on the internet and began to research. The first people on the list were Jean Houston, Sonia Choquette, Barbara Marx Hubbard and James Twyman. I saw that the ministry program with James Twyman that had started two years earlier was in a transition, changing from a two-year master's program to an intensive 3-month fast track program. The timing was perfect. I could study for 3-4 hours every morning, go deeply into the work and be finished by summer time when the summer schedule for my daughter would kick into high gear.

I was so ready! The discipline was instilled in me from two months of preparation. I continued waking up early. I studied and completed the assignments during the three-hour morning period.

The studying for me was part of a grieving, healing process that began nine months after my husband died. After 11 weeks, I completed the program and registered for the retreat where I would be ordained as a Minister of Spiritual Peacemaking. I had not consciously chosen the path of ministry. I was a widow with a broken heart. My heart was cracked wide open and ready to receive inner guidance. The official title of minister was not the reason I was doing this. Focusing on inner peace within and bringing that to the world was my intention. I never intended to be a minister.

In my grieving, the path had chosen me.

After I completed the program I decided to fly to Portland, rent a car, drive to Crater Lake for an adventure and drive a few more hours to the retreat. It was a powerful experience that opened the door to more questions.

When I arrived home I began to contemplate the question, "What is my ministry?" I didn't feel called to start a church or a business. I was home schooling my youngest daughter and the one-year anniversary of my husband's death was a month later.

Several things evolved naturally. I let go of the question and lived life, opening to the inspiration each day. The rose garden memorial I had planted to honor my husband became a gathering place in my front yard. As I weeded and pruned the roses, people stopped by. They shared in the beauty and it opened them to share their pain, struggles and stress in their lives. Sometimes people stopped to smell or pick the roses. One woman told me she drove by at the end of every workday because it made her feel better.

When the anniversary of my husband arrived, I planned a gathering at my home. We built an emissary wheel out of rocks and rope. We said peace prayers, sang songs and spread some of my husband and son's ashes. On Sept 11, 2006 we planted a peace pole to honor the 5th anniversary of 9/11. This is where I began, one step at a time to discover more inner peace and share that peace with others.

When a friend asked when I was going to start a book group with James Twyman's new book, the Art of Spiritual Peacemaking, I sent an e-mail and twelve women came to study and pray together. That group evolved into a book group called the Soul Voyagers and has continued for the last four years. Another Minister of Peace has been running it since it evolved.

For a few years, I coordinated Evolutionary Women Retreats and became the "midwife" for a book called Conscious Choices: An Evolutionary Woman's Guide to Life. Studying the peace ministry taught me about sacred ceremony and I used that to create a sacred space for a woman's voice to emerge in her writing.

Now, I have been guided to host a radio show about Grief Transformation for 44 days.

No matter where the ministry has taken me, at the core is the message of inner peace. James Twyman's program gave me tools and experiences to discover my gifts and find places to be of service. I have used the tools to marry people, to become one of the facilitators of the ministry program, to help people transform grief. Sometimes through counseling, sometimes from teaching social media, sometimes through prayer, writing, speaking to groups. I continue to open to the guidance from within.

These are the simple ways we can open our hearts to heal, to follow a deeper inner calling, to discover richer lives. Peace on Earth is not going to happen because we're looking outside of ourselves or because someone else outside of our life is going to change. Or because we are avoiding the pain of grieving. Peace on Earth happens when each of us takes responsibility to cultivate, discover, practice, and learn how to maintain inner peace.

Another experience where an outer experience forced me to look inside and heal within:

When I was in the process of studying with James Twyman and the Beloved Community, I was the coach for a Destination Imagination, creative problem solving team of girls. It was a challenging year. With all of the girls getting older, it was getting harder and harder to find times to meet. I had been the coach for the girls for six years and this was the last year we would all be together.

One of the girls blew off a meeting. When I found out that she had gone on a date with a new boy and had lied to us about cancelling because she was sick, I got so angry. It was uncharacteristic for me to be angry and the anger was out of proportion for what she had done. Because I was in the ministry program, I knew that it was an opportunity to reflect inwardly and discover why I was so angry and why this situation had disturbed my inner peace.

To be honest, I was raging, not at her but inside of me. I pounded a pillow and I took time to process the feelings over a period of five days. Instead of raging at her, I continued to explore the feelings of deep anger that were within me.

As I did the inner work of writing, reflecting and meditating, I finally discovered where it came from. When I was her age, I blew off some things that were important to me. Things that were important for my own personal growth and development. I blew it off because I was going on a date with a guy who was not treating me very well. All of that anger at Katie was really anger at myself. Because I was in the peace ministry program, I had a new awareness and I stayed connected to the emotion for days and found my way to the core. I excavated and cultivated and questioned all of the feelings.

I took responsibility for my own inner peace. The only one who can bring inner peace to you is you and your willingness to do the deep inner work.

Whenever we want to grow, to bring more light into the world, to create more peace, we will have opportunities appear to experience this.

Another experience, I had was when I was in the process of selling my deceased husband's business. For a year, I had worked with the tenant who wanted to buy the business. He stopped paying rent, making excuses and saying he wanted to buy the property. Over a process of several years, I began to take him to court to recover rent and evict him from the property so I could sell it. I let him know I was willing to sell it to him, if he would move forward with action steps.

Finally, after going through the court system and giving him every opportunity possible, I sold the property and the police had to get involved in the eviction. On the night of the eviction, the real estate agent, the buyer for the property, and the police, were all with me. The tenant and his mother were screaming at me. I actually felt complete inner peace. I knew I had done everything possible to support the tenant and I knew that I had to support myself in moving forward. The things they were saying were not true. There was nothing for me to defend. I sent them love and compassion through my eyes. This was just the next step in the process.

As a peacemaker, it was an opportunity to practice standing there and maintaining an inner peace when the outer world around me was in conflict.

Sometimes we are surprised when feelings surface that we didn't know were within us. This story is about an experience I had with a peace pole and a man on the street.

Everyday Leadership: Planting Peace Poles to Encourage People to Find Peace Within

When my husband died, I decided to plant a peace pole in the corner of our property. I planted it by the street where hundreds of cars would see it every day. It was surrounded by a garden of roses and evergreen trees. The words on the peace pole were "May Peace Prevail On Earth" in twelve different languages.

We chose the 12 languages: English, Swedish, Gaelic, and Polish for our family heritage. French, Spanish, Sign Language were languages we were studying. The original peace pole in the 1950's was Japanese and we chose that to honor the original idea. Tibetan, Animal Paw Prints, Swahili, and Cherokee for more diversity and love.

Peace within will create peace in the world. Any time we feel anger, sadness, frustration, hopelessness, or love, joy, happiness and hope, we send waves of this energy into the world. We have a field of energy that affects the people around us. We are more powerful than we realize. When each of us owns our personal power and takes responsibility for healing and finding peace within, we will create peace on Earth.

As a Minister of Spiritual Peacemaking, I work with peace prayers from 12 major religions. James Twyman created music to peace prayers from the 12 major religions. This focuses on the things the religions have in common. We develop an understanding of the differences and take responsibility for our own emotions. I am committed to spreading ideas and words of peace in the world. It is part of everyday leadership in the world.

One evening I was sitting on my porch about 200 feet from the road. A young black man walked by the house and was wearing clothing that made me think of a gang. He was walking with a pimping stroll. He stopped suddenly and turned in the direction I was sitting. I had an emotional wave of fear come over me. He stood there staring. I wondered how he could see me I was 1000 feet away from him and partially hidden on the porch. Finally, I realized he had stopped to read the peace pole. From where I was sitting I could see the young man, but the peace pole was blocked by an evergreen tree.

In that moment, I saw a clue. There was something inside of me that I needed to heal. He had not done anything except stop to read a peace pole. I had a conditioned response based on a person's clothing and walking style. I had a response of fear. I had made up my mind about him before considering that he was taking a walk and stopping to read the Peace Pole Message.

I included the man in my prayers that night and began to reflect on what I could do to heal the part of me that felt fear. The part of me I didn't even know was in me. This is the ongoing journey of healing. This is the commitment to peace on Earth. We take responsibility for our own healing.

Let's talk a moment to listen to the words of this song by Libby Roderick, "How Could Anyone."

Her website: **http://libbyroderick.com/how-could-anyone/**

As we can cultivate self-love and heal those places within that need love, we can discover inner peace and radiate that to the world. Each of us can heal memories of where we were not seen or we had a loss and we thought that our heart was going to break.

Take a deep breath right now and feel the love from Libby Roderick's song that is letting us know about the infinite possibilities within us. Allow the sadness and the hurt to just melt away. Know that you are whole within and there is a place of inner peace growing inside of you. There is a place of love that is always there. All you need is a willingness to uncover it, feeling it first, then radiating it out to the world.

In your heart, know on this evening of Christmas Eve, that the love is always present in your heart. Know that you are seen and sometimes it is by someone you would never have imagined. There is always a Spirit, a double rainbow and other miracles in nature that are surrounding you. As you can fill your heart with inner peace and imagine it radiating around the world, that one motion can make a difference.

We are healing. Blessings to all of you.

Grief Transformation Show #32
Peace on Earth and Inner Peace

December 24, 2010
http://tobtr.com/1400737

Voices of Love in the dark

Andrea Hylen

Section 2: Tools to Support Grief Transformation

"A feeling of pleasure or solace can be so hard to find when you are in the depths of your grief. Sometimes it's the little things that help get you through the day. You may think your comforts sound ridiculous to others, but there is nothing ridiculous about finding one little thing to help you feel good in the midst of pain and sorrow!"

~Elizabeth Berrien

Andrea Hylen

Chapter Twelve

Using the Body's Wisdom to Transform Grief
Guest: Anna Stookey

Show originally aired on December 20, 2010

Andrea: Do you ever experience grief as a profound ache somewhere in your body? A tightness or a shadow over your heart? How we respond and attend to grief in our bodies is an important part of our healing.

Tonight, Anna Stookey, a body-mind psychotherapist and massage therapist will share her thoughts, insights and personal experiences about the way grief moves through and affects our bodies. She'll also guide us in some experiences of contacting and working with grief as sensation in the body as well as exploring how the body might speak to us when we grieve.

Welcome Anna! I'm so excited that this is the topic tonight. Many people have celebrated Hanukkah, and celebrations of lights, winter solstice, and we're getting closer to Christmas, Kwanza and then New Year's Eve. I feel like it builds throughout the month with holiday celebrations but the grief kind of rises in the body in response to this. I am just thrilled that you're here tonight to talk about it.

Why don't we start talking about grief in the body?

Anna: It's interesting that this show is hitting around the midpoint of your series because I think there is something about talking about the body when we explore any really, really big emotions. It's very grounding because our bodies lose so much in the present moment that even if you try to talk yourself out of your grief or say that you're already past it, a lot of times, it will register again somewhere in your body.

I often tell the story, and maybe many of your listeners can relate to this, of my mother's loss of her mother who she was incredibly, incredibly close to. It was a really profound loss for her and it came early in life. She was just in her 30's when it happened. Her mother died in the spring and I was young. I was probably only seven or eight so I was barely aware of it. My mom told me years later, when I could actually understand it, that every year around the time of her mother's death, she would get a strange sort of filmy feeling around her heart. She would get moodier and more irritable. She would never know consciously what it was until she made a note of the date. And it was always within a week or so of the date of her mother's death. It was like her body was remembering it even when she thought she was past the point of grief. All of the senses and the time of year, the way the light was in the sky, had registered in her body really profoundly because it had been such a profound loss for her.

    I think we really need to be sensitive to that. We all know that grief is a *CYCLICAL* process, and we've heard that, but it's so easy to get impatient with it or to think that we're done. The truth of our bodies says that things come and go. Our bodies can't help but live in the present moment of whatever is moving through. They carry our grief for us even when we think we've put it down. I think sometimes that can be frustrating, but I hope certainly, after we explore tonight, it's also an invitation to just say, *what else is there here for me to understand.*

Andrea: I love that description and it really does bring this whole connection of who we are as human beings. How do we carry memories and how do we carry experiences in our lives? I was in Arizona this weekend. My middle daughter graduated from college. All three of my daughters and my ex-husband and his wife were together in Arizona. We were all really there in support of my daughter, Elizabeth. It was a fantastic weekend. But, what I found at times was that things came out of my mouth that I no longer believe. We have gone through all of this change but somewhere in my body, in this whole connection of me as a human being, I began to just operate out of a memory. It really brought it forward, too, that we grieve the loss of a loved one but sometimes we grieve the loss of ourselves in different ways.

    I caught myself a couple of times. I said something and my daughter, Elizabeth just looked at me, *like really?* And I said, *"I don't even know why I said that."* It just came out of some place within me. I said, *"Because I don't even believe that."*

They were just little things. Something happened and her jeans were dry. I said, *"Oh, it's going to be a good day then."* And I just looked at her and said, *"Well actually, it was already a good day and if the jeans hadn't dried, it would still have been a good day."* We both just kind of looked at each other. And I think loss and change, as well as grieving the loss of a loved one, are just stored in our body.

I am wondering if you would do a little bit of an introduction. Take a moment and do a guided imagery to help people get in touch with what is going on within their body.

Anna: Yes. And just to set this up a little bit. I think anytime there is a profound loss, and Andrea and I have talked a little bit about how that can be not just losing a person but really losing a part of your identity. If you've gone through a transition like a job loss or the loss of a relationship, what happens is we can go into a story of the loss. Whatever we think it means about us, whether or not we think that the Universe is fair to us or likes us. We can go into a lot of different interpretations. Simultaneous to that though, there is often a physical component.

Why does it matter to get into the physical component? If you can start to experience the sensations in your body, that are the root of these emotions, you can become curious about them. You can explore them and you can start to see that whatever story you make about them, whatever interpretation you've put on top of them, is a choice. They are not necessarily connected. And once you just start exploring the sensations in the body, you can watch them shift, you can see if there's a message there for you.

I want to share one experience I had a few years ago, that was not necessarily related to grief, although it was a big time of transition in my life. I was experiencing a continuous pain in my neck. I had been to chiropractors. I had tried to treat it and I was just at my wit's end. It just wasn't going away. So, I finally just decided. I already had a meditation practice at the time and I just decided and threw my hands up and I said, *"Alright, I'm just going to spend some time with the physical sensation of this pain every day and see what happens."*

I had no expectations. I felt like nothing else was working. I was going to just explore the sensations. There were a lot of feelings going on in my life at the time, just like there are in a grief process. So, I could have had a story about the pain. *Oh, this is one more thing and I don't know what I'm doing with my life.* But, I just went into the sensations. I did this for a couple of weeks.

I remember one meditation experience toward the end of that time when I just was sitting in stillness and I was continuing to feel whatever sensation was in my neck and being curious about it. I heard a voice come through the stillness that said, *"There's nothing you have to do."* It felt like the message that the pain was giving me; not the story, not what I wanted to go into, not the drama. It was what the pain was trying to tell me. It was almost like my neck was stretching and trying to move into new places in my life and this simple message was behind the pain. What happened after that was the pain went away. It really was able to shift and to move. It was a really big introduction for me: how sensation and pain speak to us in the body. They may have a message for us or something for us to know.

They also represent energy and truth that wants to move through. So, if you're feeling blocked in your body and you are feeling that your grief is really showing up in a profound way physically, which it often does. There's a reason why we have these ways of describing grief: my heart is clouded or flooded with grief. It has a really visceral quality. My true belief, and my sense, is that by really paying attention to it and listening to it, something will move through.

That was a little, long winded way of introducing this exercise but I thought it would be helpful to share an experience of actually exploring wherever you are in your grief process on a physical level. See what wants to come through.

Andrea: That was beautiful. Thank you for describing that before going into the process.

Anna: I imagine that some people listening to this are driving. So, do this in whatever way works for you. But, for those of you who are not driving and are able to close your eyes. I invite you to close your eyes and just take a few deep breaths.

Meditation 1:

(Pause from time to time)

      Settling into this moment.
      Notice what is happening right now.
      Notice what's happening in your body, as you begin to get still.
      Notice your heart beating; your breath moving in and out.
      Become aware of all the sensations that are running through your body, right now, in this moment.
      Notice if there is any tightness anywhere or constriction.
      Notice, just in this moment, if there are any emotions or feelings that you can feel present in your body.

      Create an intention to be open to the body's process, to whatever the body wants to speak. And whatever material is there to explore.
      Create an openness with your mind and your mind-body connection. To be open to exploring.
      As you do that, just call up whatever is the most pressing grief for you right now.
      Whatever that is. It's okay if you start just by calling up, the story, the image. Whatever it is that gets you in touch with the feeling that you might have in the most intense way around this grief.
      And if it's an older grief, also just check in with what residue is there. If there's anything that's still living in your body somewhere. Just take a minute and kind of check-in with the feelings.
      As you get a strong sense of the feelings, notice where they are living in your body, right now. Even though it may feel like a lot of emotion and story.
      See if you can isolate where you can feel the emotion in your body.
      Notice your breathing. Notice your heart.
      Are there any textures or colors when you focus on your body?
      What are you noticing?

Does it feel light or dark? Heavy or open?

What about your throat? Your face? Your head? Your stomach.

Find the place that feels the most central. The one that really is calling out from this grief. That is really holding the grief.

See if you can just go into that place with curiosity, without judgement. Noticing whatever is there. Becoming curious about the sensations.

Is there a pulsing? Is it dull? Does it ache?

Your only job is to become curious about the sensations that are there. If you find your mind wandering, just come back to the sensations that are there.

Notice if anything shifts at all, just by bringing in this brave awareness to your grief.

Notice how it feels to sit with this so simple practice.

Exploring and feeling the tangible quality of grief in your body.

There is often a quality to this that is so much like being held in a wordless place; the place we most needed that is beyond any story or any thinking just to attend to the sensations.

I invite you all to develop this ongoing relationship with the grief in your body. I promise you that as you attend to it, in this way and continue to be curious, something will be
moving through you that can happen no other way; that will not happen intellectually, that will not happen by having a story about it. But, that simply wants to be attended to in your body.

There is a second piece to this that I want to do and Andrea, I wonder if it makes sense to wait until the end and close with that. Just to give people another piece of this meditation.

Andrea: I think that sounds great; to let this settle.

Anna: I really encourage people to slowly come out of that experience. It takes a lot of courage to go into the sheer physicality of the grief. Just coming out and noticing how your relationship to your grief may have changed by allowing yourself to explore it in the body. Noticing what happens to your relationship to the grief by going in to the physical level.

Andrea: I really needed that. Thank you. That was so good and so powerful and profound.

Anna: I wonder if you could share a little bit, Andrea, of what that kind of exploration feels like for you.

Andrea: Well, as I said at the beginning of the show, I went to my daughter's graduation. What I was actually expecting with my mind, as you were starting this, was that I was going to find something in my body that would say something about the change in my relationship with her. We probably talked more in this last year on the phone, about this life process she was going through with her senior project and everything else. We talked much more than we had ever talked in the entire years with her. So, I thought I might be feeling some sadness about that.

But, what really came up for me was the change in my relationship with my ex-husband. And I was starting to feel this grief. I've been feeling agitated all day long not knowing what that was. As you were taking us through the exercise, it started to increase almost like butterflies in my stomach; being nervous about what was going to happen next. I would describe it as an experience I have when something is ending.
I'm excited that something new is beginning but I'm also a little bit fearful about it because I don't know what's going to be next.

I divorced my ex-husband over 23 years ago. My daughter, who graduated, was two years old when we separated. So, my ex-husband and I haven't lived together for a long time. We parented together and we had a crazy, messy divorce; we went through ups and downs and finding ways of parenting our kids. It was a very tumultuous relationship. I realized yesterday that this was kind of the end. Maybe if my second daughter gets married, that would bring us together. But she probably won't even have a traditional wedding so she might do that all on her own even. It really felt like this is the end; like the karma has been cleared and we're finished. Like, *oh, my gosh, this other level of freedom that that relationship has completed the cycle.* Yet, in my body I can feel some grieving and there is a loss of that.

Anna: That's so beautiful. It's interesting. I think a lot of times when exploring feelings in the body, there is often a layer kind of like what you were describing. The initial movement is like that butterfly feeling. Whatever gets you in. For a lot of people moving through grief or loss, there might be some real constriction or darkness or heaviness in certain places. It's really interesting what happens when you stay in the sensation being curious about it. Often these other surprises come just out of the exploration. Your energy may shift or may go, as you said, *oh, wow there's actually some sadness there, in addition to the excitement.* I frequently have that experience if I'm willing to stay with sensation long enough. It isn't always what it appears, which is why it's so profound to just stay with it and to continue to explore it.

I've had a lot of change happening and I've felt some constriction and some anxiety around my heart. Some changes in my career and wondering what's coming next. I've noticed as I've been sitting with sensations, that what's starting to come underneath, which is the flip side of what you were saying, Andrea. There's actually some excitement. There's something like what I've been interpreting as restriction and nervousness. If I stay with it and stay with it and stay with it, there's this sort of little girl quality of excitement that's starting to bubble up. I can feel that moving up through the body. So, I think it's really cool the way you described that. There was this initial concept intellectually of what you thought you were going to find. Then, there was this, *oh, I'm getting this butterfly feeling.* Then, there was even what sounds like another layer. *Oh, this is really letting go. This is really a loss.*

That is what is so beautiful about working with the body. It is that our minds can think we know what we are getting ourselves into, what this is about. And if we just stay with sensation, we start to get more layers of what the experience is for us. That really helps us move through it. We so often do not take the time to really experience how something has landed in our body. And when we do that, just like a little kid having a tantrum, and just letting him go through it. There's a whole series of feelings we get to move through instead of just the superficial idea of what we think the feeling is going to be.

Andrea: If I were to have thought with my head, I would have thought, *aren't I just ecstatically excited that it's over?* Because it's been a relationship of so many ups and downs. But, even with my children yesterday, I shared the story of how I met Bill and of course, I met him and I fell in love. And my body knows it. You're not going to just check him off the list. There is a lot of body memory here. We had two children together.

Anna: You raise such a good point. How many times have we gone through experiences where we intellectually are so glad to have left them: a challenging relationship, or a job, or even a move. But, the truth is, there are all of these layers to our experience that really are still there. And we need to attend to them. They do want our attention. They are part of the truth and the process and the healing. They are not going
to just go away. Life isn't that black and white. I mean, I can remember grieving relationships, too, where I thought I
should be over this or I was glad to be out of this relationship and almost sort of fighting about it with yourself; about the layers that are still there that bring the rest of the truth in. You need to move forward with an open heart. To really also allow that this relationship was loving and kind and beautiful, even if for a moment, it is really important in terms of whatever you allow in, in the future.

Andrea: Watching my daughter graduate in this small intimate ceremony, it is a small school and there were only 27 people graduating at this time of year. Each person who graduated spoke on the stage for a minute or so to put their voice in the room. And to have this contrast of the conflict in the relationship and to look at this beautiful human being who came forth from the two of us. So, it's layers and layers. I will also say, I don't give myself enough credit about what I'm actually going through. I will say that there are probably other people out there who do the same thing. *Oh, well that's over, let's move on.*

No, I will say to you: take some time, stay in your pajamas, drink some tea, take a hot bath, and listen to your body.

Anna: Listen to your body. I have so many clients who have gone through profound losses and we all do it. It's like being part of our society. There is such a sense of shame that there is a feeling of it in the body three months, a year later, two years later, ten years later. I would almost say, the amount of time doesn't matter.

Let's give up the concept of grief being done or not done and look at how grief is moving through my body as a teacher. You know, exploring these sensations and being in my body in a humble way with whatever wants to happen. Teach me to be different in my life. Grief at its core is really provided to us as a form of transformation. I think that is what is so beautiful about calling this grief transformation work.

Grief is like this bridge between where we have been and where we are going. There is a reason why we feel something. We don't want to make that go away. We want to embrace that as the vehicle to the next thing, if you could really honor your grief that way. And I think the reason why sometimes it is easier to do it with the body is because you can just attend to it.

You can try to stop the judgment or the story, like *why is this happening again? Why am I feeling this again? I should be over this.* Just go with whatever this is. *I'm going to go into my body right now and feel it and experience it.* So, I really encourage people listening to just develop, whether you are going through a major grief like this or not, a regular meditation practice. Explore the sensations that are happening in your body simply as a way of letting whatever is going on move through you without judgment and story. Sit with whatever the sensations are and the body will tell you what you need. So, if you can listen, you might need to slow down or you might need to be more active. The body doesn't have one language. I think it is really an important way through rather than blocking the grief and wanting it to go away and be done already.

Andrea: And to be conscious. This is holiday season and just give yourself the space. It could be that you just say, *I'm not going to bake 2 dozen more cookies for this event. I am either going to go out for a walk or I am going to get into a hot bath* or to listen to what it is that you need. Believe me. I have had so many holidays where I have had the long list of what I should be doing and what would happen if I didn't show up without that cheese ball because I said I would bring one. Oh, my gosh. I can just laugh about it now because of some of the terrible things I told myself in the past.

Anna: Yes, I think especially for people who are going through really profound loss right now. I know we all are, all the time. Check in with your body and know if you are willing to do what it says. Sometimes we are afraid to or we don't really want to, if we know our body is not going to lie to us. But, if you actually take a moment and check in, I bet you almost anything, you're exhausted. I mean, grieving is hard work.

So, what would your body ask of you right now. *Does it want to rest? Does it want to be held?* I also think the holidays are a time we tend to ignore *the knowing* in our bodies by overeating because there is a lot of emotion. It is a really big time, if you've lost someone, for feeling old feelings. It's also a time for a lot of family dynamics to come up because there is so much expectation that we all kind of want to look like Norman Rockwell families. I don't know exactly where that comes from, but it is probably starting to break down.

I think it's also really important to discern what is your body really wanting, if you are having this kind of dull ache in your chest or in your stomach. There can be an instinct to go, *I'm going to fill that with something.* And it would be a great gift to yourself on the holiday to say, *"What gift does my body really need right now? Do I need to sit and be still and cry? Do I need to journal? What are some other ways of really tending to what I'm really feeling? What does my body need right now?"*

Andrea: I want to presence something else, too. I recorded a show for Saturday night about **Healing from Divorce** which I thought was very appropriate considering I was with my ex-husband and my daughters. One of the things that happened for me was going through some craziness over the holidays during the first year we separated. I got sick with the flu the first Christmas my children were not with me. For ten years, I went through a pattern every year. It started at Halloween where I would get a cold. By Thanksgiving, it was a chest cold. By Christmas, it was bronchitis and then it would take me until Valentine's Day to get over it. And it wasn't until I really started to anticipate and pay attention to it that something changed. But, I felt like for ten years I was grieving at the holidays. Shared custody at the holidays, the changes that were already going on and this deep grief that was there. And when my children were with me, I would push through it. *Okay, we're here, we're going to have the big Thanksgiving dinner. We're going to have the big Christmas and everything else.*

    I just wanted to say that out loud because I believe that when we don't pay attention to the messages that our bodies are giving us, it can be something like that where we get sick over and over and over.

Anna: And it makes perfect sense. I'm sure that you were really grieving and there was probably some really big stuff around all those changes.

Andrea: My kids were two and three and I wasn't with them on Thanksgiving and Christmas Eve the year we separated.

Anna: It's interesting, Andrea, if you had really gone into your body and just stopped, *what do you think you would have found? What was in there then that came through as getting sick every year.*

Andrea: I think I would just have really sobbed. I know that I did let myself cry some but I don't think I let myself go into the deep pain at that point. And it showed up as flus and colds and bronchitis. The lungs are a reflection of grieving. That's why we get lung diseases during the holidays because that's where grief is carried for many of us, in the lungs.

Anna: It's interesting that there are all of these fluid, retaining bronchia in our lungs because our emotions are very watery, too.

Andrea: I could just talk with you about this topic so much because I really do believe in the importance of connecting with our bodies and listening and the work that you're doing is phenomenal work. I love your blog **http://www.bodyreunion.blogspot.com** and your "Truce" process.

We have about fifteen minutes left of the show, do you want to do the next part of the meditation?

Anna: Yes, I just want to add another piece. Before we do that, I want to say one thing about when you were talking about this huge change in your process when you separated
from your husband and your kids were young. I think we're understandably afraid that grief will overwhelm us if we let it in. I hear that with a lot of the people who I work with. *Oh, my God, if I even open that door.*

And you said, *I think I really would have just sobbed.* I just want to contain that and say, one way into this work that I think can be really helpful, is to put a time limit on it so it's not so scary. *I'm going to explore what is going on with my body and my grief and to have it be this open-ended thing.* Really. Set a timer and create a limit for yourself. Almost so that psychologically it's not so overwhelming. I will say this to clients. *Give yourself half an hour a day to sob. Just think about the person you lost, it's very containing to know it's going to happen in a chunk of time.* So one piece of advice I would say when you are doing these explorations, which I encourage you to do after the show, is to really bracket it with time so it feels safe. 20-30 minutes is fine, 45 minutes, certainly not more than an hour. So, there is a beginning and an end and when you're done, you're done for now. You can come back to it next week.

Andrea: You can do that. You absolutely can do that. You can take control of your grief and I have experienced that myself.

Anna: Yes, it's like it's right there, a reservoir. You can keep coming back to it and you can still feed your kids and put them to bed. You might not think so sometimes, but it is possible. I don't think we always trust that.

So, there's a second piece to this experience of going into our grief in our bodies which is also really listening for whether or not there is a message, a learning or something that we want to know that maybe we're not hearing. Like I shared with my story of continuing to listen to the sensation in my neck, sometimes that will just happen naturally over time.

So I encourage you to continue to listen to sensations. But, I also think there are some things that we can do or introduce into the meditation to just be more available for anything that wants to come through.

So, everyone, just let yourself close your eyes.

Meditation 2:

(Pause into between the sentences to fully connect with the sensations in your body)

Go back into that space that we contacted earlier.
Tuning into and exploring the body right now.
Feeling where that grief is in your body right now.
Having just listened to the show, it might feel a little different in there, it might feel the same.
Exploring the body and noticing if there is any sensation in the body right now, like a strong feeling is living somewhere.
It may be something other than grief. I know there are listeners who are working through a variety of issues.
Wherever the feeling is the strongest now. Go in there and explore whatever sensation is there.
Being curious in the same way you were before.
What's the texture, the quality?
Is there a heaviness or a lightness?
What do you notice?
And as you continue to explore the sensations with curiosity, notice if anything else wants to come through.

So, notice if there's an image that rises up out of being with that sensation. There might also be some words or music. There might also be a feeling, a really strong feeling that is connected to the sensations that has a voice behind it that wants you to know something.

Open to that possibility and whatever is coming through.

If you are getting an image it can be helpful to ask, is there anything you want me to know. You can also just ask the sensation and see if an answer comes from that question.

Often times there is a feeling space that is living in the body that is actually our bodies truth. So, beyond your own feelings, your body might have a feeling it is just trying to let you know about. Or something it wants you to know. See if you can tease that out.

And as you get the experience, you'll know you received something because there is often a feeling of relief.

I know we don't have a lot of time tonight. If you are getting into something that feels useful and interesting to come back to, create that intention.

Thank that image or feeling or thought for presenting itself to you. Make a commitment to integrate some of that truth in your life. You might even want to take some notes after the show on some commitments or awareness you want to bring forward.

Acknowledge that you can come back to this space, anytime you want to, by exploring the sensations in the body and being willing to listen and deepen your experience.

There's a lot of wisdom in there.

As you're ready, just taking a few breaths.

Slowly coming back into the room wherever you are.

Feeling your fingers and your toes.

Feeling your body.

Noticing what may have shifted.

Be present there now.

And again just noticing what it's like to get out of the head and moving into a different way of accessing information.

Really thanking and honoring the body for doing that with you

Andrea: I want to thank you so much for taking us through the process tonight and I want to let people know it is in the radio show archives. If you want to go back to that space and even be at a place where you can pause it.

I could feel the energy on my shoulders. It's funny because for the last week, I have been feeling this pain in my shoulders and I've been thinking it was because I have been sitting in front of the computer so much and there's been a lot of work. But, actually, it is no more than I would usually do.

What I really felt in the meditation, and the process, was that I've been carrying this weight for a long time. With my daughters, it's been really important to me even in the dysfunction and anger between my husband and me. It was
important that my daughters have a good relationship with their Dad. In many ways, I helped them negotiate and learn how to have a relationship with him that supported themselves as women. I could just feel the pain melting away, like I don't have to do that anymore. That was the ending of a time period and I can let that go. I actually felt like an angel came and put a crown on my head like a completion. I graduated, too. I had planned on taking a bath tonight, to really let myself relax. I want to bring that thought into this time period. It is the end of the year and good to really take some time to nurture myself. Find something whether it's five minutes or more. Just listening and to let this time period come to a close and to let my body heal what it wants to heal. So, thank you.

Anna: That is so beautiful, Andrea. I love that.

Anna Stookey is a psychotherapist with over twenty years' experience working with the mind and body, helping clients with trauma, bereavement and body and health issues, find peace through dynamic interpersonal work and her unique bodymind system, The Truce Process, exploring the healing power of the body relationship as a teacher and metaphor for how we live our lives.

www.annastookey.com
www.bodymindguide.com

Grief Transformation Show #29
Using the Body's Wisdom to Transform Grief

December 20, 2010
http://tobtr.com/1400734

Andrea Hylen

Chapter Thirteen

Healing with Music
Andrea Hylen

Show originally aired on December 19, 2010

During this series of Grief Transformation Shows, I have talked about a variety of ways to feel and heal grief. Alan Peterson was one of the guests who specifically talked about music and the power of love to transform grief.

    Tonight I want to share a few more ideas about using music as a tool to feel and heal and transform grief and to share how I have personally used songs in my own healing.

    Music can be used to stir memories. It can be used to help uncover feelings and it can be used to help feelings rise to the surface where you can look at them and reflect and feel deeper. For instance, have you ever felt sad and didn't know why? Did you ever feel an uneasiness and couldn't seem to shake it? Well, music can help you get to the root of it. Even if you don't know where it's coming from, music can help you feel and move the energy up and out of your body. It can help you release blocks so the emotions can flow.

    This morning I was listening to Christmas music. When Bing Crosby began to sing White Christmas, I immediately flashed back to a memory where I was watching the movie with my sister when we were children. I imagined the living room in our house and the two of us sitting together watching it on television. I imagined the Christmas tree and the smell of cookies baking. I could remember the feeling of anticipating the arrival of Santa Claus and then a thought came to me about the year we dressed my little brother in a mix and match Santa outfit with a homemade beard. All of these thoughts and images came to me in that moment and helped me to remember and feel a time period that brought me joy and happiness.

    On the flip side, I can hear the song, "Merry Christmas Darling" by Karen Carpenter and remember the first Christmas I was dating my ex-husband. I can remember feeling the joy of singing the song to record it for him. I was in California with my family visiting my grandparents that Christmas and he was in Pennsylvania with his family. I felt so much love for him and I really missed him. The song reminds of that love and passion I had for him the first Christmas we were dating. Sometimes around the holidays when I'm shopping and I hear that song playing, it brings sadness because our love died and we had a very messy, nasty divorce. I have healed many feelings, but occasionally there is a Christmas when something else has surfaced to be healed from our past relationship.

And if I felt the need to grieve over the loss, I could play that song to bring up the feelings to heal. To encourage them to rise up, giving me a chance to reflect and process what I need to. I don't need to try to dig up old memories that have healed, but sometimes an emotion surfaces and it deserves some exploration to see what wants to be healed. And I might not have been ready to heal this layer five or ten years ago.

Sound Healing is a great tool for healing loss and grief. On the other side of the healing is inspiration and joy. There may even be a feeling of relief as part of the release and healing. There is even a profession called sound healing. People have businesses where they use sounds and tones to heal emotions and restore you to balance. Sound and music can move the emotions out of your physical body. And dancing to the music helps, too!

There are several really talented, famous sound healers if you want to explore the idea of that and then look in your area for people who do this as a profession and book a session for yourself. Jonathan Goldman, Steven Halpern, and Tom Kenyon are all sound healers you can find on the internet to listen to samples.

Jonathan Goldman has a book called Healing Sounds. In his book, he describes 5 levels of listening. Using headphones can create a space to bring this into your body in a deeper way. It is like creating a container or a sound chamber.

1. The first level involves hearing.
2. A second level involves expanding your perception of the sound spectrum.
3. A third level involves imagination
4. A fourth level involves becoming one with the sound. You feel the sound in your body.

5. A fifth level is silence.

Jonathan Goldman's website: **http://www.healingsounds.com**

Music and sound can open your heart to help bring forth the tears, anger or sadness and other emotions of loss. Sometimes music can help bring forth laughter that will shake up or clear emotions. It can help you to reclaim your personal power. It can give you courage and hope and joy.

When I use the term sound healing, I use it in a broader definition. Sound can be anything from Rock and Roll to Opera to crystal bowls and chanting. It can also be sounds of nature, like hearing the sounds of the ocean at the beach or a waterfall. This is an area to discover what works for you, what music stirs your soul and helps you to feel and release and that may change moment by moment.

You may be someone who connects to classical music and a particular composer or orchestra within classical music. You may be grieving and find yourself listening to a rock and roll song from your youth. That memory could be an inspiration to turn up the volume and sing the song at the top of your lungs. It could be the music and words you need in this moment to heal. You might feel inspired to stay up and twist and shout with a memory from the 60's or 70's.

I traveled to Jonas Brothers' concerts with my teenage daughter as part of healing after the death of her father. I found the vibration from the music stirring and awakening something in me.

Here are some examples of songs I have used to heal:

Patti LaBelle- Her song "New Attitude" was the song that helped me heal the divorce from my first husband. I would turn up the volume and sing and dance in the kitchen. It helped me to reclaim my personal power. Although I was divorced over twenty years ago, I have played the song at times to heal layers of reclaiming personal power.

https://youtu.be/QWfZ5SZZ4xE

New Attitude:

Somehow the wires uncrossed, the tables were turned
Never knew I had such a lesson to learn
I'm feelin' good from my head to my shoes
Know where I'm goin' and I know what to do
I tidied up my point of view
I got a new attitude
I'm in control, my worries are few
'Cause I've got love like I never knew

Jason Mraz - The song, **"Make it Mine"** was the music I sang throughout the day when I was selling my house and preparing to move across the country. It helped me to release the life that died with my husband. I played it every day for six months. It gave me the courage and the energy to move through the feelings, get unstuck and listen to the next steps of clearing and releasing.

https://youtu.be/_r2CwihdLkc

Make it Mine:
Wake up everyone
How can you sleep at a time like this
Unless the dreamer is the real you
Listen to your voice
The one that tells you to taste past the tip of your tongue
Leap and the net will appear.

John Denver- "Perhaps Love" has helped me grieve my husband and open my heart to feel love and compassion.

https://youtu.be/c-5bMO4nMuk

John Denver's Perhaps Love:
And some say love is holding on
And some say letting go
And some say love is everything
And some say they don't know.

Nick Jonas- "A little Bit Longer" is a song I listen to when I feel like I am a failure because things haven't moved forward in my life. It gives me the courage to be patient and listen. Nick wrote this song on a day he was feeling discouraged about his diabetes.

https://youtu.be/ngJdHREjL_A

Nick Jonas's A Little Bit Longer:
All this time goes by
Still no reason why
A little bit longer and I'll be fine.
Waitin' on a cure
But none of them are sure
A little bit longer and I'll be fine

YouTube videos are an amazing resource for discovering music. Search on an artist, a topic or a song title. **http://youtube.com**
    Pandora **http://www.Pandora.com** and Spotify **https://www.spotify.com/** have a variety of options for listening and creating playlists of music.   Whatever you are guided to listen to know that there is a frequency of sound that is charging your central nervous system, the cortex of the brain and your heart. It is working on your physical body to bring harmony to your mind-body-spirit connection.

    Here is an experience I had with music and healing:
    As I said, music has always been a powerful healer for me. Songs are linked and woven into the memories of joy, sadness, and change. Music and sound opens my heart to bring forth the tears or anger or other emotions of loss.
    Many years ago, I was diagnosed with an auto-immune condition called polymiositis. My immune system began to attack my muscles. I became weaker and weaker and I was so physically weak that walking down the street and tripping on a crack in the sidewalk would send me hurtling forward and my face would land smack on the pavement. I took 3-hour naps every day just to function. My daily goal was to keep my one-year-old daughter safe during my nap and to cook dinner.

One year later I was lying in a hospital bed suddenly unable to walk at all. I was in an isolation room because the doctors thought I had a bacterial infection. I knew that I was having a reaction to a new medication that I had started taking three weeks earlier. I knew in my heart and soul that that was what was wrong with me. For a week, I was allowed to have visitors but was isolated from the other patients.

A friend of mine, Lucky Sweeny, brought a portable tape player, headphones and a tape of Kenny Loggins singing songs from "Return to Pooh Corner" to the hospital. If you have never heard of the CD it is listed under CDs for children and adult contemporary. Some of the song titles are Rainbow Connection, Return to Pooh Corner, and a Neverland Medley.

I had never heard the music before. As I played the tape I began to sob. I sobbed on and off for two days. I was grieving layers of pain and frustration. I grieved the loss of my health, the 60 lbs I had gained on prednisone, the loss of control, the quality of time with my children, and the failure to heal. Through the tears, I released the gunk that was surrounding my heart where I was so frustrated and discouraged. For two years, no matter what I did, it seemed like I was getting sicker.

I had taken the prescription medication and listened to the advice from the doctors. I tried a wide variety of vitamins. I had weekly acupuncture that included therapy focusing on the emotions and clues from my body. I prayed, and ate healthy food. I wrote about my emotions in a journal. I had daily rituals of affirmations and a positive focus.

People were praying for me.

I felt like I had fallen to my knees over and over again. *God, what else do you want me to do? What do I need to learn from this?*

As I look back now, this is what I believe happened. I had been actively doing and living my inner work. I was doing exactly what I needed to do to fully experience a health crisis. And the last huge piece was to end up in the hospital and grieve. I had to let go of a picture of my life and release the vision I was trying to control. It took time to do that. I have experienced my life turning from pain to joy in days, but not this time. The healing was deeper and required a journey deep into the core of my being.

In the hospital, I went into my heart and completely surrendered. I released through tears. The music and the words pierced my heart. I opened to more love. There were elements of forgiveness, gratitude, self-love and letting go. There was something new to discover within me.

At the end of the two days of grieving and listening to the music, I experienced a light bulb flashing moment. I knew that I was going to get well and I was going to start home schooling my kids. I stopped feeling like a victim and I woke up to the power that is within me. I had taken a deep dive into the pain and I had emerged victorious.

It was one of the most profound moments of my life. With the help of the music, I was shining a light into the core of my being. I emerged to heal and live a fuller, richer, deeper life. It did take me another year or so to finish healing physically. I continued to feel and go into the core to discover places to heal. I needed to heal on a cellular level. This was an example of the power of music to heal.

Music is such a powerful tool of inspiration and healing that I find when I wake up, almost every morning, there is a song playing in my head. I lay there for a few minutes listening. I feel it is one of the ways Spirit communicates with me and I open to the words and reflect as this is a way to receive healing and inspiration and guidance. It is a tool that can be embraced and cultivated.

I hope this has inspired you to explore the world of sound and music; to feel, heal and transform grief. I love you.

**Grief Transformation Show #28
Healing with Music**

December 19, 2010
http://tobtr.com/1438749

Chapter Fourteen

Reading Stories of Grief to Heal
Andrea Hylen

Show originally aired on November 28, 2010

Tonight, I am going to share about the power to heal while reading someone's personal story of healing trauma and loss.

There is healing, power and hope in reading stories of struggle and triumph that can also heal your story. The key is finding and **feeling a connection** between your story and someone else's story. The connection in loss then connects to hope. There is something about reading their story and knowing that if they survived the pain, I can survive it, too. There is something about realizing that someone has experienced this loss who found the strength to embrace their pain and to witness how they found the path to healing and love. Every story is unique but there are feelings and experiences that are Universal. The stories demonstrate lessons learned through adversity. The stories are a guidepost where I can see that one other person felt the feelings and survived and healed.

I separated from my first husband in 1987. It was a painful three-year process and a nightmare of a divorce and child custody battle. It was the first time in my life when I was feeling so much pain and loss while at the same time being aware of how much I was learning about myself within a short time. It was the first time I could see that the pain had a reason and it was part of the process of letting go and changing something in my life. There was an opportunity for me to learn and grow. Personal stories in books showed me the way and inspired me to stand up for myself and use my voice. Louise Hay, You Can Heal Your Life was one of my favorite books.

A few years later, I was remarried and gave birth to a son who was born with a congenital heart defect. I had some level of understanding that as painful as this was there were gifts within it. There were moments of, *"Why him? Why me?"* that awakened something else in me. My son was teaching everyone around him just by his presence. And even after he died at the age of nineteen months, the pain of his death was our teacher.

It was after his death that I began to find more books that were memoirs and stories of grief. I read them to feel the pain and find my way to healing. Memoirs and stories about grief have the potential to help us process a situation, to understand it at a deeper level.

Tonight I am going to share a few of my favorite books with you, reading short excerpts and talking about my connection to the stories. You may connect with the stories I read and you may not. If not these stories, there are others you can find that will resonate with you more. What is important tonight is to see these books as examples and to find books that resonate with you and your journey.

The first book I want to share with you is called:

The Lessons of Love by Melody Beattie, a New York Times Bestselling Author. She is also the author of **Codependent No More.**

Introduction:

"*The Lessons of Love* isn't a grief book, although that is part of it, for grieving is inherently and mysteriously connected to loving deeply. It's a book about opening the heart, living from the heart, trusting the heart. It's a learning to live again book. It's a story about love's ultimate and absolute lesson that love is the only thing in this world that cannot be lost because it's the only thing that's real.

Melody Beattie's life was tragically turned upside down by the death of her 12-year old son in a skiing accident. Her world shattered. Beattie withdrew into a dark cave of despair and nothing and no one could move her out of her sorrow. Gradually she began to see that we always have a choice between succumbing to despair and embracing life. Slowly she learned that a passion for living cannot only be reawakened but can flourish against the greatest of odds. Here was life's ultimate paradox. That while it can be unbearably clear, it is still filled with beauty and worth living with passion."

This book was published the year after my son died. It was perfect timing because I was in another deep period of grieving and I wanted to push the pain away. One of the reasons I connected with the book was because we had both lost a son. But, there was a deeper story.

There was a part in the book when Melody Beattie heard the words, *"It is time for your message to change."* She realized she needed to heal her relationship with God. She described moments when God spoke to her at the depth of her pain and she received the message that there is only one thing. Love.

One of the gifts that gave me strength as I read her words was that it was an answer and comfort to my feelings of discouragement. I questioned, *how much longer will I feel this pain? Is my life going to be filled with one painful moment after another? Divorce. Shared custody of my older two daughters. Death of a son. How much more must I endure?*

It is such a human, real feeling to want the pain to go away and to feel frustrated and discouraged that it will never go away. Her story was a model for my despair and she demonstrated the healing process. I appreciated her words and her story because they let me into her heart. And at a time when I wondered why I had to feel this deep pain again, I knew that it was a way through to more Love. She was showing me the lessons of love. Reading the story didn't take away the pain, but it made it easier somehow because I felt that someone else understood. Someone had gone to a deep place of sorrow and had made it through to the other side.

I sobbed through most of her book with several boxes of tissues by my side. And in the end, I felt some relief and hope and encouragement. I was going to survive and find the sunshine in my life again. I still think of this book as being instrumental in healing the grief in my heart from the loss of my son.

Another book, published in 2010 is called, **The Barn Dance by James Twyman.** James Twyman's organization, The Beloved Community, teaches people to be spiritual peacemakers. I met James in 1997 when he was traveling around the country singing songs of peace prayers. He had written music to connect Peace prayers from 12 major religions as songs. He had also written a book called

Emissaries of Light. My husband and James wife, both died within months of each other in 2005. My husband died of cancer and James wife was murdered. I became ordained as a Minister of Spiritual Peacemaking in the Beloved Community in 2006.

In 2007, James traveled around the United States singing peace songs at 64 concerts during the season of non-violence. The 64 days are between January 30, the day Ghandi was assassinated and April 4, the day Martin Luther King, Jr was assassinated.
http://www.agnt.org/season-for-nonviolence

James is called the peace troubadour and has traveled around the world singing peace songs in war torn areas of the world. This time he was traveling around the United States for 64 concerts and I had the privilege to go to seven of the concerts in the Washington, DC area during his US tour. One evening in a little church in DC with only 10 people present, the smallest group by far of all of his concerts, he told us some of the story that is now written in The Barn Dance and he sang a song he wrote for his wife Linda. On the day of that concert, I had received a buyer for my husband's business. It was a day of gratitude and letting go. Jimmy's song felt like a tribute to both our life partners.

Let me tell you about his book. It describes the story that James briefly shared with us that night.

"I first met Linda in 1984, when I graduated from Loyola University in Chicago. She remained the most important woman in my life until that tragic day in 2005 when she was killed. I needed a miracle and 3 ½ years later it came. This is the true story of how heaven opened a door and showed me that death isn't the end of life but the beginning. If you've ever wondered, if we really can communicate with our loved ones who have passed to the other side then this is your answer. If you've ever thought heaven and earth never met then this story will reveal a world you never imagined, a world where love never ends and life goes on forever. My intention was to honor the woman who changed my life and to reveal a mystery that is hidden to most but which is very, very real."

There are moments in the book where James talks about the sadness. For me, there is a feeling of staying connected to the person who died. Letting go can feel like, *now it's really over* if I'm not feeling the pain any longer. Reading books like this gives me ideas of how to heal and to understand a deeper awareness of the process I am going through at that time.

Another book came into my life a few weeks ago. I was at my favorite coffee shop in Toluca Lake, CA called Priscilla's. One of the regular patrons brought a book to me saying he thought I would love this story. It is a memoir written by Lauren Bacall, the actress who was married to Humphrey Bogart. It was published in 1978. Bacall and Bogart were movie stars in films including Casablanca. Her husband died of cancer and there were a few sections where she described some of the same feelings I had with my husband when he was in the hospital dying from cancer. In one section, she described an intimate moment between them that reminded me of my own intimate moment with my husband.

When I read Lauren Bacall's words about her husband, I knew that someone understood what it was like for me. It brought me comfort. It helped me cry and I felt like I released something that I had been holding onto deep in my heart. Now, I felt more connected to life because someone else knew what I was feeling.

Books like this can be found in the library in the Biography section. I encourage you to go browse and see if someone has written a story that will speak to your experience and can bring you comfort.

One of the types of books where I have received courage, ideas, strength, hope and healing are anthologies. They are books with many voices and experiences. In this next part of the show, I am going to talk about universal stories in anthologies that all written by women.

Conscious Choices: An Evolutionary Woman's Guide to Life. This was a book that was created from an idea at an Evolutionary Women retreat in 2007. Forty-four women wrote a personal story after a period of deeper listening. They didn't write the story they thought they should write but the story that was calling to them from within. They listened, waited and allowed the space for the story to emerge. That is the power in this book. Each story was written from a deep place inside each woman that was calling to be healed and shared. I was honored to be the midwife of the book.

During the process of reading and gently editing the stories, I can remember sitting in my bed at night with my laptop, reading the stories from each woman. Each story involved strength and inspiration the author had found in claiming her personal power. It was in reading their stories that I felt the women bring me to a deeper place of healing and transformation. There is an incredible power when someone is willing to share their heart, share their pain, share the struggle, be vulnerable and to share what they learned from it and show us how they came out on the other side.

Another anthology book I love is called, **Women on Fire: 20 Inspiring Women Share Their Life Secrets (and Save You Years of Struggle!) by Debbie Phillips.** Women wrote stories from deep within their hearts about when they were uncertain, times when they had lost something, times when they lost something of themselves and were able to reclaim it. As I read the stories I laughed, I cried and I felt so much of a heart connection to them.

The last book I want to share with you tonight is called, **"Saving the Best for Last: Creating Our Lives After 50," by Renee Fischer, Joyce Kramer and Jean Peelen.** Even though the authors talk about lives after 50, there is so much wisdom here for all ages. They each spoke candidly about a variety of topics, like sexuality, dating and mating, money, their mothers, loss, friendship and more. There is incredible wisdom, honesty and a heart connection. Each topic is written by all three women from three different perspectives. They talk about the loss of loved ones but also things like loss through divorce that have no finality.

The key in reading to heal and transform grief is to feel the heart of someone in the story whether it is a memoir or a book of anthologies or a novel. It is important to feel the heart of the writer where they are sharing a deeper part of themselves. **It is in our connection to the heart that we heal.**

I also want to encourage you to write your own story. Journal, blog, join a writing program for community support. I talked about the book **Conscious Choices** earlier in the show and my experience with women writing their stories. During that process, I learned about the personal power that gets tied up in an experience in our lives and when we take the time to reflect and write, we can reclaim that power and use it in other areas of our lives.

The story I wrote in Conscious Choices happened during a time in my life when I was in a marriage that was falling apart. My young daughters were 6 months and 23 months old. I felt very hopeless and helpless in my life and in my marriage. As I was writing in my journal and reflecting on what story to write for Conscious Choices, a song from the PBS children's program,

"Mister Rogers" was playing in my head. It reminded me of a time when I watched Mister Rogers with my little girls twenty years earlier. During the show, Mister Rogers would always look into the camera and say, "I love you, just the way you are." I remembered watching the show and waiting for that moment when Mister Rogers would "look" into my eyes and tell me how much he loved me, just the way I am. Every week I would wait for that moment and his words would cause me to cry with tears streaming down my face. I felt so lost and alone and it felt like he was the only person who was telling me that he loved me, just for me. It was the clue that was pointing to the pain that was in my heart. As I wrote the story, I started writing it from one perspective, an old feeling of being a victim in a marriage that was dying.

After writing and re-writing the story, I read it out loud one night and I thought, this is not the story. I was not a victim. I was a participant in the story and in my life. As I wrote the story, I saw that I had to turn within to find my own self-love. When I could tell myself, *I love you just the way you are* that was where the true healing was. It had taken time to write the story to discover that. The self-love was the story. I deleted ¾ of the story and then I wrote the story from being honest about where the pain was and how I finally reached a place of being able to look in the mirror and tell myself, *"I love you just the way you are."*

Writing in a journal, a blog, or a story will connect you with feelings that are buried. It will help you to uncover and remember. I cried, no, I sobbed as I wrote. I even got a cold where my nose was constantly running for three weeks. Old tears that I was releasing through my body. When you can write and find the words to describe the experience, it heals and changes you.

In the writing process, there is a time when you can look at the story you have been telling yourself and see something new. You can heal the story and get a different perspective. Writing your own story can be a really powerful healing tool. If you feel the joy in this idea my words to you are, "Go for it!"

A note from the editor:

After writing 70 articles in 2010 on transforming grief and hosting 44 radio shows, I founded the non-profit organization, Heal My Voice, Inc. The focus of the organization is to provide programs and workshops for women to write, speak and reclaim power. For more information, go to **www.healmyvoice.org**

Grief Transformation Show #8
Reading Stories of Grief and Inspiration to Heal

November 28, 2010
http://tobtr.com/1369277

Chapter Fifteen

Dancing with the Jonas Brothers and a Teenager
Andrea Hylen

Show originally aired on December 1, 2010

Tonight the show is focused on how to feel the feelings of grief and find ways to lighten a heavy heart. Following an inspiration to explore feelings with creativity whether it is art, writing or music will help you uncover and unlock joy and happiness.

    I am going to share part of a journey that began with one concert, one band, one grieving teenage daughter and one widowed mother. I want to warn you that this is probably one of the most outrageous stories you will hear about how to heal a grieving heart. That one concert turned into 78 concerts in less than 2 ½ years. I know! Insane, outrageous, crazy! As I begin with how this happened and some of the things that awakened in me, I invite you to notice the small inspirations that happened along the way and find things that awaken and stir something inside of you.

    To me this is the key to our own path of feeling and healing and transforming. When something in another person's story touches you in a way that it awakens something in you that is about you. It wakes you up to an AHA! Or a next step to take or a place to pause and listen. When you listen to any of the other Radio Shows recorded during this holiday season you will begin to see a pattern emerge of how every guest in every show, woke up to feeling feelings that were sad and mad and that awakened them to live a richer, deeper life of joy and happiness. Talking about grief may seem like a depressing topic. When you lean in and feel, you can see it as part of life which expands the life you can live. You can embrace all of it.

    As I look through my journal entries from July 2007, I can tell you that the idea of going to 78 Jonas Brothers concerts was not anywhere on my list of goals. I had been a widow for
two years and I had other pressing questions.
    This is what I was thinking and writing about that summer:

*What groups or programs are there to help teenagers who have lost a parent? (Underneath: *I am worried about my youngest daughter, Hannah, and I fear that I am not enough for her. My own grief is so overwhelming and my life is filled with so many responsibilities for the family, I fear that I may be missing warning signs from my daughter. I feel helpless and alone.*)

*What home schooling program will we use for Hannah's high school years? (Underneath: *Hannah has decided to home school for high school and I worry that she is disconnected from our original home school community. Where will we find activities for her to meet and socialize with other people?*)

*How do I turn my big house into a retreat center? (Underneath: *How am I going to afford to keep my home? Should I sell it? Where would we live? Is there an income source here that I am not seeing?*)

*How can I teach people about the environment, nutrition, and spirituality? (Underneath: *What kind of job can I get at the age of 50 when I have been out of the work place for 20 years? What do I want to do as a career? Should I go back to school? What would I study?*)

*What kind of fence do I want to install around the pool? (Underneath: *How long am I going to live in this house? Should I install a functional fence or a more expensive decorative fence that I want to look at for the next 30 years?*)

As you can see, my inner reflections involved helping my youngest daughter grieve, and the next steps for my house and career. Most of the questions did not have immediate answers. The questions were clues and I began to spend more
time in silence and take action steps when the answers became clearer. On some days, I wished for a magic wand that would show me the future so I could make the right decisions. Yes, I admit it. I was looking for the "right" decisions, as if they were locked away and I had to find the key or I would fail and be wrong.

Every one of these questions would take years of action and waiting, hours of reflection, tears and emerging fears, doubts and frustrations and step by step solutions. Many, many times, I prayed for the magic pill that would transform my life into clarity immediately. I felt frozen in pain and indecision. There was no one who could make these decisions for me and no one who even offered.

I showed bravado to the world about this, but inside I was crumpled in fear. The women I would have reached out to for support were all going through their own pain. Divorce, caretaking a dying loved one and difficult job transitions. We were all pushed to the maximum breaking points. They could have provided the kind of support that would have helped me to see infinite possibilities. They were the "climb out of the box thinkers," I needed at this time and they couldn't be there for me. With all of us in life transitions, I was forced to go it alone.

What I didn't know that summer was how my life was about to change dramatically. In the next three years, I would travel to 78 Jonas Brothers concerts, drive 90,000 miles, co-author a book, sell my house, and give away most of my personal belongings. I would pack a car with a teenage daughter, clothes, books, 2 cats and move 3000 miles away from a community that had loved and supported me for 25 years. Going it alone taught me I had a connection to an inner Source and there was an inner strength deep within me. Do I still need people? Of course! And sometimes part of the path you take has to be by yourself. The heroine's journey. A dark night of the soul.

When people hear that I went to 78 Jonas Brothers concerts there are two types of questions they ask me.

1. How did you afford to do this?
2. Why did you do this?

Here are the brief answers.

1. We found free resources whenever possible, even free tickets and found creative work to do along the way. We slept on couches and in the car and at the Hyatt (a gift from one of the people who worked for the Jonas Brothers.)

2. I wanted to help my daughter heal from the death of her father and I had an inner calling, one step at a time.

I can begin by summarizing each of the last three summers with one word:

July 2007: Awakening

July 2008: Healing

July 2009: Breakthrough

Step by step the journey will unfold. Let's begin with the Awakening…

My entry into the world of the Jonas Brothers concerts was motivated by a desire to help my youngest daughter, Hannah. She was the youngest of my three daughters and was only 12 years old when her father died in July 2005. My older two daughters, Mary, 21 and Liz, 19 were adults with their own grieving process. As much as I was grieving the loss of my husband, I was watching all three of my daughters to figure out how to help them in their grieving process, too.

We had all seen a counselor during the first 18 months after the death of Hurley, a husband, father or stepfather to each of us. We processed feelings, healed and did all of the things I thought we should be doing to grieve his loss. I found additional support by attending a healing service at a local church on Friday nights and going to Jayne Feldman's spiritual group in her home at Angel Heights once a week in Maryland. (www.earthangel4peace.com)

It seems like it would be so easy to grieve. Honor the feelings, cry and release. Connect with your Spirit and be present with the feelings. But, grief is an elusive being. No matter how much you grieve, you carry some memory of it in your heart always. That seems obvious, doesn't it? We carry the grief in our hearts always. Although, how many times has someone expected you to stop grieving? Or how many times have you judged yourself for still grieving, like there is a time limit on it and you should just get on with your life.

Think back on the happiest moments of your life. Can't you recall some memory of the feelings in a moment? A celebration, a birthday, a vacation and the sweet moments of a smile, a sunset, or a walk through a garden can fill our hearts with joy, happiness and connection. It is the same thing with grief. The loss of a loved one, a job, or your own health challenge can bring a wave of remembrance and grief. It is a life experience with feelings and memories.

And so it was for each of my daughters and me, as we moved back into life. The initial shock of Hurley's death was gone, but the waves of grief threw us back into a remembrance of loss and pain. We hadn't learned how to navigate and dance with the feelings, yet.

The Jonas Brothers journey began with a simple question from Hannah, *"Could we go to a FREE concert in Philadelphia."* Looking at the light shining in my daughter's eyes for the first time in two years led me to say *yes* immediately. A few weeks later, we drove two hours to Philadelphia to see a band called the Jonas Brothers on the second anniversary of her father's death. I was grateful to find something that could bring happiness back into my daughter's life.

We went to three concerts that summer. Penn's Landing in Philadelphia, Six Flags in Largo, Maryland, and the Palace Theatre in Syracuse, New York, six hours from our home. I saw Hannah connecting with a community of wonderful girls and families.

As we drove home from the third concert, I felt connected and complete. I had witnessed the power of girls and felt that my daughter would enter the school year with more confidence and fulfillment from the music and
 friendships. I really thought that was the end of the concerts. I had the feeling of coming home after a summer vacation and preparing to step back into life. I hoped that life might return to a new level of normal. The routine of school, work, and community activities would fill our lives again.

When autumn arrived and the leaves began to change colors, I could feel restlessness within me. I needed to get out on the open road. Driving long distances always gave me time to think and reflect on life. On the open road, I would breathe the trees, the sky, the clouds and the changing terrain into my heart and soul. New inspirations were bubbling.

With this inner stirring, I decided to drive from Maryland to Florida to spend Thanksgiving with my parents and my sister's family. Hannah was not crazy about the long sixteen hours of being stuck in a car until she discovered that the Jonas Brothers were touring with Hannah Montana/Miley Cyrus band. I purchased concert tickets in North Carolina for the ride home. A compromise. She willingly accepted the purpose for driving instead of flying.

Going to the concerts continued to be a carrot on a stick, a motivator and a reward over the next few months. We saw the "boys" on that tour in North Carolina, Baltimore, DC and Philadelphia. They had become part of the fiber of our lives. When I saw them in the larger concert hall, I felt like I was watching my nephews grow up and perform on bigger and bigger venues. I was so proud of them. They had touched my heart and I was really happy for their success.

As the Jonas Brothers began to share their music on larger and larger stages, there was also an expansion of my own heart that year. I released my husband's business, repaired the garage roof, and cleared out the garage and part of the basement. Memories of my husband remained. But some of the burdens were lifted as I finished details of his life that were left after his death.

For me, during this year of awakening, there was a gradual remembrance of passions I had as a teenager. That year of Jonas Brothers concerts awakened me to a part of myself that had been dormant. It helped me to let go of some of the dreams I had with my husband and a new part of myself with new dreams began to wake up even more.

To share the feelings of the beginning of that, here are two blogposts I wrote to reflect on the feelings I had at the first concerts.

Blog post 1:

The Year I Toured with the Jonas Brothers

April 13, 2008

I can't imagine a day without someone mentioning the Jonas Brothers. It started as one concert we were going to attend in Philadelphia on the waterfront at Penn's Landing. Now, it has become a habit, a daily past time.

The Jonas Brothers are like one of the family. I receive e-mails from friends and family informing me of Jonas sightings. Dancing with the Stars, The Ellen Show, Kids' Choice Awards, Jimmy Kimmel Live, The Today Show, Dick Clark's New Year's Eve. Our DVR is full of recorded programs and I watch them without my daughter in the room.

I quote words from the songs in conversations in my work and play. I can't remember life without the Jonas Brothers. What did we talk about? How did we spend our time and fun money?

In July 2007, my daughter, Hannah and I drove to King of Prussia, Pennsylvania to spend the night at a hotel located 15 minutes from our first Jonas Brothers concert. A free concert in Philadelphia. At that time, all I knew was it had been two years since her Dad had died and she was passionate about something. She wanted to connect. I was willing to hang out all day, first in the hot sun and then in a thunderstorm to see the band.

One of the first to arrive at the gate, we sat in blue cloth camping chairs eating bagels and cream cheese we brought from the continental breakfast at the Comfort Inn hotel. I found a second cup of coffee and a bathroom at the Hilton next door after we arrived at the gate. We sat there for hours comparing notes with other Jonas lovers. I listened to the heart felt information sharing about Nick, Joe and Kevin. I knew nothing about them or the music, but I was enthralled with the exuberance and passion bursting from the teens and parents around me. There was so much joy in the conversations.

There were mothers in their 30, 40's and 50's and their teenage daughters; A 20-year-old sister with her younger teen sister; A grandmother with several of her granddaughters; and an occasional
family with mother, daughter, father and a younger brother with his face buried in a hand held video game.

Friends of ours arrived from Baltimore. They were the celebrities in the group. They met the Jonas Brothers when there were small groups coming to concerts and hung out with them at a dance studio talking past midnight. Becca, the youngest daughter, also had the most enviable moment with the Jonas Brothers. Six months earlier, they chose her to come on stage and receive their attention, as they sang, "Hello Beautiful" to her. With tears and a shaking hand, her mother, Kim, recorded this event and posted it on YouTube.

In anticipation of the gates opening, I put the chairs back into the car and braced myself for girls running and screaming for the front row spots in front of the stage. After the sprint to victory, they stood in their claimed spots for two hours. They were waiting, watching and dancing to the music from two other bands. Rolling waves of giggling and screaming burst from the crowd when they thought they caught a glimpse of one of the "boys."

Then, a thunderstorm arrived. Dark clouds looming over the Delaware River that slowly made their way over the stage. Thunder and lightning so big and bold and loud and dangerous that the girls had to leave the stage area. Can you feel the pain of that? Waiting since early in the morning, running to claim your spot and then a thunderstorm comes in to ruin it all?

We all stood in the rain, getting drenched, waiting to see if the concert would go on at all. After all of that time of waiting and expecting and hoping and wishing for the moment to dance with the band it might be over now. Oh, the pain, the trauma, the frustration, the groans and protests from all of the girls.

I describe it this way with, exaggerated drama, from the memory of what it felt like when I was a teenager and also, as a mother whose heart had been breaking watching her daughter grieve for two years and feeling helpless to take this pain away. The disappointment was palpable and added to the pain that was already in my heart.

After 30 minutes, the storm moved on and the girls ran back down to the stage area. This time my daughter was a few rows back. I watched from the top of the pavilion looking down on a mass of bobbing bodies and heads. Girls holding tightly to keep their space in
*the crowd. They were there to see the band and **to be seen** by the band.*

As soon as the Jonas Brothers came on stage, I felt the power and natural magnetism oozing from them. Girls dancing, screaming, jumping up and down. I could see how incredible they were as performers. I was reminded of Mick Jagger from the Rolling Stones and Paul McCartney from the Beatles. I saw my daughter alive and passionate and full. I was witnessing a moment in her life.

I was hooked.

Blog post 2:

Heartthrobs from the 60's and 70's

April 20, 2008

The teen years of my generation happened during the 60's and 70's. I am part of the famous baby boomer generation who caught this ride and experienced some part of the 60's. Born in 1956, I remember more of the late 60's with an occasional memory of seeing the Beatles on The Ed Sullivan Show, but too young to have experienced Woodstock.

Our first three Jonas Brothers concerts were general admission. First come, first served. Sitting in line for six hours in Philadelphia, eight hours at Six Flags, in Largo, Maryland, and ten hours in Syracuse, New York

Even though we had tickets, we waited in line for the possibility of front row seats where, maybe, the Jonas Brothers would look into my daughter's eyes and tell her that they love her and everything is all right. (Okay, this is a song, in case you have missed this: **When You Look Me in the Eyes** *by the Jonas Brothers)*

The mothers waiting in line with their daughters reminisce about the bands they adored when they were teenagers. One mother in the line says none. She didn't have a band or a singer she liked.

What?!?

We don't believe her! What about the Cowsills, Bobby Sherman, David Cassidy, the Monkees, or the Beatles? Okay, she finally admits Frankie Avalon and Bobby Darin. She is a little older than the rest of us and they were the heartthrobs in her era.

We all sigh, roll our eyes and clutch our hearts, as we think about pictures from Tiger Beat magazine taped to our bedroom walls with dreamy eyes smiling at us. We try to remember the words from the songs that still make our hearts beat a little faster.

A flash back! I am 14 years old holding a picture of John and Barry Cowsill to my chest. It's the middle of the night and I'm rewriting one more version of the letter I know they will love. I hear lyrics from a song playing in my head. "But, I knew-I knew, I knew, I knew, I knew- She could make me happy, happy, happy. Flowers in her hair. Flowers everywhere." –The Cowsills.

My parents let me choose the wall paint for my room when I was 13. One wall blue, one green, one yellow, one orange with corkboard and mirrors. Bright, bold colors. I stay awake late into the night, in that room, dreaming about the life I will have when I am all grown up.

I was convinced The Cowsills would read my letter and know I am so wonderful, they would write back to me. They would want to write back to me even if they have never written back to anyone else, ever! (This is the only fan letter I ever wrote and no, I did not hear back from them.)

And now, it is 2008. I am sitting in lines all day, making food runs so my daughter doesn't lose her place in line, singing Jonas Brothers songs and when the doors to the venue open I hold my daughter's purse so she can run into the concert hall for a front row seat.

Run, Hannah, run! Inside my soul, I am still 14 and I run with her.

In the 8th Jonas Brothers concert in Reading, PA, during the month of March 2008, something totally unexpected happened to me. As I danced and sang with a group of teenagers, my heart burst wide open. Tears began to stream down my face. I was beginning to heal my own heart. More than healing from grieving, I was opening my heart to feel again. I was alive and ready to live life, to feel deeper passion and dream new dreams.

The first nine months of the Jonas Brothers experiences had opened a deep, raw place inside of me that was ready for more feelings, healing and love. I had been grieving for three years. I was learning more about how to grieve the loss of a loved one and at the same time learning how to support each of my daughters in their grief. While I was doing things to support the emotional healing, I had also been in a steep learning curve with physical action steps to clear things that were left unfinished by my husband.

I was learning about details of my husband's business and how to winterize our home, the things that my husband took responsibility for when he was alive. The pressure of that was even greater because of the grieving. The cloud of grief can make it difficult to concentrate, to absorb new information and to take risks out of your comfort zone. My internal energizer bunny was operating at about 50% and everything felt like an effort. At times it felt like I was doing tasks while walking through sludge, mud and quicksand.

Every time I thought I was nearing the end of clearing there were more details like hiring people to do more house repairs or finding places to sell, give away or dispose of all of my husband's unfinished projects, including two truckloads of polyurethane and a half-finished ultra-light airplane. I fell to my knees over and over again in frustration and despair, curling up on the living room couch to retreat and sob. I was a single parent, a single home owner of a large home, and I was a solo business owner of a business I knew very little about with piles of stuff I couldn't even identify.

The timing of concerts during the summer of 2008 was perfect. I had worked so hard for three years. I was exhausted emotionally when we left for the trip. I had been so focused on everyone's needs I was burned out. I just wanted to get on the open road and rest from everything. The death, the letting go of our life together, the clearing of physical possessions, the care of a home, a business and challenge after challenge after challenge.

Blog post 9:

The Bridge

June 3, 2008

My daughter, Hannah and I are finding our way back to each other. Since the death of her father, we have occupied the same house, living our lives in parallel time continuums, crossing paths when necessary or when one of us wasn't looking. She needs transportation; I inquire about schedules and details. We share an occasional moment of laughter or a shared interest that is over in a blip. On this journey of concerts, I hope that we can find our way back to each other.

It began with a dream to see more Jonas Brothers concerts. At the eighth concert, Hannah asked to go to ten concerts. My immediate response was, maybe five concerts. I thought that would be an easy goal with all five concerts within driving distance of our home in Baltimore, Maryland. When my heart opened to another possibility during the concert, everything changed.

With travel, photography, and the Jonas Brothers, we are weaving our separate passions into places where we can connect again. We have decided to travel around the USA this summer. It will be a continuation of the passion for travel we shared before her Dad got sick.

We have always traveled with purpose. One of my friends, Karen created a Celebrate the States Club when Hannah was five years old. The club opened a door to travel and learning about the states in person. We traveled to 36 states in six years with her sisters, friends, family and just the two of us. The focus was fun, food, history and nature. A visit to the capital in Kentucky allowed us to meet the governor and have an official photograph. Vermont was where we sampled maple sugar candy and spent the day on an alpine slide. In Ohio, we visited the Rock and Roll Hall of Fame and took an evening walk in Findley State Park with a park ranger who showed us owls and fireflies. We would bring our personal experiences back to the Club with reports, pictures and samples of food. Hannah has sketched the state capital building in over 20 states.

Photography was one of her father's passions. As a falconer and skydiver, he photographed his other interests and developed the pictures himself in a photographer's dark room.

Now the Jonas Brothers have given us a reason to get back in the car and drive to more states. Here we go. Traveling most of July and August. Ten Jonas Brothers' concerts; a Shaklee convention in New Orleans; visiting with Hannah's sisters in NYC and Arizona; stopping at bookstores with information about the Evolutionary Women book release in the fall.

We have two months to prepare. Camera equipment, tickets in hand, packing lists, and learning words to the new Jonas Brothers songs. There is conversation, purpose and fun.

We have found the bridge that connects us once again.

The awakening that had gradually happened in Jonas Brothers concerts over a nine-month period, had prepared my heart to feel more love and passion. I was ready to live again during the summer of 2008. Like a child in a candy shop, I looked at every mile, every part of nature, every stop to see
history, museums, and peace memorials with fresh eyes, the beginner's mind. My heart had been cleared and emptied for new experiences.

As we wove our way across the country we eventually drove 10,000 miles and went to 15 concerts.

The music in the concerts was a form of sound healing for me. Every song carried the energy of love and passion and the desire to live a dream. The vibrations from the instruments in the arenas and the dancing all connected me to my heart, soul and my physical body. Exercise, music and youthful audiences created a sort of euphoria and freedom.

At the end of the summer, as Hannah and I approached the east coast after being on the road for two months, we both shared how we wanted to keep going. Our car had become our home. The death of my husband had changed everything about our life in Baltimore. I now knew that wherever I lived I would carry my home in my heart. I would carry the community, my friends, the teens I had mentored in Girl Scouts with me forever. I had lived in Baltimore for over 25 years.

During the summer of 2008, I learned about Facebook. I also connected with friends from Baltimore who happened to be visiting other parts of the country when Hannah and I drove through for a concert. All of these pieces began to help me let go. Travel always changes you in some way. This time when we returned, the house did not feel the same. I spent time walking around the property every day wondering what I would do next. Was it time to sell the house and let go of this chapter of my life? Or would it transform into a retreat center where I would lead retreats for women and open my home to other groups for retreats. I could build a smaller house in the backyard and open the big house to others. For months I went back and forth with the choices.

All of these feelings led me to drive west in November 2008 for Thanksgiving in Arizona, Jonas Brothers concerts in Las Vegas and an Evolutionary Women retreat in California to celebrate the release of my first co-authored published book, **Conscious Choices: An Evolutionary Woman's Guide to Life.**

There is more to the story and I will save that for another time.

In January 2009, I flew to California for the Freedom Formula event where I received a vision in a meditation. There was a U-haul truck in my driveway. I knew it was time to release all of my personal belongings.

The Jonas Brothers concerts had helped me to awaken and heal my heart. It was time to create new dreams, feel the gratitude for the first 50 years of my life and leap into the next 50 years.

Grief Transformation Show #11
Dancing with a teenager and the Jonas Brothers

December 1, 2010
http://tobtr.com/1369280

Chapter Sixteen

Nature Ceremonies to Release Grief
Andrea Hylen

Show originally aired on December 31, 2010

Tonight is New Year's Eve. This is a great time to reflect on the year and to participate in ceremonies either alone or with someone else.

For the past few days, I have been feeling and thinking about what I wanted to share on this last night of the year. I have been asking myself questions. *What did I want to say about 2010 and 2011? How did my exploration of the year connect with grief transformation? What topic would serve the listeners and myself tonight?*

Words like honoring, appreciation, solitude, grief, and joy bubbled up within me. As I look back at the year 2010, a great part of my year was spent in solitude, listening to my inner voice. It was a year of self-discovery. And since every year is a year of self-discovery, I asked myself what made this year unique. I learned at a deeper level that grief is a part of the cycle of life. It is a part of traditions and celebrating and remembering every year. I learned more about the gifts of grief. I connected with more of my voice. How about you?

Today is my deceased husband's birthday. This is the sixth birthday since he died. December 31 is the end of the year, New Year's Eve and the birthday of Hurley Cox. It has been his birthday since he was born and even though he died, it is still his birthday. I loved him and we had a real relationship that was complex. I have grieved and healed and processed. I have even cried on the radio about the loss and his death. And I can tell you that I know that someday there will be another man in my life. I can also feel that I have moments of grieving that still come in waves even though I am fully living my life. I believe that will continue because he was an important person in my life. We have loss and we also have the memory of the person or an event.

And here it is, his birthday. I can feel a heaviness in my heart even though I felt joy around some of the activities in my day. Maybe you can relate to this. Call it a body memory or a habit or the rhythm of life. Most of us have that around the holidays. There is always a rhythm and routine to the events of the holidays. For me, the holiday begins with Thanksgiving, then my wedding anniversary with my husband on November 23. Many years I have had a Hanukkah party as a reminder of a beautiful story of light, so we added that in as a tradition. Then there was the winter solstice and Christmas. Both of my parents have birthdays on, December 29 (yes, they share a birthday.) Next is my daughter, Mary's birthday on December 30 and then Hurley's birthday, December 31.

That has been the rhythm for many years. And even with six birthdays without him here physically, it still feels like there is a step missing in the dance of the holidays. It is just the way it is. So, today I thought, *okay, what am I going to do with the feelings of grief?* I declared that I am going to remember, appreciate, breathe, and honor him. The bottom line I reached today is that it will always be his day. I was here with him for a long time and December 31 will always be his birthday. So, for a moment, I pause, close my eyes, hand over my heart and I say, *"Happy Birthday, Hurley."* It is as simple as that.

Tonight with New Year's Eve, people are focused on New Year resolutions or reflections or intentions, whatever you want to call them. There are other times throughout the year that you could reflect and set intentions, too. It could be your birthday or a loved one's birthday or anniversary of their death. It could be a day that represents an ending or a new beginning.

So, the focus tonight is about ceremonies to help us release feelings of grief. And even as I say that I want to remind you that there is really nothing you can do to take away all of the grief around any loss, disappointment or sadness. You can learn to dance with it, honor it, and explore why it has returned again. And you can learn to live with it. Ceremony and ritual can be used as honoring everything in your life. Births and deaths and double rainbows; honor the seasons or anything else that is meaningful.

Every night I have a ritual before the show to set the intention and build the energy and focus. I set up about an hour before the show starts. I print notes from the computer and post the link reminders on Facebook and Twitter. I check-in with my daughter, Hannah to remind her the show will begin soon and to see if she needs anything from me. I feed my cats and put them in my bedroom with the door closed. I call in to BlogTalk and set up the switchboard and chat line. I make a cup of tea, light a candle, say a prayer and I clear the space and set the intention. No matter what has happened today or how I am feeling right before the show, I take a few breaths, connect with my heart, open to guidance from Spirit and set the intention that I'm here to serve whoever is going to listen to the show. We can set a ritual like this with anything in our lives for honoring and setting a clear intention.

As I share different ceremony ideas with you tonight, I am going to weave in peace prayers from 12 major religions tonight as part of the ceremony.

I am a Minister of Spiritual Peacemaking and I like to share the prayers whenever possible. The first prayer is the Hindu Prayer for Peace:

Hindu Prayer for Peace

Oh God, lead us from the unreal to the Real.
Oh God, lead us from darkness to light.
Oh God, lead us from death to immortality.
Shanti, Shanti, Shanti unto all.

Oh Lord God almighty, may there be peace in
celestial regions.
May there be peace on Earth.
May the waters be appeasing.

May herbs be wholesome, and may trees and
plants bring peace to all.
May all beneficent beings bring peace to us.
May thy Vedic Law propagate peace all through the world.
May all things be a source of peace to us.
And may thy peace itself, bestow peace on all
and may that peace come to me also.

Ceremonies with Nature:

Whenever I connect with nature in a ceremony, the first step is to focus on myself. You begin with you. Think of yourself as a light being or as creating an environment to purify and to connect with your heart first. When you start with yourself and then radiate love and healing from that place, anyone or anything you are sending healing towards has the free will to receive it or not.

Let's begin by connecting to our own bodies and take a few deep breaths. Just imagine that you are standing on the Earth. It is okay to sit or lie down, but imagine a connection to the Earth. Imagine sending roots from the bottom of your feet deep into the Earth. This will help to anchor the energy and allow the Earth to support you in this process. All you have to do is intend for this to happen.

Focus on the top of your head and imagine it opening up to receive light. A gold healing light will enter into the top of your head and allow it to flow down through your body. The light is clearing away anything that is in your way and preventing you from connecting to the Earth. Anytime you are in a ceremony, you can connect with spirits and ask your loved ones to connect with you here. I sometimes ask my loved ones to wrap their energetic arms around me and give me a hug. I ask them to be with me.

Now that we have connected to ourselves and we have called in our loved ones and any guides or angels for support, let's talk about the four elements of nature: Air, Earth, Water and Fire. I will discuss each one of them and there will be a burning bowl at the end.

Ceremonies with Air:

Balloons- When my son died 18 years ago, my family would buy a balloon on his birthday and release it. Because of a new awareness about the environment and the potential harm to wildlife, when I purchase a balloon now I do not release it. I tie it to a pole or keep it in the house and bless it as his balloon.

You can also go into a meditative space and imagine a balloon and place your emotions into the balloon and release it. Fill the balloon with your emotions and keep filling it. Have a conversation in the meditation until you feel the pain or grief or has filled the balloon and release it to fly away into the cosmos. You still have the love in your heart but you are releasing the pain.

Spreading the ashes of a loved one is another way that I brought in the element of air. This is a personal story about two of my loved ones who were cremated. I share this as an example of the infinite possibilities of deciding when to release or keep the ashes. I hope it will help you see how every situation is different. The best decision is the one that works for you and your loved ones.

When my son, Cooper, died at the age of 19 months, my husband and I bought an urn and kept the ashes with us. The thought of releasing my little boy was too much for me. I had every intention of keeping him with me for the rest of my life.

My husband died 12 years later.

At the one-year anniversary of my husband's death, I was ready to release some of the ashes of both my husband and my son. I chose a corner on my property next to the street where a peace pole with the words, "May Peace Prevail on Earth," in 12 languages was placed. The garden in that area had roses all in full bloom. The names of the roses were Passionate Kisses, Love's Promise, Peace, Glowing Peace, Our Lady of Guadalupe, and the Mary rose. After I had placed their ashes in the hole, my brother shouted and pointed towards the east. There was a hawk. It flew straight towards us, circled over our heads and turned to fly to the north.

Amazing! My husband was a falconer and we had named our son Cooper, for a Coopers hawk.

It was two years before I was ready to release the rest of the ashes. All I can tell you is I was ready. Nothing was forced. I think it was a part of releasing our life in Baltimore
because two months after releasing the ashes I was ready to sell my house. A year later, I moved to California to begin a new life there.

The final release was with a community of skydivers. My husband was also a skydiver from an earlier part of his life. A gathering was organized at a drop zone, a place for skydiving, on the Eastern Shore of Maryland. On the day of the release, I gathered things to give to the skydivers as a gift; Hurley's parachute and jumpsuit, pictures of people skydiving, his log books, pictures of falconers.

My youngest daughter and I drove two hours to the drop zone. The drive was a trip down memory lane for me. I thought about how much Hurley loved the Eastern Shore and living on a farm where he raised dogs, planted trees, raised hawks and so much more. This was also the route we took for almost ten years of family summer vacations at the beach and for the best milkshakes in the world at Holly's Diner.

When we arrived, the weather had changed. The temperature dropped to 55 degrees, overcast, and windy. There was a question as to whether or not this would even happen. I had asked for prayers from people around the world on my status line on Facebook.

As Harry, my husband's best friend, was talking with different people about the weather, I trusted that everything would happen at the perfect time. I released the need to control this and opened to the possibility. The decision came back as yes. Because of the weather, they did something called a "hop and pop." Instead of free falling, they jumped and pulled the chutes right away. Nineteen men and women of all ages went up in the plane and jumped. It was a quick dive, but I did see the stream of ashes, a combination of Hurley and Cooper. My guys, both flying free together.

At that moment, the sun popped through the clouds and you could feel the warmth of the rays. I took a picture of some of the skydivers with the sun in the background. It only stayed like that for a few minutes and then went behind the clouds. I felt gratitude for I knew it was a sign from them.

The suggestions I offer for releasing ashes:

1. Release the ashes when it feels right to you
2. Create a ceremony that is meaningful to you
3. Feel all of the feelings
4. Connect with your loved ones in spirit
5. Look for the messages that connect you forever

When we scheduled this, I didn't think about the significance of the day. It was November 1, All Saints Day or the Day of the Dead. This is the day when people traditionally remember their loved ones in Spirit and the "veils" are thinner between the living and the dead. And for us, they were.

Buddhist Prayer for Peace

May all beings everywhere plagued
with sufferings of body and mind
quickly be freed from their illnesses.
May those frightened cease to be afraid,
and may those bound be free.
May the powerless find power,
and may people think of befriending
one another.
May those who find themselves in trackless,
fearful wilderness---
the children, the aged, the unprotected--
be guarded by beneficial celestials,
and may they swiftly attain Buddhahood.

Zoroastrian Prayer for Peace

We pray to God to eradicate all the
misery in the world:
that understanding triumph
over ignorance,
that generosity triumph over indifference,
that trust triumph over contempt, and
that truth triumph over falsehood.

Ceremonies with Earth

With the Earth element I want to talk about using stones for grieving: Apache Tears are called the "Grief Stone." Apache Tears are a type of Obsidian, which appear rough and opaque at first glance, but are often translucent when held up to a light source. Apache Tears are created when hot lava is forced directly into the air and quickly solidifies before hitting the ground. Made from the fire energy deep within the Earth, this mineral is wonderful at grounding energies into the Earth before, during and after energy work. Apache Tears help one to see into the core of an issue to assist with deep healing.

If you are drawn to working with the energy of stones and healing work, this is a very powerful stone to assist you with feeling and healing grief. I had something happen earlier today when I had a conversation with someone and it brought up some issues from another relationship that I have been working through. Some deep emotion and grief came over me. I sat quietly, holding the Apache tears and within fifteen minutes I could feel some clarity that I hadn't had before. It felt like a veil was lifted and I felt calm.

Apache Tears have an uncanny ability to lend support during times of sorrow. They will gently help one to accept and then release their grief, thereby releasing and removing blockages. Holding the stones will allow for tears to be shed, stimulating emotional spontaneity and the release of barriers that prevent you from experiencing deep sorrow. This stone is excellent for transmuting one's own negativity under stressful situations. As I said, the Apache Tear is a dark black stone of obsidian and when held up to the light appears transparent. It has been noted that the grief one feels, enters into the stone and can turn it opaque.

One of the ways of working with a stone is to pick up any stone from the Earth or use a stone or crystal you may have in your home. Think of something you want to release. Pour the thought, the negative emotion into the stone. Sit with it until you feel you are complete. It might take 30 seconds, or five minutes or 15 minutes.

The stone is now holding onto the emotion. Next, you can release the emotion from the stone and cleanse it.

If you are outside, throw the stone as far as you can throw it, as a symbolic gesture or throw it into a bonfire or put it into a stream.

If you live in an apartment in the city, you can also bury the stone in the earth or even in potting soil in a pot and ask the earth to transmute this.

Or fill up the sink with water or put water into a bowl and place the rock into the water. Ask the element of water or earth to transmute the emotions.

You can also visualize all of your emotions going into the earth and ask to have them transmuted.

Jainist Prayer for Peace

Peace and Universal Love is the essence of the Gospel
preached by all the Enlightened Ones.
The Lord has preached that equanimity is the Dharma.
Forgive do I creatures all,
and let all creatures forgive me.

Unto all have I amity, and unto none enmity.
Know that violence is the root cause of all miseries in the world.
Violence, in fact, is the knot of bondage.
"Do not injure any living being."
This is the eternal, perennial, and unalterable way of spiritual life.

A weapon, howsoever powerful it may be,
can always be superseded by a superior one;
but no weapon can, however,
be superior to nonviolence and love.

Ceremonies with Water

One of the ways that you can use water in healing is to take a bath. Soaking in a bathtub with Epsom salts and essential oils can help feelings surface. As you become aware of them, you can imagine releasing them into the water. You can even do this while taking a shower. Imagine the water washing away the pain and it all goes down the drain. Being in water can help us to release tears, too.

I love to go to the ocean. It is a 30-minute drive from where I live right now and I feel a strong connection to my intuition and Spirit there. It is easier to tap in and listen for guidance. Every time I go I have a different experience. I may feel like I need to take a walk on the beach and feel the connection to the Earth. Being close to the water can bring a healing as I feel mist from the water wash over me. Sometimes I feel guided to go to the water's edge and to lie down and take a nap and I wake up feeling refreshed and healed from being there.

I recorded a Youtube video one day I was there with sounds of the water and the birds and the wind.
https://youtu.be/6JpXde7e5uU

A friend recently recorded the ocean sounds on her phone and placed them on a CD. It is a great energy to connect with for healing. As we feel full and healed, send that energy back to the water. It is a cycle of healing. Use the image and memory of the ocean in a meditation to bring in the healing energy.

This website is dedicated to water and healing around the world. **http://www.waterconvergence.com/**

Some of the words from the website:

To water and to all who are called to work with water in energetic and practical ways...
As we listen to the earth's waters, we know that now is the time to share and collaborate. The many urgencies around the earth's water catalyze us toward unity in our human experience and toward collective opportunities to bless our waters, cleanse our oceans, and provide clean drinking water for generations to come.

Water makes up 85% of the human body, and is essential for all life. It is literally true that we are One with the waters of the planet. It is time for humanity to hear the call of water and come together, even as our many bodies of water flow together around the world.

Focus on the words: Unity, Love, Gratitude, Humility, Flow. These energies are first coming through us as a healing to anything we are feeling or grieving. Things we are ready to let go of and to be healed in this moment. Then radiate the healing into the water.

The Net of Light is another organization that does water blessings at the beach. Some of the words from the website:

The Grandmothers say, "Each person is a point on the great Net of Light and each point of light forms a network to which all life is connected. Yin and yang have now begun to shift and during these difficult times, the Net of Light will hold the earth together. Meditate on the Net of Light; use it to support one another, to support the earth, and to strengthen the energy of yin on the planet. Know the reality of this Net, for by knowing it and being at one with it, you will do untold good."

"Cherish the daughters as you cherish the Mother," they say, "as all are her daughters. Pass this on, to the younger ones, the older ones, to others who don't have it. Pass it on."

Tonight we started the show in a very intentional place, connecting to our hearts and to the earth and bringing in light and peace into this moment of completion of the year 2010 and setting an intention for 2011. You are a clear being of light on the net of light. Imagine these energies going into the water as a healing. **http://netoflight.org/**

Jewish Prayer for Peace

Come, let us go up to the mountain of the Lord,
that we may walk the paths of the Most High.
And we shall beat our swords into ploughshares,
and our spears into pruning hooks.

Nation shall not lift up sword against nation –
neither shall they learn war any more.
And none shall be afraid,
for the mouth of the Lord of Hosts has spoken.

Shinto Prayer for Peace

Although the people living across the ocean surrounding us,
I believe, are all our brothers and sisters,
why are there constant troubles in this world?
Why do winds and waves rise in the ocean surrounding us?
I only earnestly wish that the wind will
soon puff away all the clouds which are hanging
over the tops of the mountains.

Native African Prayer for Peace

Almighty God, the Great Thumb,
we cannot evade to tie any knot;
the Roaring Thunder that splits mighty trees:
the all-seeing Lord up on high who sees even
the footprints of an antelope on a rock mass here on Earth.
You are the one who does not hesitate to respond to our call.
You are the cornerstone of peace.

Ceremonies with Fire

Abby Wynne is an energy healer. She wrote a note about how to energetically burn what no longer serves you.

Focus in on something you no longer want in your energy body. It can be an emotion. It can be a behavioral pattern. It can be a stuckness. Let it flood your body and lock into it. Really feel it strongly in yourself.

Place a stick right up to your mouth and blow the feelings into it. Keep repeating that until you feel your energy shift. And let the feelings be transmuted. You can do the same thing with the paper. Repeat until you feel an energy shift.

Her website: **www.abby-wynne.com**

The Burning Bowl ceremony is a way of releasing something. It is a ceremony where you write something on a piece of paper and burn it to release.

A few years ago, I was at a campground with a bonfire. I was in a retreat space with a group of twenty people. We each wrote some things onto our own piece of paper. I decided I wanted to release anything that was hanging on in my life from past relationships with men. Anything that was unresolved that I might be carrying in my head or my heart or my body. Then, we all burned them in the fire.

About two weeks after the bonfire ceremony, I received a Facebook message from the first guy I ever dated. He wrote me a note and said, *"I want to say that I'm sorry for anything I ever did that caused you pain. I know we were young, but that's no excuse, will you forgive me?"*

I thought that was pretty cool and a great completion of forgiveness and release over mistakes we both made. Things do come back to be healed when you are ready to heal another layer.

Native American Prayer for Peace

O Great Spirit of our Ancestors,
I raise my pipe to you.
To your messengers the four winds,
and to Mother Earth who provides for your children.
Give us the wisdom to teach our children to love,
to respect, and to be kind to each other
so that they may grow with peace in mind.
Let us learn to share all good things that you provide
for us on this Earth.

Muslim Prayer for Peace

In the name of Allah, the beneficent, the merciful.
Praise be to the Lord of the Universe
who has created us and made us into tribes and nations.
That we may know each other, not that we may despise each other.
If the enemy incline towards peace,
do thou also incline towards peace,
and trust God, for the Lord is the one that
heareth and knoweth all things.
And the servants of God,
Most Gracious are those who walk on the Earth in humility,
and when we address them, we say "PEACE."

Baha'i Prayer for Peace

Be generous in prosperity,
and thankful in adversity.
Be fair in thy judgment,
and guarded in thy speech.
Be a lamp unto those who walk in darkness,
and a home to the stranger.
Be eyes to the blind, and a guiding light unto the feet of the erring.
Be a breath of life to the body of humankind,
a dew to the soil of the human heart,
and a fruit upon the tree of humility.

Sikh Prayer for Peace

God adjudges us according to our deeds,
not the coat that we wear:
that Truth is above everything,
but higher still is truthful living.
Know that we attaineth God when we love,
and only that victory endures in consequence
of which no one is defeated.

Christian Prayer for Peace

Blessed are the PEACEMAKERS,
for they shall be known as the Children of God.
But I say to you that hear, love your enemies,
do good to those who hate you,
bless those who curse you,
pray for those who abuse you.
To those who strike you on the cheek,
offer the other also, and from those who take away your cloak,
do not withhold your coat as well.
Give to everyone who begs from you,
and of those who take away your goods,
do not ask them again.
And as you wish that others would do to you,
do so to them.

As I end the show tonight, I want to stop for a moment to appreciate all that we shared and learned in 2010. I feel gratitude for all of the places that our souls have grown in this year and gratitude for our hearts being big enough to feel sorrow, sadness and pain and our hearts are big enough to love and send light into the world.
  I send you blessings into 2011. Happy New Year everyone!

Grief Transformation Show #38
Nature Ceremonies to Release Grief

December 31, 2010
http://tobtr.com/1440659

Andrea Hylen

Chapter Seventeen

Saying Goodbye to a Home
Andrea Hylen

Show originally aired on December 5, 2010

Tonight I am going to share my personal experiences with moving from home to home and different ways to create a sacred space to say goodbye to your home.

I moved twelve times in the first fifteen years of my life. First, my Dad was in the Marines and then he worked for Pillsbury as a sales manager. Every time he was promoted we moved to a new state. In addition to my Dad's work, my parents also renovated several of the houses we lived in and sold them which meant moving again. It was real estate boom time in the 60's and 70's!

There are always good and bad things about moving or about anything that happens in your childhood. But, one of the things I learned from moving so many times was how to create a space and time to honor your home before you move on to the next one. To bring this time in your life to closure. To pause and reflect.

Sometimes you move because you initiate it. There might be a job offer or you choose to move to a different location for a variety of reasons. You may be ready for a bigger house or a smaller house because life and your needs change. Sometimes a move is thrust upon you because of life circumstances that are out of your control, like a divorce or death of a loved one or even a change in the economy. Whatever the reason for the move, I have found it is important to feel the feelings of loss and change. You are letting go of a part of your life and moving on to something new.

When I was nine years old, we moved from Dallas, Texas to Minneapolis, Minnesota. I loved everything about Dallas; my house, neighborhood, friends and my school. My Mom was involved with organizing the selling of our house, packing and moving. My Dad was already working at the new position in Minneapolis and I was emotionally devastated. Who had time to notice the feelings of a nine-year-old? This was 1966. We didn't have Phil Donahue or Oprah to talk about how this could be impacting a child emotionally. And it was survival linked to our survival. My Dad's job was dependent on the move which meant financial support for our family. That was the number one priority.

The day finally arrived when we would all move to Minneapolis. As we pulled out of the driveway, packed like sardines into a green Chevy station wagon, I began to cry and sing the state song of Texas. My younger sister, Joanne, age 7, joined in with me. We sang it a few times and then sang louder with more sobbing as we saw the sign, **Leaving the Lone Star State of Texas. Come back soon,** and crossed the border into Oklahoma. The memory of the house and the loss stayed with me for a long time. Forty-five years to be exact. When I returned to the house on a road trip across the United States, I did some of the rituals and practices to reclaim a part of myself that I left in that home in Texas.

Now, as an adult, every time I move, I create time to go through the house and say goodbye. I walk through every room. I think about the joy, laughter, sadness and pain. I think about the things I learned about myself and others while I was in the house. Some moments are bittersweet like the house I lived in before I separated from my first husband. One of our daughters was born there and there was also lots of pain as the marriage fell apart. There's something really powerful about taking a few minutes to appreciate the life you have lived in a place. Everywhere we go, we live life and create memories. Because I have an awareness of what it feels like to leave without saying goodbye, I always take time, no matter how long I stay in a place, even a hotel room. I take a minute to look back, appreciate the memories, feel gratitude for the experience before moving on to the new.

My daughter and I traveled for 11 weeks one summer driving 24,000 miles in the United States and Canada. As we left each home or hotel we had stayed in as a guest, I always took a moment to reflect on what had happened while we were here. A meal that had been shared. A concert we went to. A moment of connection. It helps to bring in appreciation for all of the experiences of life, to connect more with the present and it also brings in a sacredness for the places that we stayed on that 11-week journey. It was a reminder to feel gratitude for where we laid our heads to sleep and the journey that we had while we were there, even if it was one night in a hotel.

Leaving a home is usually filled with moments of joy and sadness; memories, the reason you are moving, the timing in your life. All of these things play into the emotions of grief. Even when you are ecstatically thrilled with the idea of moving, there is a change. A loss of the old to release and then embrace and move into the new. It is common to feel waves of sadness and grief when you leave the past to move into the future. It is important to create some space to feel so you don't bury them. Even when you are excited and happy about where you are going next, there is a need to release the space. It is a sense of creating an empty space within yourself to move from one part of your life to the next.

When my second husband and I found our dream house, I was thrilled to be moving. It had taken us nine years to find the perfect house that would fill the needs of our family and I couldn't wait to move! But so many things had happened in the house we were leaving.

This was the first house I lived in with my husband. This was the house he lived in when we were dating. Our son was born and died while we lived in the house. My husband left a job to start his own business while we lived there. There were nine holiday seasons of Halloween, Hanukah, Christmas, Thanksgiving and New Year's Eve parties. Our youngest daughter, Hannah was born while we lived here. We started homeschooling there and so many more memories. As we packed to move into the new house, I spent time alone in each room recalling some of the precious moments. I talked with my kids and created space and time for them to share their own memories. And then we moved.

Ten years later, I sold our dream house after my husband died. As much as I tried to transform the space and energy of the home without him there, it was time to let it go. I spent six months writing in a journal, feeling the joy and deep sadness before I put the house on the market. It had been four years since my husband died.

This time I created a ritual to share with my kids. My daughters were 25, 23 and 16 when we decided to sell our house. We had cleared out the 3rd floor where my two older daughters shared the two bedrooms and a sitting room. The four of us sat up there on the floor with our two cats, the only animals left from the menagerie of dogs, cats, fish, birds, and leopard geckos who had lived here at one time. We lit a candle and sat quietly together. I said a prayer of gratitude. Then we each shared some of our happiest and saddest memories. We laughed, cried and appreciated the journey in the house. Then, we walked through every room of the house doing the same thing together.

We had renovated this house, room by room. When we bought the house, it had three falling down ceilings and twenty-seven boarded up windows. Most of the work on the house we did ourselves. One of my daughters wrote poetry all over the walls and ceilings of one of the attic rooms. We took pictures, read some of the poems and continued to share.

One evening, we cooked a favorite meal. We looked through pictures in a scrapbook. We had a variety of indoor and outdoor yard sales, inviting friends to come over to say goodbye and share their memories. I posted the information about the house sale on Facebook and group e-mails. Several people asked to come over and say their own goodbye to the house.

It may seem like we did a lot to say goodbye but it was probably one of the hardest moves for all of us. I thought this was the house I would grow old in. My kids loved the house and the land so much they had talked about living in the house with their kids and building more houses here. It was on 3.5 acres near the city and the country. There was already the foundation for a small house in the back yard. This could have been a place where we would lead separate lives but share a common plot of land for gatherings.

It was important to sink into our feelings and take the time to say goodbye. We were all moving into new, exciting places for the next part of our lives and there was still a wide range of feelings. There is always sadness, and grieving as you let go of one part of your life to move into the next.

Honoring the inner feelings will help you remember and release the past to make room for the new possibilities. Your life is a tapestry of experiences to be remembered and cherished. It is the path that has awakened you to yourself.

To highlight some of the steps that can be applied to releasing anyone or anything.

1. Write your memories in a journal
2. Write a letter to the house or your loved ones
3. Create a scrapbook
4. Talk with friends and family to look back and have moments of appreciation and gratitude
5. Create a piece of music, art, poetry
6. Reflect on things you learned about yourself in the home

7. Create a ceremony with candles

Two years ago I went back to Dallas to say goodbye to the house I left 45 years earlier. Until I created the space to go back and say good-bye to the house, I didn't realize that I had left a part of me back there. I went to the house and knocked on the front door. I didn't feel like I needed to walk through the house but I wanted to tell the people who lived there now that I was going to take a picture in the front yard. For someone else, seeing the inside of the house may have been important and it is okay to ask the current owner. No one was home the day we stopped by Queenswood Lane in Dallas, Texas.

My daughter, Hannah was with me and took a picture of me in front of the house. Then, I took time to walk around the neighborhood and drove to a couple of places. I stood in the circle where we had played kickball and where I had "married" Peter Myers when I was eight years old.

And as I toured the neighborhood, I realized that this was not the life I came here to live. I did not come here to live in the same neighborhood for all of my life, to marry Peter Myers, give birth to children who would attend the same schools I attended. That was not my life. I came to live a life where I lived all over the United States and connect with people of different cultures.

I thought about what my life would have been like if we had stayed here. As I created a sacred space to say goodbye to this home, I felt more of my personal power return to me. I was able to appreciate the life I had there and see that my path was to move and live in a variety of places. Maybe there is a home for you to say goodbye to from your past. You can go there physically or look at a photo of the house and of yourself or bring the feeling into your heart and mind. Do a ritual and bring it into completion.

I know that in the future, I may have an image of another house come into my mind as needing healing. When that day comes, I can write about it and connect my heart with that space. There is a lot of power in taking some time to say good-bye and to claim those parts of yourself.

And even though I focused on a home tonight, you can use the same ideas for saying goodbye to a job, a relationship or anything that involves letting go of something, someone, some way of being in the past, as you prepare to move into the future.

It is never too late…

**Grief Transformation Show #15
Saying Goodbye to a Home**

December 5, 2010
http://tobtr.com/1369284

Chapter Eighteen

Writing as a Path to Healing
Andrea Hylen

Show originally aired on December 3, 2010

Tonight I am going to talk about the power of writing as a path to healing. Writing is one of the ways I have healed grief and loss by tapping into my creativity over the years. There is a power in writing your own story.
    I am going to talk about writing in three areas:
Private Writing- Just for yourself
Writing with Support
Sharing in public forums
    My earliest memories of writing were in diaries. Does anyone out there remember having a diary with a key? My diary was a place for secrets that I felt I couldn't tell anyone. I don't think anyone ever read my diary. My parents were busy with their own lives, I was the oldest child and we moved 12 times by the time I was 15. And I don't think anyone would have thought I had anything to say that would be worth reading. I felt free to write whatever I wanted to.
    I lived in an era when people wrote letters. Remember letter writing and snail mail? Most of the letters I received while I was growing up were from my maternal grandfather and my paternal grandmother. Each of them had their own style of expression. My grandfather became a writer later in life. He studied the craft of writing in college and realized he didn't have enough life experience to write about anything. So, he became a fisherman. When he became a writer in his 40's he had a column in the local Cape Cod newspaper called The Cape Codder and he wrote books with fish tales and non-fiction books about shellfish farming. He wrote letters with limericks and encouraged me to write to him, too.
    My grandmother wrote letters of inspiration and encouragement. She also asked me to write to her. Both of my grandparents encouraged me to express myself through words.
    The letters to my grandparents and my diary gave me a place to put my feelings. It gave me a space to process and look at

different situations. It gave me a place to put emotions that sometimes felt so big, I was afraid of them. What would happen if I really expressed the anger, the pain, the frustration, or feelings of betrayal in open dialogue?

      A couple of things really opened my world of writing as an adult. One of the books that encouraged me to write was, "The Artist's Way," by Julia Cameron. The book was published around the time my son died and a few years later after I recovered from a life threatening illness, a group of home schooling moms formed a book group. We worked and played with this book together and followed up with Julia's next book, The Vein of Gold. Being with the group of women in an environment that felt very safe opened me up to hidden creativity, dreams and passions. The subtitle of the Artist's Way is A Spiritual Path to Higher Creativity.

      To me, grieving is a path to open ourselves to more creativity and to discover hidden gems of who we are.

      I want to share a few things from this book. If it peaks your interest, it is in libraries and there is an on-line support. **www.theartistsway.com** In the front of the book, Julia lists her Basic Principles: There are ten in the book. Here is the first one.

#1: Creativity is the natural order of life.

This is a good place to begin reading because it may spark something to hear some of the words.

      One of the non-negotiable tools in participating in The Artist's Way program is something Julia calls morning pages. This is one of the basic tools in the book. You sit down first thing in the morning and write three pages of whatever is on your mind. It is a way to open you to words that may be trapped inside. I highly recommend this resource. It helped me to see my life experiences with a detachment to the events and to find a deeper connection. It was like looking at my life with a telescope and a microscope.

This next one may seem to be a little weird to be on this list. I encourage you to use E-mail and the internet. When I first started to e-mail in the mid 90's, not a whole lot of people were using this for personal reasons.

I was coordinating groups like Girl Scouts and Destination Imagination teams. It was easier to write an e-mail and send details and thoughts and descriptions to people. It also gave me a place to work within a structure. To provide information, thoughts, and to sit with the thoughts for clarity allowed me to learn to process and focus.

When my husband was sick with cancer, it was one of the ways I communicated with my friends and family. I would sit with my private thoughts staring at the computer at the end of the day. I wanted to give them details about my husband's cancer treatment but I also wanted to bring them along on the journey of sickness, health, healing and open my heart. It gave me a place to really record the journey. E-mail gave me a way to share the experience from a fuller way. When I knew that my husband was not going to survive, it helped me grieve. After my husband died, it gave me a place to share and to say thank you. The internet became a place of healing for me.

Note from Editor: Now, we have **www.caringbridge.org** *a forum to share a journey of health where family and friends can receive information and make comments. You can also set up schedules for people to help with care.*

Now, let's talk about you writing your own story. I was fortunate to have the opportunity to be co-author of a book in which 44 women each wrote a 1500-word personal story to explore a conscious choice in their lives. The book Conscious Choices: An Evolutionary Woman's Guide to Life was written by women who had attended an Evolutionary Woman's Retreat.

This was the first time I shared my deepest thoughts on paper and someone else was going to read them. For the first time, I was going to share my thoughts with the world. In the process of writing, we created a sacred space and an honoring of their words.

When each author e-mailed her story idea, I printed the e-mail, rolled it up in a scroll and tied a ribbon around it. I had a large jar on an altar I had prepared with pictures of goddesses, nature, angels and minerals and rocks. As I placed the scroll into the jar, I said a prayer that the woman would write a story that wanted to emerge from her right now. The story would heal something in her and provide a healing for anyone who read it.

There were a few things I learned in writing the story that I would like to share with you.

1) Create a sacred space. Create your own ritual. Saying a prayer, lighting a candle, preparing a cup of tea, turning on some soothing music, as you begin to write. The ritual is a way of honoring your words and your healing. The sacred jar of stories I described with the scrolls and prayers is another example of honoring your words.

2) Find Support: If you want to write your story in the expectation that someone else will read it, you can create support by asking friends who can truly hold a space for you. Your words are precious. It is important to find someone who can gently hold your words. In Conscious Choices, we called them gentle readers. A woman who held the words of another woman close to her heart.

Writing a story can be a way of remembering your loved one or a situation of loss and sadness in your life. It could be the writing of the end of a relationship or the loss of a job or your health. You can even write about a project you were involved with that has come to an end. Any time you put your heart and soul into anything, it is important to respect all of the feelings. Writing the story can help you recover a part of yourself and help you come to a completion.

When I wrote my story for Conscious Choices, I wrote about a time I had already processed with a life coach, in journaling and in personal growth seminars. Each one of those experiences healed a part of the story. When I sat down to write the story, I spent three weeks writing. It was a 1500-word story about feeling unloved and unseen in my first marriage. I was ready to heal it at a deeper level. After three weeks of writing, I deleted ¾ of it and realized that that was not the way I wanted to tell the story. In writing it, I moved from a feeling of being a victim, to reclaiming, healing and forgiveness. I wrote about the raw vulnerability and I took responsibility for my choices that led me from despair to triumph, one step at a time.

If you want to write your own story or write a book. You could publish it using a self-publishing site or by joining a book program or by submitting it to a publisher.

Lulu.com is an on-line self-publishing site. You can create a book, an e-book, Calendars, Photo Books. This is a way to honor a loved one or an experience and a way to honor your words. It may be something you want to share with family members and with friends. **http://www.lulu.com/publish/**

*Note from Editor: I have used **https://www.createspace.com/** for all of the Heal My Voice books and this book. I have formatted the document in word and hired a graphic person to do the book cover.*

    The last thing I am going to mention is blogging. Blogging was a place for me to put words and ideas and feelings over the last few years. I have always blogged publicly but there are ways to create it as an on-line private journal. I have used **www.blogspot.com** and **www.wordpress.com**. Take a look at those and see what feels right to you.

    There is a website I joined recently called http://www.onlinegriefsupport.com/

    You submit information about yourself and wait for approval. It is free. You can start a topic or read things people have started. There are groups within the site with specific losses like the loss of a mom, dad, losing someone to cancer, sudden loss of a spouse and more. You can start another group to meet your needs. Use discernment in meeting people and connecting. Loss can have so many emotions. It feels like a great space to share and to learn and support. Be careful with anything on-line and enter into it slowly. Set a boundary when all you want to do is share and you are not looking for advice.

    In each of the various writings I have shared with myself and others, there have been reasons for each one. When I started blogging I could feel a need within me to share the story. Something was urging me to write. I wasn't really sure if anyone would read it, but I needed to write it as if someone was listening. It was in each of these that I healed something within me to open to new deeper places.

    Your Life is a Story. It deserves to be told.

    If there is something that is calling you to write, I encourage you to follow that calling. Each of us carries a different vibration. Sharing your story will help you heal and it helps others heal.

    When I think back on some of the losses in my life, I am so grateful that there were many books to read. People were so willing to share their hearts. In reading their stories, it helped to heal my heart. I am eternally grateful for the writers out there and I am eternally grateful for the desire in my own heart to write my own stories and to share some of them with you.

**Grief Transformation Show #13
Writing as a Path to Healing**

December 3, 2010
http://tobtr.com/1369282

Chapter Nineteen

Grieving the Life You Thought You Meant to Live
Guest: Elizabeth St. Germain

Show originally aired on January 6, 2010. Liz Draman changed her name to Elizabeth St. Germain. In the radio show, I called her Liz. In this written format, I have changed her name to Elizabeth.

Andrea: Tonight my guest is Elizabeth St. Germain and the topic of our show is called, "Grieving the Life You Were Meant to Live".
   Elizabeth will share a variety of ways for you to connect with your Higher "Self", the divine creative force within you, and recognize how the "self or Ego" offers you many opportunities to live the life you are meant to live in every moment.
   We are going to talk about making choices, claiming your life and she will honor us with an energetic healing on the show. She will introduce us to the Violet Flame, a spiritual tool that has changed her life and accelerated her own path toward living the life she is meant to live.

Elizabeth: Thank you for that beautiful description. I am so excited to be here just by virtue of being in this time and place with you. This being the first radio show I have been invited to speak on is absolute proof that living the life you're meant to live is possible. It is possible in every single moment because this is living proof of it. I thank you and I'm honored to be here with you. I want to send out great big hugs to everyone who is sharing this special moment with me in the audience.

Andrea: Thank you and Welcome!
   Elizabeth, why don't you share your own experience of **grieving the life you want** to help bring people into this conversation. Tell us your own experience.

Elizabeth: There is so much to gain just from this one topic. I believe we travel lifetimes to understand it all. I do believe, also, that in this lifetime, in this moment, in this hour, we can actually get it all. Tonight, I would like to share a process that has come from my own desire to live a life that I'm meant to live. That is the remembering and the reconnecting and the realigning of the divine spark that lives in our hearts. That divine spark is who we are. It is in the remembering of who we are that brings us in every moment to living the life we were meant to live.

I am sure everyone in this audience can relate to the many, many life challenges that have caused us to expand, to grow and at times, to re-evaluate our life. I know that there have been times in my life when I felt, maybe my light was lost. I also share with you the experiences of losing loved ones through grief; losing pets, losing relationships. So loss in itself is a life challenge. You've been talking about grief for 43 nights consecutively on the radio. I'm sure you have heard some amazing stories, life stories about grief and loss. My understanding of grief is that it is a deep sorrow, something we have perceived as being lost.

Have you heard that similar reaction to people you have talked to over this series of shows?

Andrea: I have. It is a deep sorrow and it is a loss of so many things. People have talked about the loss of a loved one; this deep sorrow. But, they've also talked about parts of themselves that were dying and that part of deep sorrow. You know, Elizabeth, in this moment, the thing that comes to me the most is how in every show, I am absolutely filled with joy and awe and amazement. It is absolutely amazing how people go into this deep place of loss and sorrow and discover something new about themselves. Each person has their story and their experience and deep feelings that were discovered when they went into this place of sorrow. They talk about resistance and still go into healing.

Elizabeth: I believe the spirit is so resilient. You bring up a good point about resistance which is something I really wanted to talk about. I talk about this a lot in my private coaching and classes. The degree to which we are enjoying our life or experiencing discomfort in our life is determined by whether we are resisting or allowing. It's how we perceive each experience.

For example, we live in this vibratory Universe. We are vibratory beings. This physical body that we have is only a fragment of who we really are. If you were able to see yourself energetically, you would see the beauty of your essence and your soul and it is not this physical body. This physical body is only a vehicle and you have your Spirit that emanates in order to live the life you came here to live. You have this human experience that reminds you of exactly who you are. Sometimes we are reminded in the beauty of things. Sometimes we are reminded from joyful experiences. Those experiences are experiences of love.

Think about that for a moment. Close your eyes and think about experiences you have had that have brought you love, a feeling of love. How do we describe love? We describe a lot of things by labels, by names and so the emotions are exactly that. If we were to talk about emotions that elicit love: Happiness, joy, peace, harmony. There are many descriptions.

So close your eyes for a moment and imagine an experience in your life where you felt love, you felt peace, you felt joy. Allow yourself this experience. Go back to that moment. Was it a time in nature when you saw a beautiful sunset or sunrise or you were at the beach and you were just taking in the ocean air? Maybe it was when you were holding a newborn baby or possibly looking into the eyes of someone you love. Whatever it is, go back to that moment, in this time and bring all of that feeling and emotion to this moment. Breathe it in. *What does it feel like? What do you feel in your physical body? Where do you feel sensations in your physical body?*

My heart is opening and when I breathe that in, my heart opens even more. Now, I have a memory of a fragrance. When I say that, you may smell something, a beautiful fragrance. *What does it feel like?* This is who you are. This feeling is who you are.

And it is in the remembrance of that in every moment. This is who you are. We are truly spiritual beings, reflections of God. We can describe God in many words, Creator, Divine, Source. However, you choose how to describe a higher power is perfect for you. If we are a reflection of that, then everything in our experience is a reflection. Love and also fear. Our emotions are our spiritual compass; they are a barometer. They will remind us when we are in alignment with the high vibration of love or when we are in misalignment and we are in the vibration of fear.

What then determines our experience is how we judge it. If I say, *I love this experience and I'm having a wonderful interaction with someone and it feels good,* I allow that. Yes, it feels great. I want more of that. But, if I'm having a conflict with someone, it doesn't feel so good. I'm like, *okay, see you later, bye!* Resistance. I believe that we are groomed for that. We're taught that by our society, by no fault of anyone, other than we are all growing and learning and expanding. We are reprogramming these patterns that we have of resistance. And that means to allow even the contrast, the discomfort, and the disappointment; to allow them into your experience, as it is an expression of the Divine, as well.

So, if I am in a relationship with you and you and I are having a conflict and I truly believe that everything is a reflection of the Divine. Then, if I can see you, even in this conflict as an aspect of me, a mirror reflection of something that is in me. You are a reflection of something in me that is choosing to be expressed, Then, I can learn from it. I can remember. *What are you showing me? What are you reminding me of about myself that maybe I really need in my life?*

For example, if you and I are in a relationship and you are having a conflict about accepting me and accepting the type of life that I live or the beliefs that I have and I really, really want you to accept me and you are resisting that and showing me contrast and I react to that, *what am I really reacting to?* You're mirroring back to me, something in me that maybe I really need to accept within myself.

Andrea: Someone on the chat line just asked a question you might be able to bring into this: *How can we get through resistance, especially with a teenage son?*

Elizabeth: What I invite you to do is open your heart rather than your mind, look in your heart to what rings as true. I may express some things tonight that are new. Philosophies you have never heard, beliefs that are new to you. I share that and invite the entire audience to look in your heart to what rings true. I invite you into that space. I would say to the listener that I would look at what discomfort my teenage son is causing in me. *What is my resistance in that particular interaction, particular experience?*

If I believe, and our children absolutely are the clearest mirrors of ourselves, then *what is my son reflecting back to me.* Because they will teach us; they will remind us by being so clear even in their very animated reactions to things.

Andrea: The person on the chat line says it is extremely difficult.

Elizabeth: And, let me go back to say, to what degree you are enjoying or to what degree you are experiencing discomfort is determined by whether you are resisting or allowing.

Andrea: It makes perfect sense and there are times I have been in the moment when I couldn't see a place to back off from something because of safety, for instance, or some immediacy in the moment. But then there have been other times when I could hold a space of separateness and even see that one of my children was having a breakthrough. It was time for their soul to grow.

It was time for one of my daughters to move from Maryland to Arizona. She had been accepted at a college as a transfer student and it was a huge move. It was a huge emotional break from the family. It was a big leap for her to do that. She had been accepted into a school and she had resistance to going. She was able to delay it for a few months and then it came around again and it was time to go. There were moments when she was screaming at me. *"How can you be a peace minister when there's no peace in this house?"* I remember looking up at her with confusion. I was sitting in a chair quietly reading a book and I thought, *what just happened? The house is quiet and no one is here right now.*

I recognized in that moment that I just needed to hold a space for her. The, *no peace*, was in her. And during that time of inner turmoil, I offered to help her pack, drive the U-haul to Arizona and she could fly. I offered assistance. Ultimately, she and her boyfriend packed the U-haul and drove it to Arizona. I nurtured my own inner peace to be able to hold a space for her.

With the same daughter, I can remember one night, pretty much pushing her up three flights of stairs physically so she wouldn't leave the house with a friend. There was a crisis in the friend's household and I had taken responsibility for her that evening when there was a lot of insanity. I needed to keep her indoors and safe. In that moment, I couldn't just say, *sit down and read a book.* There was a safety issue and they were trying to leave the house and it was really a challenge.

I just want to say to anyone on the phone. In this conversation tonight, both of us are parents and have had our moments when something immediate had to happen. I wish it could have been different but in the moment I didn't know any other way.

Elizabeth: Your stories are wonderful examples of the resisting and allowing. For instance, if someone is reflecting something back to me and I'm having an emotional reaction to it, it's hitting me somewhere. And children know exactly where to go. They're masters of hitting the right button at exactly the right time. Why? Because they are mirror reflections of us. They are doing exactly what they came in and agreed to do with us, which is to remind us of who we are. To push us and to push the limit for us to expand.

What I would say and I didn't always do this with my own daughter because it has taken me a lot of those experiences to expand and grow. There were plenty of times I wasn't coming from my higher self. What I learned is the more contrast we have in our life, the more challenges, the more discomfort, the more we are going to push ourselves to grow and expand.

Why? Because it gets so uncomfortable sometimes we have to do something. And the hope and the desire of our soul is to expand and to grow toward greater love. There are times when we may have to spiral down into a fear based emotion and that may describe itself and express itself as unconsciousness, apathy, grief, anger, fear. All of those emotions that are so important to our growth because they are the barometers and the compass to tell us when we are in alignment with love or out of alignment with love and all we have to do. It's a beautiful thing, in any given moment, to make a shift to a better feeling. At any given moment, we can make that shift, there is an opportunity to change.

If someone is presenting me with an experience or life is presenting me with an experience where I'm having an emotional reaction to it and I feel it in my physical body, I see it in my outer world in maybe some chaos or anxiety. Things aren't happening and going the way I want. What I would say is, *what is that reflecting back to me? What am I feeling so uncomfortable about? What is in that person that really bothers me? What is it in their behavior that is really affecting me?*

I had something happen this week. I was looking for assistance with a particular business task. I was interviewing some people. I am a bit of a creative person and sometimes I have an inspiration from the Divine and I have to do it now! Not everyone functions like that. I had this idea and I wanted to make it happen within 48 hours and this particular person decided to pass and said, *I can't work like that.*

Now, in the past that would have really bothered me when someone has a definite boundary and they own themselves and they own their stuff and they say, *no, that doesn't work for me.* And I'm like, *why? Let's do it. It's a great idea.* In the past, I may have reacted to that because I was, in the past, working on boundary issues myself. So, when this happened this week, it was really interesting. I recognized it and I said, *oh, wow. I recognize that and it doesn't even bother me right now. I am actually honoring that person's choice.*

People ask me, *how do I know when I'm healed of the situation?* You're healed when you don't have the same emotional zing you had in the past. You can stand in your peace, you can stand in your power, and you can be in that situation and in that chaos and all is well.

As opposed to in the past, when you were working through that. When the Divine in you was desiring to be expressed and desiring to express itself as more love. When you were in that process of growing and expansion, it may have bothered you in the past.

Now, back to the Mom on the chat line.

Andrea: She is saying, *"Also true, and when the breakthrough of light fails without notice. I think the only way to get through to him at this point is via e-mail. He's wired like me and has a tremendous consciousness."*

Elizabeth: I am going to agree with that, if you feel you need to keep a boundary in that way for yourself. I think that is a really good, healthy idea. I am going to take a leap of faith here and share something else about my own personal life at a time when I was going through some expansion and changes and growth with my own daughter. We chose to do that as well because the need for healing was so intense that when we had a conversation we were definitely not hearing each other. Sometimes it's good to use e-mail and technology. I've heard that the tech thing is actually a good thing because you can think about your response rather than being live with the person. Time to think about it before you respond. So, I agree with that.

Andrea: One of my daughters and I e-mailed back and forth for a time. One of the things I appreciated, because she was a kid who really held her emotion in. that in e-mail she really let it rip. I was really grateful that she was able to express anger, frustration and really intense emotion. I was able to then filter through the words of anger to discover what the issue was underneath all of that and I appreciated when she shared her opinion and perspective because it helped me to make some changes. She had a lot of anger built up and it was a situation where I was able to change some things and things got better.

My oldest daughter and I had a journal where we would each write an entry to the other one. Sometimes it was things that we appreciated about each other and sometimes it was things that were really pissing us off.

Elizabeth: That's a really nice thing to do and even just the recognizing. We have these experiences of love and fear. We expand through contrast and we expand through loving experiences and sharing what you love about someone is a wonderful way for you to bring that into your life.

If you desire more love in your life, then act loving. If you desire more abundance in your life, then act as if. I don't mean to be reckless and charge up to the limit of your credit cards. This is going all the way back to remembering who we are, remembering that feeling of who we are. Love and expansion. You truly are a magnificent, creative being within every cell of your body. You could create a Universe. Think about that; that is amazing.

To look in the mirror and to say, I see you. You don't have to be an Avatar to say that. *I see you. I see who you are. You are beautiful. You are magnificent. You are fabulous. Who are you not to be fabulous?* So act that way and life will reflect that back to you. We've heard a lot over the last couple of years about the law of attraction and I'm really thankful that The Secret brought it mainstream. However, that again is only a fragment of what the universal law of attraction really is. You don't really have to do anything. You don't have to really try to be wealthy. You already are. You don't have to try to have perfect health. It's already within you. It's in every cell of your body. The only thing that keeps you from actually experiencing it and materializing it is your belief of separation that it's outside of you. And that's what happens and we experience grief. We are perceiving this experience as a loss. And yes, there are times when it is a physical loss, as in those times when we lose a loved one.

I believe losing a loved one is probably the most challenging loss of human experience. However, it is our perception that although this person is not here physically that they are gone. They are more alive than they were in their physical body. And they are present. They are here. If we are a reflection of the Divine and we are part of all that is, then we are a part of them as well. And fortunately, science is beginning to prove this through many theories. One is called the M theory, the membrane theory, and they have taken us down to the essence of our membranes. We are literally connected at the energetic membranes. And if we were able to see, feel, believe accept there is no loss. It is only our perception that keeps us in pain. And in this moment, we can experience freedom.

Andrea: It's part of a process. There are so many different layers of this thing called loss. It is such a big topic. The loss that I'm really feeling right now is what we're talking about that is more than the loss of a person. We are really talking about when we lose parts of ourselves. When we are in a conflict with our child, in a relationship, there are actually parts of ourselves that have to die. I put that in the same category as losing a loved one. You might have more a shock initially with the death of a person. But, when you are really letting go of layers of yourself or looking at a pattern of behavior, there is loss. I am 54 years old and I was just looking at a pattern with a friend of mine. I was thinking, *okay I'm feeling better about that but there's still a little more to release with that.* It can feel like free floating through air and can be as painful. I have lost so many loved ones that I can tell you losing layers of myself and letting go of them to really discover the shining light that's underneath some of the crap can be just as painful. I want to presence that in case there is someone who is saying they haven't lost a loved one. If you have let go of parts of yourself, yes, you have experienced loss. If your life has changed in a way that changes who you are and you feel lost, take time to feel the feelings as the old dies and the new emerges.

Elizabeth: I agree with what you're saying. However, what I am inviting everyone to do is bring it up to a higher perspective. Imagine that you are an eagle in flight and you are looking down at the landscape of your life from a higher perspective. Loss is loss and it does express itself in many, many different ways. But, it's our perception of loss, even when we talk about the deaths of ourselves. If we are all energy and everything is energy, then we are a continuum. Energy cannot be destroyed. It will only transform and that's what we talk about when we use tools like the Violet Flame. We are transforming energy from one vibration to another.

Imagine that there is a beautiful symphony and in that symphony there are all different notes in the octave. They are strung together to make this beautiful sound. Well, that's who we are. We are the Low C, the high C. The only difference between them is not a judgment. It's a vibration at which they resonate. So when we think of emotions and we think of love, love is being the highest vibration. Love being the higher Self, the Divinity. And the low vibration of fear that expresses itself as grief, anger, sadness, separation all of those feelings that are heavy, if you will. We think of them only as energy, all we have to do is transmute, transform that energy. We literally transform our physical body. We can transform not only our physical body, but all of those around us. We literally can lift this planet up in a chalice of love. So, we can talk about all of the experiences.

One of the things that I've been getting from my own guides in the past four months is detaching from the expectation of an outcome. And Spirit is challenging us to even take that a little bit further by detaching from the stories of life. We get caught up in these stories, these beliefs. Well, this is the way it is supposed to happen. This is the way it should be or this is what I was supposed to do. This is what it is supposed to feel like.

We are transforming. We are evolving. Mankind is a species and we are evolving. In order to evolve, we have to be willing to allow new thoughts, new ideas, new concepts, new beliefs, to transform the archaic old ones, and we've been seeing that happen over the last twenty years in our society. So, as above is below, and we are being asked to do that ourselves.

One of the tools I have experienced, through you, Andrea. I want to acknowledge you for that and thank you for that. Delivering it to me and reminding me of this spiritual tool of the violet flame. It literally will transform energy in your life. It is basically a spiritual light.

It is something we have around us, in us, through us, all around us in the Universe and all we have to do is invite it into our lives. Just as we invite the light of God, it's just another aspect and expression of the Divine.

We talked about doing a meditation tonight. If you are ready and everyone else in the audience is ready.

Meditation...

I invite you to get yourselves comfortable.

Close your eyes and I would like you to think about an experience in your life now that is causing you to feel loss. Is it a relationship, job, or the loss of a loved one? I want you to allow those emotions that surround the feelings and experience of this loss to emerge.

Take a few deep, cleansing breaths, breathing in through the nose and out through the nose.

Breathe in light.

Breathe in to every cell of your body.

Breathe in beautiful, crystal, rainbow light.

Imagine it coming in through the crown of your head, from a beautiful orb that is floating above your head.

Imagine a light coming in from this orb, coming in through the crown of your head and spiraling down, all the way down your spine, out the base of your spine, all the way down to Mother Earth.

Take a nice, deep breath.

And as you breathe, allow your body to relax. From your head, all the way down to your toes.

Allow the feelings to emerge.

Notice in your body, where are you feeling sensations?

Imagine this light with its Divine intelligence touching any area of your body, where you are feeling discomfort.

This light magically knows exactly where to go. And as it touches you, all the way down to the cellular level, it dissolves all discomfort, all pain, all disharmony, all stress.

Breathe that in.

Feel your body relax, deeper and deeper.

Now, with your attention and focus, imagine a beautiful flame, deep within your heart.

Within this flame, there are colors of beautiful luminescent pink, sparkling gold, and beautiful vibrant blue.

See these flames swirling and merging together and as they do, they begin to shine the color violet. Beautiful violet light shining in your heart.

Feel it expanding now in your heart, through your chest, down your arms. Throughout your entire body.

Breathe in this light.

Within this light, there are sounds, there is vibration, there is love. There is a song in your heart. And it's a song that we sing with beautiful words and melodies of the soul. Some are spoken whispers. Some are shouted at the top of your voice. All come from the same place, the one Source that is in all of us. Whether it is a song of love, song of pain, song of memory, song of dreams, the foundation is in Spirit.

That is in all, everyone and everything.

Raise your voice, your song.

Sing the purity of light and let that resonate from your heart.

The perfection of living in the Garden, of loving all of God's creations and all of the emotions come with it.

Sing the praises to those that cause you to stretch.

See them in your mind's eye now.

Send them love from your heart.

Beautiful violet light, from your heart to theirs.

Imagine in your mind's eye now, any person, situation, experience that is causing you discomfort, causing you to stretch.

See a beautiful violet light, flowing like ribbons from your heart to theirs.

Breathe in.

See that light begin to swirl within them.

You begin to merge with that image in your mind.

You are them and they are you.

You are One.

You are Spirit.

You are Love.

You are Light.

Breathe in.

In the quiet of your mind, deep within your heart affirm these words:
> I am created by Divine Light
> I am sustained by Divine Light
> I am protected by Divine Light.
> I am surrounded by Divine Light.
> I am ever growing into Divine Light

And I share that with everyone and everything in my experience.

Take a breath of Violet Light in the Golden heart of Father, Mother, God and exhale it into your body and throughout all of Creation.

Breathe in, beautiful, effervescent golden light and picture yourself standing in a blazing column of golden light.

This is your inner life stream.

This is who you are.

I am in-breathing the violet light.

I am absorbing violet light.

I am expanding into a violet light.

I am projecting the violet light into this world.

And as I do so, I am freed of all Karma, of cause and effect.

I am free.

I am love.

I am light.

Breathe in.

This is who you are.

In every moment, of every day.

This is who you are.

No matter what circumstances are in front of you.

No matter what life is mirroring back.

This is who you are.

Take a deep breath in and know that you can connect this feeling, at any given moment, through the breath.

And so it is.

Andrea: And so it is. Wow. That was beautiful Elizabeth.

Elizabeth: I am honored and I am blessed and humbled to be in all of your presence.

I would like to invite you, if you are in your body, to type in a word. What you are feeling now. Anything. I am feeling pretty delicious at the moment. That felt really good. And please know, if I can leave you one thought.

You are Love

The journey you are living, the life you were meant to live is a choice away, a thought away, a shift of energy away. It is in you. It is you. You are already living the life you were meant to live. If you weren't you would be doing something different. Wherever you are on your journey, personal evolution, I would be honored to meet you there. Together we can create your tools through exploration and expansion, through love and through laughter, the life you desire to live.

Andrea: There are some words being shared on the chat line: Ecstasy, serenity, bliss, thank you, and love sent to you Elizabeth.

Thank you so much for coming on the show.

Elizabeth Saint Germain *is a contemporary luminary whose message of Living In Love has touched the lives of thousands through private coaching, transformative workshops and speaking engagements. Elizabeth believes the great work of our generation is transforming fear to love, separation to unity and masterfully supports people to love themselves free of pain, suffering, limiting beliefs and separation, to live life fully in the power of Love.*
Connect with Liz: www.elizabethstgermain.com

Grief Transformation Show #43
Grieving the Life You Thought You Were Meant to Live

January 6, 2010
http://tobtr.com/1460072

Chapter Twenty

Healing with Laughter
Andrea Hylen

Show originally aired on December 4, 2010

Tonight's show is about healing grief with laughter. I'm going to share some personal stories about how to bring laughter into your healing process and to understand the power of accessing, allowing and receiving this emotion.

As I was preparing for the show, I noticed Facebook Profile Pictures were changing to cartoon characters. It started as a way of bringing awareness to child abuse, something we can all feel in our hearts to grieve and heal and change.

As I looked at profile pictures of my friends, it stirred memories of some of the cartoons I had enjoyed as a child. I chose Felix the Cat as my cartoon picture. Then I searched on Youtube for songs and found the theme song for Felix the Cat, the wonderful, wonderful cat. I continued to search and I found songs for The Jetsons, The Flintstones and Batman. I found people who began to share joy and laughter by listening to cartoon songs. This is one of the paths of healing. Looking at the past and thinking about moments that were special can help us to remember joy and laughter. Uncovering challenging, painful situations and transmuting the pain to joy.

Laughter can support the healing process and lift us up. You may not think of laughter as a way to transform grief because the natural reaction is tears and sadness and heartbreak. One purpose of laughter is to release grief from your physical body. It raises the endorphin levels and it can move this feeling of sadness out of your physical body. You can support your healing by immersing yourself in opportunities to laugh or embrace them when they happen spontaneously.

There have been studies about physical illness and the healing power of watching funny movies and laughter.

I first really understood the power of laughter and healing right after the death of my son. Two days after our 19-month-old son died, my husband and I were lying in bed watching Saturday Night Live. We were numb from the pain of losing our son after 19 months of open-heart surgeries, therapies and in the end a neuro-blastoma cancer that took his life. Neither of us could sleep that night even though we were exhausted physically and emotionally. After channel surfing, we found Saturday Night Live. It was the only thing on television we could both agree to watch.

I remember lying in bed watching the show when all of a sudden I started to laugh. I was laughing so hard I had to get out of bed and stand up. I was 8 ½ months pregnant with our 4th child when our son died. I had a belly full of a new baby, a new life. There was no more room in my belly to laugh. Standing up gave me more room to breathe and keep laughing. The strangest thing is that I rarely laugh like that. I am more of a silent laugher or giggler. I can think something is funny but I don't laugh out loud. I knew on that night, I was releasing grief through a deep, rolling belly laugh with tears rolling down my cheeks.

There have been times I have been so sad and I needed a break from crying. Have you ever had that feeling where you thought, I just cannot cry anymore? I had a pain in my heart but my tears had gone dry. In those times, I have looked for something funny to release and rest. Laughter can also shift your perspective when you are feeling sadness.

Here are a few examples from my own life:

1. Transform a sad experience into something funny

    a. One year my daughter, Elizabeth created a song to sing about an ugly Christmas sweater that brought her adolescent sister, Mary to tears of laughter. There was a history with a distant relative and receiving the sweater was emotionally painful. So, Elizabeth cut through the pain by making up a song that brought humor to the situation. We still sing it in times of grief and sadness. "Yes, we're sisters and we're chillin' in our ugly Christmas sweaters."

2. **A funny movie**

    a. I ordered a free video with box tops from a breakfast product one year. Paula Poundstone, a comedienne, was highlighting three new comedians. It became a classic movie for the family. My older daughters memorized the scripts and would randomly perform skits. The video became a family joke and my older daughters still recite the lines.

3. **YouTube videos are great for a dose of laughter.**

    a. Our family loves cats and the funny things they do naturally. Here is a link to one of the videos on-line. **https://youtu.be/IytNBm8WA1c/**

4. **Laughing at yourself**

    a. We are all so precious and we do the funniest things. Finding something you can laugh at about yourself can help to lighten the seriousness of life. Some days I really crack myself up!

5. **Memories of a loved one**

    a. When my son was alive, his sisters would find a way to make him laugh every day. We called it the laugh of the day because when the "thing" was introduced he would laugh every time someone did it on that day. For example, you could make a funny noise and he would laugh all day. But, the next day, he would just stare at you until you came up with something new. It still brings a smile to my face to think about that.

    b. My husband had a booming, throw your head back kind of laugh. Thinking about his big laugh makes me smile. He was an out loud laughter.

Sometimes you can bring laughter into the memorial celebration of a loved one. When my husband died, my youngest daughter was twelve years old. The last year of his life was devastating for us all. There had been cancer treatments and drugs that had changed his personality and he had a lot of anger and rage. I don't blame him for that. Cancer, drug treatments and dying. That's a lot to be dealing with and I have a lot of compassion for what he was going through. And as a child, it was hard and confusing for my daughter to watch her father dying. I wanted to remind my daughter of who her father really was throughout his life. The fun, laughing, adventurous, intense guy.

Because he was cremated, I was able to postpone his memorial service for five weeks. During that time, I decided that I wanted to create a party of celebration to honor his life with rock music in the church and asked people to wear bright colors. I wanted to have a party afterwards that would be a celebration of his life. We had a moon bounce and a chocolate fountain. We held it outdoors where people could enjoy the land that we lived on and enjoy the projects my husband did over the years.

It was a very conscious decision to have that kind of memorial because I wanted to remember the laughter and the joy we had in life. I wanted to imprint joy in my daughter's memory of her father. I wanted her to remember who he truly was in life. I wanted her to remember that he was a fun guy.

Sometimes we forget to celebrate someone's life because we are so sad and grieving that they are gone. By remembering things from the past and bringing up and letting yourself laugh and remember the joy it is a way of remembering that part of life. You can complete a person's life by honoring the good times, too.

As I was writing about laughter a few months ago, I posted a question on Facebook:

What makes you laugh?

Some of the ideas:

"Laughing at the actual thing that is breaking you in half." **Finding some sort of irony in the situation.**

"My husband loves to tell dorky jokes and he is always laughing at the punch line before he gets to it. The childish joy on his face always makes me laugh and smile."

"Farts." As I say, natural bodily functions can be funny.

"A husband's perpetual puns and sense of humor."

"Remembering walking down Samoset Road as a child and getting cookies from Ina Rogers and from Great Aunt Jean."

"Tickling my 6-month-old grandson and hearing him giggle."

"Remembering a song my mom sang to wake me up. I didn't like it then, but it makes me smile now. "It's time to get up, it's time to get up, it's time to get up in the morning! do do dododo do do dododo do do dododo dododo-do!"

Looking at the list reminded me of how easy it is to find something that can make me laugh and smile. As much as I can look back at the loss and the sadness, I can also find a memory that connects me to joy.

Here are a few more ideas:

A funny picture or image

    a. When I was in second grade, I took a tissue box to school for my desk. Why we all needed a full box of tissues on our desk, I have no idea. On the bottom of my box was a picture of a man blowing his nose. For some reason, I thought it was hysterical. I even got in trouble one day for laughing at the man uncontrollably and my teacher sent me to the principal's office. That moment reminds me to laugh at the little things and to lighten up, even if it upsets some people.

b. Cartoons in the newspaper, magazines and on the internet.

Singing songs and listening to music

c. As children we have songs that make us laugh or smile. Find some songs that fill your heart with joy.
d. As a teenager, I used to walk to the park at night and swing on the swing set and sing songs from musicals like the Sound of Music. It brought joy and laughter into my heart sometimes through tears first, then lifting me up.

Make yourself laugh

e. Laughter Yoga Clubs were started by Indian physician, Dr. Madan Kataria, in 1995. Now there are laughter clubs all over the world. There are exercises to help you find laughter. If you are having a day when you want to break through the feeling of laughter, you can do an exercise. It is healthy for your soul and your body.
f. Exercise: make the noise Ha Ha Ha from your belly. Keep making the noise until the sound brings on spontaneous laughter. I love to do this with kids, too and tapping into your own inner child.

Follow a funny person on Facebook or Twitter.

g. The laughter is fresh every day.

h. @conanobrien (Conan O'Brien, the comedian) started an account with one tweet a day. Simple and funny!
i. Google "funny people on twitter" Get an account just to follow the laughter.

Spend time with a child. Become like a child
j. Look at the world with fresh eyes
k. Tickle and giggle
l. Play a game

m. Kick a ball/Throw a Frisbee
   n. Feel the joy
   o. Skip down the street. It is hard to skip and be serious.

Grieving is a natural part of our day-to-day lives. We lose loved ones. We have disappointments. When my son and then my husband died, I made the decision to live life for all three of us. That includes finding the joy in life. Feel all of the feelings and remember to include laughter as one of them.

These are my simple ideas and at the same time, remember to be gentle with yourself. There are no magic pills for grief. We heal one moment at a time; one day at a time for the rest of our lives. Make time for laughing.

I hope some of these ideas will inspire you to create an environment for laughter. The idea that every day has the potential for bringing waves of sadness and balance and finding moments of joy no matter what is happening in your life. As human beings, we do have the ability to feel grief and to feel joy at the same time.

The most profound example I can share with you is something else that happened when my son died. A week after his death, we had the memorial service and a week after that was the birth of our 4th child. I learned at that time of intense grief and joy how absolutely incredible human beings are. We are capable of shifting our emotions from one moment to the other and to honoring all of it.

In a short period of time, I could feel this deep loss for my son and I could turn at look at my daughter with her sparkling eyes and her smile and I could feel incredible joy.

Just like with anything else, we feel the sadness, we can grieve and we can also find a moment of joy throughout our grieving. Let yourself remember the joy in life, too.

I wish you days of laughter to bring a balance to your life.

Grief Transformation Show #14
Healing with Laughter

December 4, 2010
http://tobtr.com/1414056

Andrea Hylen

Chapter Twenty-One

Staying Balanced as You Grieve
Guest: G. Brian Benson

Show originally aired on December 29, 2010

Andrea: Brian, I know we were talking before the show about all of the shows I have hosted since November 21 and tonight is #36 of 44 shows. I have talked with guests about grief, people losing loved ones, discussions about spending time in a hospital with a loved one or just being in the holidays with a loved one with new feelings coming up and old feelings that are arising. With Hanukkah, Christmas and New Year's, this is the perfect time to talk about this topic. **Staying Balanced as You Grieve.**

   I want to share one thing with you about your book. My 17-year-old daughter read it and really liked it. She asked who was on the show and when I told her it was you and I showed her the book, she said, *"Oh, I really liked that book."* So, there you go, you have an endorsement from my 17-year-old daughter.

   So, what inspired you to write this book, *"Brian's List – 26 ½ Easy to Use Ideas on How to Live a Fun, Balanced, Healthy Life."*

Brian: I will try to make this story semi-short. Basically, there is a quote I really like *"We are here to teach what it is that we need to learn ourselves."* I'm going to tell you how this came about to play a part in the creation of my book. A couple of years ago, I was running a family business: my Dad and I. And in the back of my mind, I always knew that it was not what I wanted to do for the rest of my life. I had just gotten to the point where I was really burned out and I was ready for a change. I wasn't growing there anymore and I was pretty out of balance. I'm a pretty driven person. Through the years, it served me well with the triathlon and some of the other stuff I've done.

Being a driven person, I thought, let's do a couple of things about this. I did not like being out of balance. First of all, I wanted to see why I was feeling out of balance. It was pretty obvious. It was because of my job. What I decided to do then was come up with a handful of things that I knew would keep me in balance.

I scribbled some notes down on a piece of paper and I stuck them in my wallet. Every day thereafter, when I would begin to feel out of balance or out of sync, I would pull that list out and I would read it.

1. Drink more water.
2. Daily exercise
3. Get enough sleep
4. Alone time each day (that's how I re-energize myself)
5. Be creative each day (for me, that means play my guitar or write

I really stuck to that and it helped me get through that period. It worked so well I thought, why not expand the list and make it into a book, to help others in the same way that it helped me.

It's been a really great experience in a lot of ways. I learned a lot about myself. I've met some amazing people doing workshops. The book won a couple of awards, which I'm still kind of pinching myself. But most importantly, I know the book helped others in the same way it helped me. I'm very proud.

We ended up selling the business. I feel like I am doing what I was meant to do and I'm very happy.

Andrea: Was this a family business?

Brian: Yeah, we had a big golf center, driving range and a retail store. Taught lessons and the whole works up here in Oregon.

Andrea: I'm fascinated. I didn't really know that part of the story. I knew things had changed. Were there things you had to go through with other family members being ready to sell the business also?

Brian: I was very fortunate. It was just my Dad and I who were involved. He had another business so he didn't really do any of the day-to-day stuff. I'm very fortunate. He supported my decision. It wasn't that big of a deal. I can totally see why it would be very difficult for somebody whose father or sibling didn't want to sell. Then you come into a whole lot of potential problems.

Andrea: I think this is an important key, Brian. When a person does the internal work to discover where they are out of balance. It feels like you got in alignment and you got really clear. Then you had the conversation with your Dad and it flowed easily for this ending. I don't know if you have had this experience, but I'm sure some of the listeners have. An experience when you, have this inner feeling that is letting you know you were out of balance but you kept on going. Then, the little whispers became a shout and it could have ended with a big drama around the whole thing. So, I really think that is an important piece of the whole message here, Brian. You took responsibility for your whole out-of-balanced-ness.

Brian: Thank you. I appreciate you saying that. I have always been the one to work on myself and read and self-analyze, probably too much. I have wanted to become the best that I can be. What you touched upon. **Listening to an inner calling**; that's one of the most important reasons for why we need to stay in balance because we can hear our intuition and guidance come through clearer. When we're scattered, it's a lot harder to listen.

Andrea: Why do you think it is harder for some people to live a balanced lifestyle? You are on a path of growth and you took responsibility and you did that. What about the rest of us out here who are resisting? Why is it hard to have a balanced lifestyle?

Brian: There's more than one answer but we can go over some of the different ones. Balance is a moving target. Each day our own point of balance can change depending on how much energy we have and what our focus is. Every day is kind of different.

But, I think in a broader sense our lives have become busier. We may be trying to do too many things. We allow some of those things that aren't as important become habit in our lives. And we just try to fit too many things in our schedule, kind of like the old juggler. He keeps adding balls and we just keep adding more and more to the act and pretty soon they're going to drop.

The same thing happens to us if we try to do too many things in our lives, in our daily schedule. I am one that really believes many of the things we have made habit in our lives aren't really as important as we think they might be. They just have become habit, you know.

Andrea: I love everything you just said. But one thing you said in the beginning, *"Balance is a moving target."* Wow! I wish you had told me that twenty years ago. (Lots of Laughter) Okay, I'm glad I'm hearing it now. I will keep it in mind for the future. Yes! Balance is a moving target, like making the choice every day of being balanced. What worked yesterday is not necessarily going to work today. It must be why you have 26 ½ easy to use ideas.

Brian: There's a few other reasons, too; Why it's hard to find balance. Part of it is self-awareness. We don't know ourselves well enough. That's one of the workshops I do. It's called, *"An Introduction to Balance."* It's really all based on self-awareness. Once we really take a closer look and see what works for us, to keep us in balance and to see what knocks us out of balance. Once we are aware of them, we can really begin to try to eliminate them from our lives. That makes it a lot easier.

There's one other thing that I think is important. We might be involved in something that doesn't suit us. And that was the case with me, with my job. It could be a job, a relationship or whatever. You can fill in the blanks. We're doing something that we don't enjoy or isn't right for us. We're going to be swimming upstream.

Andrea: How do you think people can find balance on a regular basis? How do you even find balance within that?

Brian: First thing we have to identify. Common feelings are feeling stuck, feeling overwhelmed, stressed. Health can come into play. Sometimes we'll get sick. We'll get colds because we're out of balance. Once we can identify those, that's the first step.

Once we've identified those it's really about getting to know yourself better. Become more self-aware and begin to implement the things that will work for you into your daily life and make them a habit, instead of those things that don't suit us. It can also be that if you find that life is too intense, balance it with some lightness. Maybe it's listening to music or going for a walk. There are lots of things. If you find yourself working too much, make sure you find you balance it with some play. If you find yourself giving too much, I know that this is an issue for some people, make sure you balance it with some receiving. There are lots of different ways we can fall in and out of balance.

Andrea: I think for a long time part of the reason I was out of balance was I didn't love myself enough to put myself before anyone else. I would say, if there is a lesson for me throughout my life, it is self-love. After the death of my husband and completing things like selling his business, I spent the last year taking time to listen to my own inner voice again. This
year really strengthened that muscle. Helping people is just a passion of mine and it was a role I played in my family of
wanting to help people feel better and feeling responsible for people's emotions.

The whole self-love part can really come into play when there's someone in the hospital with a chronic illness who might even be dying. Well, forget giving myself anything. I should feel grateful that I'm not the one dying, right? Do you have any tips for someone who has the list but still isn't on the priority list?

Brian: Well, it's not always easy but, as you've learned, for us to really be there and to support people and to help people in a positive, helpful way we need to be whole ourselves. We need to be in balance. We need to be loving ourselves as you've mentioned. When we're not, it feels different. It is received differently.

Is that how it felt to you? It does all start with us and I think it is very important to really realize that we are very valuable and full of amazing things, gifts, and really just honor ourselves. If you're not feeling up to doing something and you need to take care of yourself, do it. You have to do that. Or eventually your body will force you to take that time off due to sickness or something else.

With that said, I think it is important to find those things that really make you happy, that give you relief that bring you happiness. And then just honor those things and do them. Make them part of your lives so you can be whole and you can help people in a positive way, not in a desperate seeking love angle.

Andrea: Well, definitely with grieving, there is a tendency to put someone ahead of yourself. When you talk about illness, I know that personally, I did get an autoimmune condition. My immune system began to attack my muscles. It was a condition called polymiositis. I had very weak muscles and I also felt very powerless in my life. I felt that was what my body was telling me. It was time to do inner work and strengthen my inner power. It was a whole healing journey and I ended up healing myself because I did the inner work connected with the illness.

So, right on. That is correct. That is what happens when we don't put ourselves first. One of the things I have had people say to me is, *"Well, you lost a son so my loss is not that great."* It feels like people are forgetting that we are all here for different experiences in life. At least, that's the way I look at life.

Brian: I believe it revolves around love and we are here to learn about ourselves and grow and share our gifts and try to be the best that we can be. Help others and enjoy life. I am one that feels that life is not meant to be a struggle; we just get in our own way.

I know through the years, and our families will teach us, we need to work hard. We need to find the line and we need to find the work that we are meant to do here. When we do that, it doesn't really feel like work.

And I think that we're supposed to have fun, as well, and enjoy the ride, enjoy the journey. Tap into that aspect of it.

Andrea: I think that really speaks to the whole idea of what having balance in our lives is about. Finding balance is not learning how to juggle things in a better way. *Okay, I have these ten things, I'm holding onto them. I'm stressed. I just need to learn how to juggle better.*

What would you say to someone like that? I've got these ten things and I can't give any of them up. Teach me how to juggle.

Brian: First of all, I would ask the person to write down everything that they thought they needed to do. And then have them go down the list and talk about each one and see if something they really thought they needed to do can be changed.

A lot of times, it is just habit. Just because it is a habit doesn't mean it's right.

Andrea: That is a great exercise. Become aware and get clear.

You know, Brian, in some ways, your message is so simple but I'll tell you that even as you are talking, I keep getting these aha's. Then, I think, *do I really not know that*? I try to make it really complicated. I'm exposing myself here because I really don't feel that I'm unique in that way. I think there is this underlying feeling that life is complicated. Or staying in balance has to be complicated. I want to reflect on one thing about your book right now because I thought this was so brilliant.

I was telling you before the show that I was just exhausted. I couldn't figure out why I was exhausted other than I've hosted 35 shows in a row. But, really, the holidays have been very low key. I made the decision that this was where I was going to put my time. I have a tiny little plant that we used for our Christmas tree. I didn't exchange presents with my family this year. I really cleared my plate. So, I have not done the holidays with any hoopla, the way I would have done them in the past.

Yesterday, I had a whole list of things I wanted to do and I had some writing and things I wanted to do for my business and I just felt exhausted. So, I took a nap at 10 a.m., which I never do. Then, I went for a walk and I wanted to take another nap later in the afternoon. At one point, I picked up your book. I had a bookmark in it and I opened it up and it was on #13, which says, **Get more sleep.**

I want to let the listeners know that this is the kind of book that it is. You can just pick it up and open it to a page for an inspiration. I really felt like Spirit was talking to me. *You want to really know what's wrong? Pick up Brian's List and I'll give you a clue.*

So, I didn't have to figure out why, I just needed more sleep. So, I took two naps, went to bed early and slept for eight hours. Today I feel energized.

Brian: It's amazing. Sometimes I will really push myself. I won't get the sleep I need and I will just push, push, push and I will get sick. I don't get sick very often but I will. Once I am forced to take that time off and once I am forced to take my health back, it's amazing how many things will come back in that I really felt I had to do three, four, five days before.

It is so important to stay on top of that. We can't avoid some of those times. Good for you for honoring that yesterday.

Andrea: Believe me, I went through many levels of resistance. I'm just going to be honest. I was already tired at 8:30 am after being awake since 4 am, but I finally gave in at 10 am because it just wasn't going away. I could barely keep my eyes open.

Maybe my body just needed some time to catch up. I have been doing a lot of writing and thinking and sometimes the body just needs some downtime to integrate.

Brian: I totally agree with you. Mental work is probably harder than physical work. Our bodies do need to catch up sometimes and process.

I want to touch on the comment you made about the book being so simple. I did that on purpose. I really feel like my purpose here is to help people who are already kind of self-aware and working on some of their self-worth. So, I really want to make my books fun and entertaining and simple.

A lot of people have told me they like to read one chapter a day and kind of chew on it during that day. You can also read it all the way through. They are things that we know about but we just need to be reminded. In their simplicity, they just elude our everyday thinking about them.

Andrea: One of the reasons I keep focusing on your book is because it really is this underlying idea of simplicity to balance your life. Finding simple ways. And I can tell you, having spent numerous days, weeks and months supporting loved ones who were in the hospital with serious illnesses and operations and taking them to physical and speech therapy and being the main caregiver for my son and husband during their illnesses, I didn't really find ways to take care of myself. I know there are people who have come to this show because they are in similar situations.

When you and I connected, it was one of the things that was so appealing to me about your message, the simplicity. That's what I love about your book. It's not about sitting down and memorizing things. It is a great book to keep in a handy place to just open it and see what the message is.

Brian: Sometimes when we are in the grips of grieving or having a lot going on in our lives, there is almost a misconception that we think it is going to be harder than we think it is to maybe find a bit of balance amidst all of the stuff that's going on.

If we just did a couple of simple things like going outside and sitting on the grass. Taking some deep breaths or going for a short walk or just listening to some music. It doesn't have to be a huge production to find that relief.

Andrea: Again, that is the message. The simplicity to find the little things and that is what my daughter and I both felt about it. I love the audio recording you have on CD. We keep it in the car and listen to it on car rides and pause it to reflect on certain messages. I think that is another way for people to find these moments to support themselves during a grieving process and during all of these holidays.

Let's briefly walk through some of the Easy to Use Ideas of your book.

Brian: Did you have any other favorite chapters?

Andrea: Treat yourself with respect. It is important for an over giver who is always working on self-love.

Brian: That's a good one for everyone. We need to be whole before we can give support to others that we want to.

For me, the original five: Drink more water; Get daily exercise; Get more sleep are very, very important for me. If I don't get enough sleep, then I don't go to the gym. If I don't go to the gym, then I don't have that snap in my step I'm used to having. Everything seems to flow better for me when I get a little bit of exercise.

A little bit of alone time each day is important for me to re-energize and re-generate. I think some people can get energy from being around people, but for me I really need some quiet time.

A bunch of people like the tip about clearing out items. I think a lot of us have a bunch of extra stuff floating around the house. Even though we don't really think about it, it does put a weight on our shoulders. Maybe we see it when we come into our home. I know how good I feel when I get rid of stuff I'm not using anymore. Donating items or giving them away is important. I get a lot of comments on that one.

Andrea: That was a big one for me. I went through a huge clearing. I had an eleven-room house in Maryland and it was filled with stuff. Because I had such a huge house and I was a Girl Scout leader, I stored things for other people, too. Part of the process of clearing was for me to go through an emotional release with all of this. There was a lot of crying. And there was a lot of readjusting after finding my balance again after the crying.

The stuff was connected to my value and feeling important. Storing things for other people had become an energy drain.

Now, my daughter and I live in an apartment in California and everything in our house can now fit into our car except for the two beds we bought here. I got rid of a lot of things I thought I would never be able to let go of. It freed up a lot of energy.

I'm sure you get a lot of response to that because when people really wake up to that and realize they don't need everything. It does bring in more balance. Even just trying to live with less.

Brian: I got rid of a lot of stuff a few years ago when I moved to Nevada. I honestly don't remember what I got rid of. There is one thing I remember, but most of it, I don't. It's a good thing.

Andrea: Yes, there is probably going to be one or two things that you say, *"I can't believe I got rid of that."* But, just let it go. If you get rid of hundreds of other things, the couple of things you regret will be okay. And the things you regret, that is an exercise unto itself. Why does it really matter? It's only a thing. And when I die, it won't matter anyway.

Brian: One of my favorite chapters is **Chapter 18: Try something new. Take a chance.** The last couple of years for me have been very interesting since I left the business. I moved and I really had to step out of my comfort zone in different ways. I was doing workshops and speaking, I hadn't really done that before. I had to force myself into Toastmasters and speech classes. It really makes you feel alive. The really neat thing is the feeling of accomplishment of doing something you didn't think you could do or really have thought about it. It's really important to do different things. It doesn't mean you have to go speak in front of people but just do something you haven't done before and watch your vibrational level grow and rise.

Last fall, I had yet to do a workshop and I just knew I was going to set up this little tour. My intuition was telling me. So, I picked up the phone before I could talk myself out of it and figured out this little route through Utah, Colorado, and New Mexico and Arizona and southern California and started calling different stores, bookstores, churches, you name it, to set up this little workshop tour. In the space of about a week and a half, I had it set up. It was about fifteen different stops. I was terrified but it worked out just fine. And I would never have known that if I hadn't taken the chance.

Andrea: Live Life. What are we here to do, if we are not going to live life and stretch out of that job? *What lights you up? What's crossing your path? What's crossing your mind that you're interested in?*

When I turned 50, I decided I had wasted too much of my life wishing I had taken more tap dancing classes when I was in college. I learned how to tap dance in a musical in high
school and I totally loved it. I hadn't done anything about it
again but I would think about it and wish I had. So, for my 50th birthday, I bought myself a pair of tap shoes. I signed up at a
local college class and started tap dancing again because it was just fun.

What are you telling yourself you can't do?

Brian: There really is nothing that we can't do. We just have to put aside our fears and just do it. I've really made it a point to do things like that for myself for the last year and a half and it's been great. I still have some work to do and that's why we're here.

As long as you are moving forward and remembering you are alive. It's all good.

Andrea: I wanted to ask you about your next book, **"If Brian Can Do It, I Can Do It!"**

Brian: Thanks for asking. In a nutshell, the book says that everyone has the answers if they just get quiet and listen. I think a lot of self-help books out there have this one-size fits all protocol. If you read it, then you're going to become happy and successful.

In my next book, the readers must follow their hunch, their intuition, their gut, their inner GPS. I just feel that it's never wrong. If we just get quiet and listen, use meditation, get outside and go for walks, and get yourself in balance, it will come through. I have been really blessed in using my intuition for the last 20-25 years. And it really has been magical.

Andrea: I love it. I think that's it. That message is about taking care of yourself and finding the balance, too, and listening within.

What do you want people to really take away from this discussion?

Brian:

1. It doesn't have to be difficult to find balance in your life.
2. It is so important to be in balance so that you can find your fulfillment and happiness on your path by listening to your intuition and guidance.

I think those are the two main points.

Andrea: The ideas from the book are simple ideas that are very powerful. Some of them do not take very much time at all. Check out Brian's website for his current adventures.

G. Brian Benson, founder of Reawaken Media, is an award-winning author, actor, filmmaker, and inspirational speaker. His mission is to wake up the world with conscious, thought-provoking media that inspires. As a 4x Ironman triathlete, Brian knows the value of hard work and never giving up on his dreams, a message he shares with audiences. www.gbrianbenson.com

Grief Transformation Show #36
Staying Balanced as You Grieve

December 29, 2010
http://tobtr.com/1424642

Andrea Hylen

Chapter Twenty-two

Angels and the Angel Lady
Guest: Betsy McMahan

Show originally aired on December 25, 2010

Andrea: The topic tonight is Angels. I had this inspiration about a week ago. I knew I wanted to be here live on the show on Christmas for a variety of reasons. One is I know I have had Christmases that have been lonely and it would have been nice to have heard a voice in the dark. And the other reason is it has been 33 nights of shows in a row and I can't imagine not being here with you tonight.

Betsy, I am so thrilled that you were willing to come on the show on Christmas.

Betsy: And I have to just say that I have been so blessed to have been on the show on Christmas. And to be able to spend this time with you and with all of your other friends.

Andrea: I was thinking that this morning and how excited I was that I was spending Christmas with Betsy.

Betsy: I was thinking that on my way home, too. We are on separate coasts and we are wrapping the United States and wrapping the coasts with angel love. I am on the East Coast and Andrea is on the West Coast and it just seems perfect.

Andrea: There are a lot of things I could say about Betsy and the amazing work that she does with angels. The one thing I want to say about you, Betsy, is how I have always seen you as someone who works with the angels and who acknowledges angels in her life. The first time I met you was when you owned your store, **Heavens to Betsy**.

How did you start knowing they were in your life? How did you start acknowledging angels in your life?

Betsy: It's different for everybody and I think their presence becomes known to different people at different times in their lives. For me, I was an early teenager 12, 13, 14, somewhere around there. Before then, I had read about them. I grew up Methodist. So, I certainly had read about them in Sunday school. They were sort of more religious beings that may or may not be around. They were there in emergencies for people. But, I didn't see angels as being an active part in my life at that point.

And then my grandmother, who is very insightful, started talking to me about angels and how I could ask angels for help whenever I needed it. She told me I had my own guardian angels and up until that point I hadn't given much thought to that.

There is a book by Terry Lynn Taylor called, *Messengers of Light*. That was the very first angel book that I read. She really opened me to the fact that angels could be an integral part of your life every day. Whether you need parking spaces or you can ask your angel team to make sure you wake up every morning. Just sort of nudge you, you don't even need an alarm clock because they will just sort of nudge you when it's time to wake up. There were lots of techniques in that book. I read it many years ago and I remember just starting to use them one at a time.

One angel story that really resonated with me when I was working for a corporation. There was a lot of movement and I had a new boss. We just weren't seeing eye to eye. So, one of the techniques I used from that book was to sit down and before I went to bed at night, I asked my angels to talk to her angels and just work everything out. To just have a little conference while we both slept and take care of working everything out.

I think that is one of the first angel things I asked for. The amazing thing happened the next morning. We had a corporate meeting and everyone was there. This woman, who I felt I had a bit of a challenge with, was telling everyone what a phenomenal job I did and that I was one of the best people in her department.

From that point on, I said, *this angel thing really does work*. They are there to help with anything we need help with. We'll give a few more examples later in the call.

Andrea: I love that, to be able to just call on them and know that they're always with us. Sometimes I think people put a limitation on the availability of angels. I know I've done this myself when I think I don't want to trouble them with this little thing. And yet, they're here for us.

Betsy: Exactly. I would say we each have a guardian angel, if not a whole guardian angel team. And if you're not asking for help with the big things and the little things…if we're not talking to an angel team and asking for help, they're just standing around kind of watching us as we live. And they would much rather be a part of our lives and enjoying the journey with us. But we definitely need to ask for their help. It can be a whole lot of fun.

Andrea: I know and that is why people call you the angel lady because you have so many ways that you've called on the angels and they respond.

I want to share one experience. I decided to sell my house back in 2009 and this year, a year later in Jan 2010, I moved across the country and I felt such a strong calling to do that.

There have been times when I have really enjoyed the solitude and times I really questioned whether I was making the whole thing up about feeling guided to be in California. There have been a couple of times I have felt really low and I have actually asked the angels to just come and hold me. It is usually at night. I'll be lying in bed and I say, *I just need an angel to hold me* and I really feel so much comfort in that. Sometimes it's not even an action or insight or anything other than, *I just need to feel your presence to know that you're here.*

And I feel it immediately. It feels like someone just cuddling up to me and I feel my fear or anxiety or whatever I am feeling in the moment. I relax and I feel calm. I feel totally loved and supported.

Betsy: And often times you may even feel the warmth of their presence. I have to share something with you. Right when the call was starting, I pulled a card for our call. I have some really simple angel cards that have one word on them. And the card that I pulled said **Reassurance**. For this specific call and knowing that you've done a series of calls up until now on grief, as you were talking about asking the angels to hold you and give you a hug, it just all seems to be weaving together.

There is a book that goes along with the card and this says that *drawing this card will restore confidence in yourself. It signifies a yes answer. Let go of doubts and fears, proceed forward. Perhaps someone around you needs reassurance or validation. Find a friend and give them a big bear hug. It is so fun when you invite the angels into your life that little by little you'll see.*

One other thing I think might be helpful. As we're learning to communicate with our angels, sometimes, being a human being, it helps to see physical things. For the most part, we can't touch them, we can't see them. How do I know they're really there?

I would invite all of your friends who are listening to: **Ask their angels to show them signs that they're really around.**

As I was driving home tonight, I was inspired to tell you, all of you, to tell the angels what you want to see. So, for me, they show up in two different ways. The numbers 3, 6, and 9 just seem to appear in my life more frequently than all the other numbers. In fact, probably about a month ago, when I was doing a lot of focusing on angel work I had an experience. Every morning for about two weeks when I woke up and looked at the clock, it was 6:39. Every morning it was 6:39 when I woke up. I'll look at the radio and it's 6:39. Or I'll look at a license plate and its 369. I go to get gasoline and the total when I'm not even looking at it is $33.69. So, 3, 6 and 9 show up a lot. And more than anything, it is reassurance telling me, *smile, we're here.*

I would say whatever it happens to be is all good. I also look at license plates. I could be driving along, ask a question and a vanity plate tag would go by that speaks to the question that I asked. Because I know that I look at vanity plates, I decided to have a vanity plate of my own that says, **U R LOVD**. Because if anyone out there is wondering if they are or not, I want to be the car that reassures them they are loved by angels, by God, by their loved ones.

One story. I was going through a rough time in life and I was driving along the Baltimore Beltway. I remember saying out loud, *"I give up!"* The next car that drove by, the license plate, the vanity tag read, never give up. **(NVR GV UP)**. I just had to look at it and smile. *Well, okay, but I need a little help!*

The more that you invite them to participate in your life, the more fun that life can be. Life can be easy, if you ask them.

Yesterday, I had to go to a big store. The day before Christmas! I was in and out of there in ten minutes and the parking lot was absolutely full. On my way in, I said, *Okay angels help me find exactly what I need and help me get through the line.* One of the store managers walked up to me, as soon as I walked in and said, *"How can I help you? What do you need?" "Okay, this is what I need."* Life can be so much fun when you invite them to participate.

Andrea: You have your own shopping angel. I love it!

I get messages from angels in license plates and billboards, also. I wrote a story that I put on-line about a time I was really frustrated. I had jury duty about 45 minutes north of where I lived and my daughter had a home school class with a really interesting storyteller and writer who had come from the West Coast to the DC area. I really wanted my daughter to take this class. One of the grieving tools I wanted her to use around the loss of her Dad was writing. I thought it would be a great healing outlet for her to write more. I was
frustrated because I couldn't change the jury duty. None of my friends were available to drive my daughter, 45 minutes
south of our home, in the opposite direction of the jury duty. Finally, the mom who had organized the class said I could drop Hannah off early. Even with that, I would be driving to DC and to Baltimore in some of the peak rush hour traffic areas. I asked for guidance. I asked for support with this. We arrived at the woman's house easily and early. There was no rush hour traffic either way. And on the way back to Baltimore, I was feeling so much gratitude and saying thank you to God. I saw a license plate on a car with the words **GODS GFT (God's Gift)**.

I took that message into the day. I looked at the jury duty as a way to give back. When I was taken into one of the selection processes, I sat there sending light and love to everyone who was involved to come from the highest place. I talked with God and I said *I am willing to serve. If I need to be here for days, I will find a way to work out my schedule. I'm here to serve.* I wasn't selected for any of the jury duties but I felt it was a whole day of God's Gift.

Betsy: I also believe, wherever I am, because I am in cahoots with the angels, even if I think I am lost in that moment of time, I am in the perfect place. Especially when I think I am somewhere that I shouldn't be and *how did I end up here?* I take a breath and I just know for some reason that God needed me to be there for some specific reason. I offer a blessing to the area around me. That would include being there for jury duty. Maybe you really didn't want to be there and you found yourself there and being grateful for the chance to be a blessing to those around you; to be a light in that area at that point in time.

Invariably, if I think I'm lost and I do that blessing, all of a sudden I will see a sign that will lead me back to where I need to be. I just take a moment and take a breath. It helps me relax. Sometimes when you're lost you can get anxious. It helps me to know I am exactly where I'm supposed to be. The angels will help me back to where I want to be but right now I am going to send a little blessing to the people in the cars and the community right here because they must have needed it. That feels good, too.

It just feels good to be doing good things. I don't know how better to say that. *It just feels good to be one of the good guys.* I think when I am working with the angels I am one of the good guys. Whenever I can be an Earth Angel for people, I take on that role, too. I feel that I am here in this moment. This person needs my help. I am being an Earth Angel. I don't expect gratitude or anything in return. It just feels good to be helping.

Andrea: Do you have any stories about when you have been an Earth Angel to someone?

Betsy: I remember a person at the post office. For some reason, their credit card wasn't working. It was almost 5pm and the post office was going to close. They had a whole lot of boxes. I just came up behind them and said, *I will write a check for that and I know they will pay me back.* The post office wouldn't trust them writing a check but the gentleman wrote me a check and I wrote a check to the post office. And the check cleared and all was well. He thanked me.

It's those kind of things. Believing in the best in people. I like to randomly pay the toll for the person behind me once in a while. Those kinds of things aren't as easy these days with the EZ Pass, but you find a way to be a blessing in people's lives. I really think if you are a blessing to one person, they may bless ten other people. It's sort of a ripple effect.

Andrea: Last night I was talking about peace on earth and finding inner peace. I really believe this is what it is, too. When we can be Earth Angels to people and to do these things as part of our day to day life, it can really shift someone's belief in the world.

They might feel that there is no one here for them and then, all of a sudden, there you are paying for something or holding the door open.

Betsy: Even just smiling at people when they pass you by, saying, *Good morning*, just those little things. I choose to be a light. I choose to be positive. The more I'm positive, the more positive things will be in my life and that feels good.

Andrea: Do you ever have moments when you've had something happen and you feel discouraged or there's been a loss of some sort or the day's not working the way you wanted it to work? Do you have a way that you connect to the angels at that time? To honor what you're feeling first of all. You can't just stuff it down or ignore it. But to honor it and then do something to shift it with the help of the angels?

Betsy: I've realized over the years, with some of the spiritual work that I've done, that how I feel is basically a reflection of the thoughts that I'm thinking. How I'm relating to what is happening in my life. Icky things do happen. It could be just a challenging day or it could be that you really had a significant loss in your life; the loss of a loved one, the loss of a job, the loss of a home. I don't want to make light of them. For example, the loss of a loved one. I honor myself and I choose to be thinking the thoughts that will make the tears flow. I understand that that's a choice and I'm choosing to do that. Sometimes you need to have tears flow. I know sometimes you feel sort of refreshed at the end of a good cry. There's something to be said about a good cry.

But, I also know I can ask the angels to inspire me with thoughts that will help me feel better. So, as I'm feeling really icky, really down, really discouraged, I ask them to help inspire me with something that will feel a little bit better. I don't expect to go from depression or anguish or desperation to bliss. That's a pretty big step to make. But, you can go from something that feels really desperate to a thought where you feel a little bit of a relief from the really bad thought.

And then I work my way and I keep looking for a thought that feels better and then a thought that feels better than that. And within a short period of time, if I choose to, I can be feeling better than I did a half hour ago. I know with loved ones, to feel the void of their presence, that can be such a heavy feeling. Tears can really flow around that feeling. I also know there are memories I have the capability of retrieving that would make me laugh, that would honor the presence they were in my life. And even make me feel, I believe there is life after life after life. So, as I think of happy things, I imagine my loved ones smiling along with me. I'm certain my departed loved ones don't want me to be feeling pain and anguish. They want to be here as I'm remembering fun times that we had together. So, in this process, I ask my guardian angel team to help me to remember those things that will put a smile on my face. Those things that will help me remember that laughter and bring that joy back. As we are remembering and honoring the people that we loved who are still in our hearts. That's my process.

Andrea: I really believe the same thing. Sometimes those feelings come and we do need to sink in to let the tears come because that's part of the healing that needs to happen. To move the feeling through our body. But, then, we can ask for support. We can ask for a hug from the angels. We can ask for support in moving to more laughter and joy.

I was listening to a DVD today by Abraham Hicks. The topic was the description of incrementally moving from depression to a better feeling one step at a time.

Betsy: When I'm in my car, often times I don't have my radio or anything on, because I have this dialogue with the angels. I was laughing out loud because I was just having this dialogue with the angels getting ready for this show. Asking the angels to inspire me with what to say. I'm sure the people next to me thought I was on my blue tooth phone because I was talking out loud.

If I'm in the car, I choose to be listening to some sort of spiritual material. It is generally an Abraham Hicks CD that I'm listening to. If people aren't familiar with them…their website is **www.Abraham-Hicks.com** I do believe their information is profound. They have helped me a lot in the process of knowing that I have personal power and can impact everything I am experiencing. Thank you for bringing them up because I do really resonate with their material.

They do have an hour CD that is free to download on their website and it is a good foundation of them from the beginning. They talk about the law of attraction and the law of intention. One of the things I was going to bring up was segment intention. If you are picking up the phone and you want this outcome to happen in the phone call, you intend that. Or if you're getting in the car and you are heading somewhere you set the intention that you want to arrive safely. When you wake up in the morning, you set the intention you want it to be a good day. I set the intention for this phone call that I wanted it to be fun and I wanted it to be informative and helpful and healing to people.

Andrea: With the conversation of angels and weaving in the Abraham-Hicks work, it brings in choosing these thoughts and asking for support. Setting the intention and expecting that you are supported in your life. Knowing that you can shift from one way of thinking and being to another. And there is always support available there.

Do you ever ask for guidance and information to show you the meaning of a situation or what's next in your life?

Betsy: That is one of my intentions every morning: **to be inspired with anything and everything that would make my life better on that day.** It goes along with asking them to be a part of your life. I have found more of that in the last two months because I really have been asking to feel their presence more and more. It's not just about seeing the numbers 3, 6, 9 and seeing the license plates.

Ask them to be a part of your life and tell them, *"Okay, I would like to see symbols."* Whether it is pennies on the ground or dragonflies or roses or whatever it happens to be. Just see these things. Whatever you ask for, you'll see the presence of these things in your life more and more. It is just nice to know that they're there with you.

I have been inspired lately. I'll be walking out the door, headed to a meeting and something makes me go back in and pick something up. When I get to the meeting, I have this thing that I went back for and it ends up being exactly what I needed. Somehow it makes a difference to the person I'm meeting with.

I have a couple of examples of that.

I had a picture that I took at a spiritual retreat center of a fairy. And something made me go back and get this picture of this fairy. In talking to a woman in the middle of this meeting, she started sharing with me that she really believed in fairies. I said, *Oh, let me show you this picture.*

Another friend of mine was going on a long trip. I was going to say goodbye and wish him Bon Voyage. I was inspired to go back into my house and get a bag of candy out of the cupboard to put in a little gift package for his trip. When I gave it to him, he said, *How did you know I wanted to stop and get a package of this specific candy but I didn't have time to stop?*

I sent a Christmas present to my nephew. My brother was telling me today that my nephew had seen this item somewhere and really wanted it. But my brother didn't know where to find it and he opened the present from me and it was exactly what he was looking for.

This is the kind of stuff that happens again and again and again. Somehow I am being inspired to do what I'm doing in my everyday life. It is really neat to feel that you're in the flow. To feel that you're in the right place at the right time.
You're pressing the *"That Was Easy"* button.

I do invite angels to inspire me. Whatever that looks like to you. Some people actually see angels. I don't have that gift. Some people hear them speaking to them. Some people are inspired with thoughts. I think more of us are inspired with a thought or a feeling. You think about, *Andrea*, and call her. She says, *"I really needed to talk with somebody. Thank you for calling me."* I think that is her angels and my angels being in cahoots with each other. If we are open, we are inspired to do many things in life. Life is more fun when you feel like you are in the flow.

Andrea: It's funny. I have such a connection with Facebook. I feel like I waited my whole life for Facebook. I find that I will be doing something and I am drawn into the computer and the newsfeed and a friend will have just posted, what a difficult day it is at that moment. I will just say, *"I'm here. Take my hand."*

I think that is another way we are angels in each other's lives and that we listen to that angel whispering to us. Trusting that we are saying the words that the person needs to hear.

Betsy: Opening up to be inspired. Allowing it to happen. Believing it will happen. All of these things help you to get closer and closer and closer to see some of these everyday miracles happening in your life. Just opening and allowing is an important part of the process.

Andrea: I feel that doing these 44 radio shows over the holidays was an inspiration from my angel team. I was awakened in the middle of the night, several nights in a row and I sort of resisted it. I never really saw myself as a radio show host with guests so I thought, *Why would I do this?*

Every night there would be another little piece of information that would come. *Okay, I could just get on and read articles that I'd written.* Then, I let people on Facebook know that I was going to do this and people started contacting me and saying that they would love to be on the show. I thought, *Oh, I'm going to have guests on the show.* I felt that there was divine inspiration. Luckily, I was already in it before I actually knew what it meant and saw the enormity.

Betsy: Sometimes they see the big picture but they know that we are not ready for the big picture and they give us little nuggets. *How does this feel? Start with this. Well, as long as you are doing that, why don't you add this.*

The updated version of my website was like that. I kept being inspired with other things that people needed. It is fun seeing the pieces come together. It is like peeling an onion and little by little by little, more things are added. I'm enjoying it. It's really fun.

I believe we work with different angels at different times in our life. I believe we have an angel team. But, we have angels that come when we are working with specific projects. We have a guardian angel team that is always with us.

Let's say, you have to go to court one day and you are really anxious. I believe there is a team of angels that is really good at helping people in court situations. And you just have to ask them to show up and help.

Or you need to speak in front of a whole group of people and you don't feel comfortable about that. So, you call on the angels who are really good at public speaking. I ask the angels to whisper in my ear so I know what I need to say to the people.

Whatever it is that makes you a little bit nervous or a little bit fearful. Invite an angel team that is good at doing that specific test. They are there to help us.

In my journey here, I might be able to trace this back to the beginning of the summer when my friend, Andrea Hylen, (laughter) sent me an invitation to invite the Archangels into my home for five days. I believe that's when I reconnected with them strongly again. I took it as an opportunity to prepare the space for their arrival. While they were with me, we did all sorts of things. We went to the ballgame together. I was a tour guide of Baltimore with the Archangels. They also helped me clear out a room. I wanted a wonderful meditation healing space and at that moment in time, it was filled with boxes.

The week they were here with me, they helped me to empty that room. It was a fun time together. We meditated together and we went to parties together and took them to meet my friends. I included them in my life like they were friends who came to visit. It was really fun. And that was the beginning of this resurgence of feeling really connected especially to the Archangels. More than any of them during that week, I really felt the presence of Archangel Raphael. His focus tends to be healing. Raphael means God's healing love.

One of the first menu items on my website is Archangel Raphael's Prayer list. You can click on that specific link. If you are in need of prayer support or there is something in your life you need a healing around, I invite you to write your first name and share whatever information you want on the website. Keep in mind, it is open to the public.

On the flip side of that, I invite everyone to go there to look at the request for healing, look at the requests for blessings. Give gratitude and help the people. Know their prayer has already been answered. You can go there if you need help and you can go there to help others. It would be awesome to see lots of entries on this prayer list. That is one of the things that's there. There is also information about angelic healing and emotional release healing sessions that I do with people. I live in Maryland and I do them in person and I also do long distance healing.

Andrea: It is profound and powerful long distance healing. I have known Betsy for a long time but we had not talked very much during this year of solitude in California. It was a couple of weeks ago that we connected over an angelic healing and emotional release. Releasing trapped emotions.

She was guided to three different emotions. She had no way of knowing the specific situations and the time period. As soon as she would focus on the emotion and the time period, I had a situation pop into my mind and I knew exactly what she was talking about. They were things she knew nothing about. I felt lighter. I encourage you to go to her website. **www.betsymcmahan.com**.

One of the listeners on the chat line said that when she travels she asks Ganesh and her travel angels to travel with her. And she can tell the difference when she doesn't ask.

Betsy: Wonderful!

The more you can resonate with the feeling of gratitude, it can bring absolutely magnificent things into your life. If you are in a spot and you are really down, if you can feel one thing that you are grateful for and really focus on that one thing, I can almost guarantee you that you will think of another thing that you are grateful for. It is funny the way the angels and God work in our life. It's almost like when you thank the angels and God, the response is, *if you think that was good, let me show you something that's even better than that!*

Finally, relating back to healing specifically. One of the things I do for myself is just focus on the top of my head, the crown chakra and feel God's love and light pouring in through the top of my head and filling every cell in my body. At some point, you will just feel like you are glowing like the top of a lighthouse. And knowing that that healing light and love is helping to heal whatever it is you need help with. It could be emotional. It could be physical and that is the best thing right here in this moment I can share with people. And surround yourself with white light.

Andrea: Betsy, thank you so much for bringing your light and angel team to the show tonight. Merry Christmas.

Betsy McMahan is a minister, angel lady and healer. For more information and to connect with Betsy, go to her website: http://www.betsymcmahan.com/

Grief Transformation Show #33
Angels and the Angel Lady

December 25, 2010
http://tobtr.com/1400738

Guest Websites in Book 1

G. Brian Benson: www.gbrianbenson.com

Jeff Brown: www.soulshaping.com

Carin Channing: http://doodleoutreach.com/

Andrea Hylen: www.healmyvoice.org

Betsy McMahan: www.betsymcmahan.com

Alan Peterson: www.alanpetersonmusic.com

Debbie Phillips http://www.womenonfire.com/

Andrea Raynor: www.Revandrearaynor.com

Elizabeth St. Germain: www.elizabethstgermain.com

Anna Stookey: www.annastookey.com

Voices of Love in the dark

Andrea Hylen

44 Radio Show Links:

(I have included links to all 44 shows from Books 1 and 2. This is the order of the shows with show dates, titles and guests and the Book and Chapter.)

Show One:
Honoring the Feelings of Grief
Andrea Hylen
Nov 21, 2010
Book 1: Chapter 1
http://tobtr.com/1369270

Show Two:
Grief Relief: Finding Comfort After Loss
Debbie Phillips
Nov 22, 2010
Book 1: Chapter 2
http://tobtr.com/1369271

Show Three:
The loss of a life partner or spouse
Andrea Hylen
November 23, 2010
Book 2: Chapter 20
http://tobtr.com/1369272

Show Four:
Thanksgiving Eve: Remembering
Andrea Hylen
November 24, 2010
Book 1: Chapter 4
http://tobtr.com/1369273

Show Five:
Thanksgiving: Gratitude
Andrea Hylen
November 25, 2010
Book 1: Chapter 5
http://tobtr.com/1369275

Show Six:
How to Stay Open to Feelings and Take Control of Grief
Andrea Hylen
November 26, 2010
Book 1: Chapter 3
http://tobtr.com/1369275

Show Seven:
Stay Open: Spiritual and Self-Care Space
Carin Channing
November 27, 2010
Book 1: Chapter 8
http://tobtr.com/1369276

Show Eight:
Reading Stories about Grief
Andrea Hylen
November 28, 2010
Book 1: Chapter 14
http://tobtr.com/1369277

Show Nine:
The Journey of Building a Heart Based Business
Kathryn Yarborough
November 29, 2010
Book 2: Chapter 5
http://tobtr.com/1369278

Show Ten:
Messages from Beyond
Ellen Kittredge
November 30, 2010
Book 2: Chapter 9
http://tobtr.com/1369279

Show Eleven:
Dancing with a Teenager and the Jonas Brothers
Andrea Hylen
December 1, 2010
Book 1: Chapter 15
http://tobtr.com/1369280

Show Twelve:
The Transformative Power of Love
Alan Peterson
December 2, 2010
Book 1: Chapter 10
http://tobtr.com/1369281

Show Thirteen:
Writing as a Path of Healing
Andrea Hylen
December 3, 2010
Book 1: Chapter 18
http://tobtr.com/1369282

Show Fourteen:
Healing with Laughter
Andrea Hylen
December 4, 2010
Book 1: Chapter 20
http://tobtr.com/1414056

Show Fifteen:
Saying Goodbye to a Home
Andrea Hylen
December 5, 2010
Book 1: Chapter 17
http://tobtr.com/1369284

Show Sixteen:
The Voice that Calls You Home
Rev Andrea Raynor
December 6, 2010
Book 1: Chapter 4
http://tobtr.com/1369286

Show Seventeen:
The Loss of a Parent and Forgiveness
Susan Gardener
December 8, 2010
Book 2: Chapter 12
http://tobtr.com/1385916

Show Eighteen:
Memories of a Friend
Shelly Rachanow
December 9, 2010
Book 2: Chapter 15
http://tobtr.com/1385906

Show Nineteen:
Listening to Your True Voice
Sherryl Lin
December 10, 2010
Book 2: Chapter 2
http://tobtr.com/1385907

Show Twenty:
Letting Go of the Old You
Asha Ramakrishna
December 11, 2010
Book 2: Chapter 1
http://tobtr.com/1385908

Show Twenty-one:
A Journey from Grief to Peace
Kathy Perry
December 12, 2010
Book 2: Chapter 13
http://tobtr.com/1385909

Show Twenty-two:
The Art of Grieving
Claire Perkins
December 13, 2010
Book 2: Chapter 18
http://tobtr.com/1385910

Show Twenty-three:
Loss of a sibling
Sally Laux
December 14, 2010
Book 2: Chapter 22
http://tobtr.com/1385911

Show Twenty-four:
Loss of a child
Andrea Hylen
December 15, 2010
Book 2: Chapter 17
http://tobtr.com/1433629

Show Twenty-five:
Surviving the Dark Night of the Soul
Kater Leatherman
December 16, 2010
Book 2: Chapter 7
http://tobtr.com/1385913

Show Twenty-six:
Embracing Life after a Loss
Andrea Hylen
December 17, 2010
Book 1: Chapter 7
http://tobtr.com/1436200

Show Twenty-seven:
Divorce and the journey of healing
Andrea Hylen
December 18, 2010
Book 2: Chapter 10
http://tobtr.com/1437627

Show Twenty-eight:
Healing with Music
Andrea Hylen
December 19, 2010
Book 1: Chapter 13
http://tobtr.com/1438749

Show Twenty-nine:
Body Wisdom and Grief
Anna Stookey
December 20, 2010
Book 1: Chapter 12
http://tobtr.com/1400734

Show Thirty:
Journaling the Journey
Lee Forest Knowlton
December 22, 2010
Book 2: Chapter 14
http://tobtr.com/1400735

Show Thirty-One
Healing from a Loved One's Suicide
Connie Cornwell
December 23, 2010
Book 2: Chapter 19
http://tobtr.com/1400736

Show Thirty-Two:
Peace on Earth
Andrea Hylen
December 24, 2010
Book 1: Chapter 11
http://tobtr.com/1400737

Show Thirty-three:
Angels and the Angel Lady
Betsy McMahan
December 25, 2010
Book 1: Chapter 22
http://tobtr.com/1400738

Show Thirty-four:
Gender Transition
Jay Lee
December 26, 2010
Book 2: Chapter 6
http://tobtr.com/1400739

Show Thirty-five:
A parent with Dementia
Renee Barnow
December 27, 2010
Book 2: Chapter 4
http://tobtr.com/1400740

Show Thirty-six:
Staying Balanced
G. Brian Benson
December 29, 2010
Book 1: Chapter 21
http://tobtr.com/1424642

Show Thirty-seven:
Writing and Reading as Healing
Frank Mundo
December 30, 2010
Book 2: Chapter 21
http://tobtr.com/1445660

Show Thirty-eight:
Nature Ceremonies to Release Grief
Andrea Hylen
December 31, 2010
Book 1: Chapter 16
http://tobtr.com/1440659

Show Thirty-nine:
I AM STILL ALIVE!
Yvonne Gonzalez-Baez
January 1, 2011
Book 2: Chapter 16
http://tobtr.com/1457143

Show Forty:
Heeding Your Call
Jeni Shaw
January 2, 2011
Book 2: Chapter 3
http://tobtr.com/1385912

Show Forty-one:
Welcome Change and Move Forward
Cherry-Lee Ward
January 3, 2011
Book 2: Chapter 8
http://tobtr.com/1454732

Show Forty-two:
Cell Your Soul: Soulshaping
Jeff Brown
January 5, 2011
Book 1: Chapter 6
http://tobtr.com/1422820

Show Forty-three:
Grieving the Life you Thought You Were Meant to Live
Elizabeth St. Germain
January 6, 2011
Book 1: Chapter 19
http://tobtr.com/1460072

Show Forty-four:
A Summary of 44 Days
Andrea Hylen
January 7, 2011
Book 2: Chapter 11
http://tobtr.com/1457160

Andrea Hylen

Resources from Radio Shows

12 Peace Prayers
Abby Wynne
Agape Spiritual Center
Caring Bridge
CreateSpace for publishing
Masaru Emoto
Stan Grof: Holotropic Breathwork
Hospice
Jack Kornfield
Lulu for Publishing
Macy's Day Parade
Net of Light
On-line grief support: http://www.onlinegriefsupport.com/
Peace Pole
Priscilla's Gifts and Coffee
Season for Non-Violence
Stacy Robyn, creator of The Gratitude Experiment
Violet Flame
Water Convergence

Andrea Hylen

Books

*Melody Beattie: Lessons of Love and Codependent No More

*G. Brian Benson: Brian's List – 26 ½ Easy to Use Ideas on How to Live a Fun, Balanced, Healthy Life, Finding Your Voice, Steve the Alien

*Sara Ban Breathnach: Simple Abundance

*Jeff Brown: Soulshaping: A Journey of Self-Creation, Love it Forward, Ascending with Both Feet on the Ground, An Uncommon Bond, Spiritual Grafitti

*Julia Cameron: The Artist's Way: A Spiritual Path to Higher Creativity, Vein of Gold

*Carin Channing: 365 Days of Doodling (Discovering the Joys of Being Creative Every Day) and Doodle Book Junior – 101 Creative Prompts for Kids

*Course in Miracles

*Ram Dass: Be Here Now, Be Love Now

*Erich Fromm: The Art of Loving

* Louise Hay: You Can Heal Your Life

*Andrea Hylen, Conscious Choices: An Evolutionary Woman's Guide to Life, Heal My Voice books on Amazon

*Abraham-Hicks: Ask and it is Given

*Kater Leatherman: The Liberated Baby Boomer: Making S P A C E for Life

*Debbie Phillips: Women on Fire: 20 Inspiring Women Share Their Life Secrets (and Save You Years of Struggle! Volumes 1 and 2.

*Rev. Andrea Raynor: The Voice that Calls You Home, The Choice, Incognito

*Terry Lynn Taylor: Messengers of Light

*James Twyman: The Barn Dance, The Art of Spiritual Peacemaking

*Neale Donald Walsch: Conversations with God

Films and TV

Ghetto Physics
Law of Attraction
Saturday Night Live
The Secret

Music

Beatles: In My Life
John Denver- Perhaps Love
Bob Dylan
Jonathan Goldman: Healing Sounds
Grateful Dead
Here to Here
Elton John
Nick Jonas- A little Bit Longer
Kingston Trio
Patti LaBelle – New Attitude
Kenny Loggins: Return to Pooh Corner
Tim McGraw: Live Like You Were Dying
Jason Mraz: Make it Mine
Pandora: playlists
Alan Peterson: World In Love, Music Of The Heart, Circle Of Love
Libby Roderick: How Could Anyone
Simon and Garfunkel
Spotify: playlists
YouTube videos

Andrea Hylen

Heal My Voice Book Series

http://healmyvoice.org/

Fearless Voices:
True Stories by Courageous Women
2012

Empowered Voices:
True Stories by Awakened Women
2012

Inspired Voices:
True Stories by Visionary Women
2013

Harmonic Voices:
True Stories by Women on the Path to Peace
2014

Tender Voices:
True Stories by Women on a Journey of Love
2014

Feminine Voices:
True Stories by Women Transforming Leadership
2014

Sensual Voices:
True Stories by Women Exploring Connection and Desire
2015

Andrea Hylen

www.ingramcontent.com/pod-product-compliance
Lightning Source LLC
Chambersburg PA
CBHW070546050426
42450CB00011B/2740